Hope & Change
for
Humpty Dumpty

Successful Steps to Healing, Growth & Discipleship

Gary Sweeten
and
Steve Griebling

Cover Design and Graphics: Copyright © 2001 by Linda Crank
Creative Team: Betty Reid, Linda Crank and Steve Helterbridle
Back Photo: Copyright © 2001 by Judith Haag

Scripture taken from the *Holy Bible,* New International Version. Copyright © 1973, 1978, 1984, International Bible Society. Used by permission of Zondervan Bible Publishers

Also Quoted: *The Holy Bible,* New King James Version (NKJV) © 1984 by Thomas Nelson, Inc.

1stBooks - rev. 04/18/02

Contents

Acknowledgements v
Preface vii
   1. Seeking Solutions to Life's Problems 1
   2. The Church as a Healing Community 11
   3. Four Essentials of Effective Helping 23
   4. A Road Map for Helping 35
   5. Love Really Works 49
   6. Genuine Love that Heals 61
   7. Love with Skin on It 73
   8. Tuning in to Others 85
   9. Respecting The Golden Rule 97
   10.How to Host a Visitor 109
   11 Learning to be Concrete 119
   12. Moving to Action with Affirmation 129
   13. Looking For Good and God 141
   14. Setting Good Goals 153
   15. Going on with Goals 163
Appendix 173
   1. Depression Checklist 173
   2. Marital Happiness Assessment 174
   3. Is Your Child Angry? 175
   4. Pictorial Chart of Lifeway Principles 176
A Structure for Equipping the Local Church 177
Group Questions, Exercises & Real Life Models 180
References 189
About the Authors 191

Acknowledgements

We are thankful for the many people who made this project possible. Some of them are named in the text, but many are silent partners in this team effort. Anyone who has ever attempted to write a book knows that some of the most hidden people are the most important. Such is the case of Betty Reid, a friend and editor/critic for many years. Betty has helped us design many of our seminars, articles and books over the years and we are all richer because of her input and prayers.

Linda Crank, whose illustrations appear throughout the book, used her gifts and talents with skill, gentle resolve and creative acumen. Steve Helterbridle gave us much important computer advice and Jim Weible continues to provide computer, design, video and spiritual support. Dorothy Faye Geverdt, is a wonderful actress, friend and encourager.

The team of wonderful men and women from one of the most generous large churches in America are greatly appreciated. The Vineyard Community Church in Cincinnati provided space, volunteers, advertisements, finances and encouragement for the video taping that is the companion for this text. Pastor Steve Sjogren, Rob Reider and the video team, Mark Stecher, Nancy Dodson and Elaine Hanson made it all possible.

Harvest Fellowship Church of Cincinnati, Ohio and Pastor Rich Femia, prayer, financial support, love and encouragement.

Many brothers and sisters helped us develop this material through input at seminars around the world: Faith community Baptist Church, St. Andrew's Lifestreams, Church Of Our Saviour, Girl's Brigade in Singapore with Valerie Chan, Esther Tzer Wong and others as key supporters. The Pastoral Training Center in Taiwan; Ansgar Seminary in Norway; Kristen Callesen in Denmark; Dr. Galina Chentsova in Russia; and Larry Chrouch, Butch Ernette, Jim and Brenda Dyer and Richard Kidd in the USA.

Our supporters support our travels around the world with the good news of Christ's love, truth and power. Without the individuals, churches and businesses that believe in Lifeway we could not carry on.

The Lifeway Counseling Center team provides technical support, love, office space, and all the things that help us operate smoothly. Martin Re and his team make it possible to minister with freedom. The board of Lifeway Ministries loves us, prays for us and helps us find the money to carry out His ministry.

Our wives are longsuffering, patient and kind, modeling the behavior we promote.

In memory of John and Kathleen Kantz by their son Rich Femia.

Preface

No group of persons on the earth desires to bring about changes more than Christian leaders. It is our daily food, our constant companion, the content of our dreams and the energy behind our hopes. Almost every magazine, television program, ministry, sermon, Sunday school and Bible study either begins or ends by calling for a response, a change, a commitment, a movement. Can you ever remember a sermon that explicitly or implicitly asked the congregation to remain passive? Nor can we.

The title of this book lays out in metaphorical terms the problem of Adam's Fall and the hopelessness of all secular humanistic "answers." Yet, it proclaims the bold belief that there is hope for Humpty and all his offspring. The subtitle reveals the three groups who are the focus of our work.

- Healing focuses on those who are broken by the fall.
- Growth in Christ is for all believers.
- Discipleship brings Christians under the lordship of Jesus Christ.

Care and Counsel

Everyone is a problem, has a problem, lives with a problem, works with a problem or makes problems. We all have days when we wish we knew how to find solutions to the problems of life and living. Despite the best intentions or the greatest amount of motivation, we are often lost or confused about how to help troubled people.

During Gary's college years, Mrs. Betty Ann Ward, a counselor, inspired him with her compassionate ability to motivate students. She modeled a caring heart and a listening ear to all her students and friends. He saw the power of "heart ware" to captivate, motivate and celebrate the lives of all people. A never-published guidance counselor in a small junior college who rented worn-out facilities from a regional high school, showed Gary how to love people in ways that enabled them achieve greatness. Her legacy lives on in hundreds of people around the world. She made a difference.

Are you also involved in helping people grow? Are you asked for advice or a listening ear? Do you sometimes get frustrated when people do not take your counsel and yet return for more of the same? Do you say to yourself, "*I tried to tell them, but they just would not listen to me?*" Do those you advise sometimes do the opposite of what you recommend?

If so, you are in the same boat we have been in most of our lives. Being helpful was so important that we got advanced degrees in counseling. *Surely,* we thought, *somebody has the expert answers to people's problems.* Unfortunately, graduate training sometimes made things worse because professors taught so many unrealistic and contradictory theories about helping. We wanted to offer clients effective ways to stop the pain in their lives but we were frustrated by failures.

Adding to our stress, were the books, articles, theories, and suggested solutions that promised great results. Even professionals can become overwhelmed with all the data and all the competing answers from celebrity "experts." In the early 70's, Alvin Toffler wrote *Future Shock*. In it, he predicted a time when the amount of new information would be so great that the leaders who needed the knowledge most would be unable to use it to make good decisions. Toffler said that it was not the content of information that would fry our brains but the rapidity of the change itself. He predicted that by the year 2000, the pace of change would reach exponential proportions.

Exponential is the term applied to any change that grows geometrically rather than by addition. For example, if we fold a paper forty times, we are causing exponential growth. Additive growth is stacking forty sheets of paper, which would reach the height of one half inch or less. However, a doubled paper would be much higher. How much higher? You probably won't believe it, but it would reach 277,000 miles! Addition gives us a half-inch of growth but doubling it each time would take us past the moon.

The Thirty Years War

From the sixties through the nineties, we, in America, have witnessed the greatest social and cultural changes imaginable. Toffler's ideas about *Future Shock* have not only come to pass in technology and information but also in the ways we live, relate to one another and construct our family life. Dr. Richard Swanson in the book, *Margin*, notes that there have been exponential changes in five areas: Technology, Information, Psychology, Sociology, and Spirituality.

> *Perhaps the changes in information and technology have been, for the most part, positive. However, the issues and changes in the other three have had damaging effects upon both individuals and families. We see the unhealthy results all around us in society, in families, the workplace and even in the church. Many people want their lives to be different but do not know how to change. Because of the breakdown of our basic institutions, the church, schools and extended families, our nation faces challenges more daunting than any time since the Civil War.*

You will learn how to cut through all the psychobabble, competing theories and contradictory strategies to be a successful change agent in a sinful, hurting, confused society. Leaders need to be able to access these insights efficiently. After applying the information learned here you will experience a great leap forward in helping people mend, grow and submit to Christ.

C. S. Lewis in God in the Dock: Christian Apologetics, summarizes our attitude toward books on the topic of psychology and Christianity. Although he was pointing to books written with a latent faith, we think there is a similar focus in this book.

> *Any Christian who is qualified to write a good popular book on any science may do much more good than by direct apologetic work. We must attack the enemy's line of communication. What we want is not more little books about Christianity but more little books by Christians on other subjects. The first step toward the re-conversion of this country is a series, produced by Christians to … compete with secular books on their own ground. Its science must be perfectly honest. Science twisted in the interest of apologetics would be sin and folly.*

This book is the service of Lifeway Ministries Incorporated International
a non-profit organization in the United States of America

The stories and anecdotes are a combination of real events and creative interpretations with names and places changed to keep the information private.

For additional course material (including vcds, videos, manuals) contact
Lifeway Ministries Inc. Int. 4015 Executive Park Dr. Suite #305 Cincinnati, Ohio 45241
Ph: (513)769-4600 www.lifewaycenters.com E-mail: lifeway@lifewaycenters.com

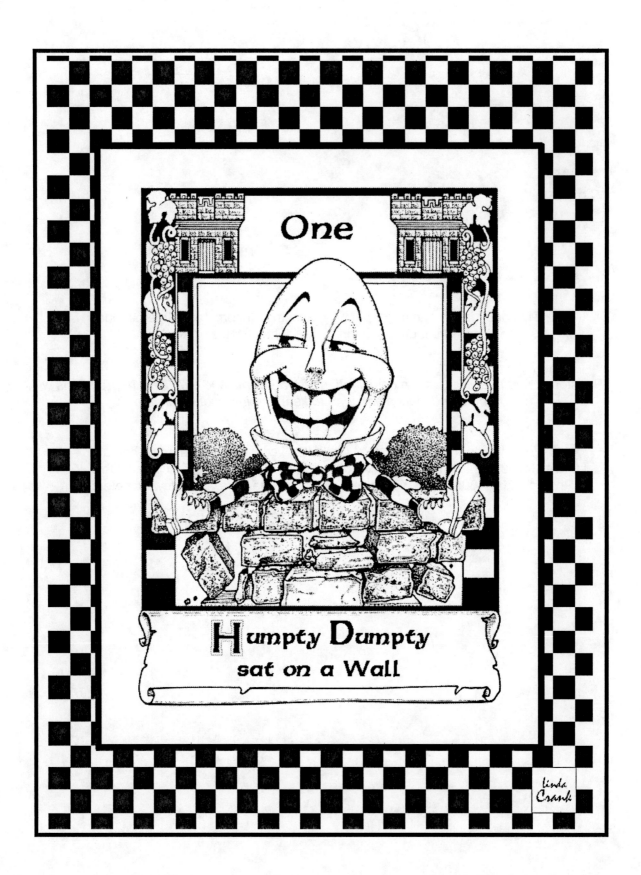

1

Seeking Solutions to Life's Problems

I will ask the Father and He will be with you forever, the Spirit of truth.
You know him for He lives <u>with</u> you and will be <u>in</u> you. John 14: 16-17

> *Humpty Dumpty sat on a wall.*
> *Humpty Dumpty had a great fall.*
> *All the king's horses and all the king's men*
> *Couldn't put Humpty together again.*

This famous old rhyme offers a remarkable comment about the situation that faces people who seek help and healing from the church. The church has always had hurting members, but more of them are now coming out of the closet. The pre-war builders tended to suffer silently with pain, disappointments and dysfunction. However, younger Christians are different. They are better educated, more widely traveled and generally more assertive than their parents about customer service. Humpty Dumpty is not only fallen; he is demanding quality help from the church. If he does not get it, he will leave in order to find another place to minister to his needs.

Additionally, there has been a revival in the numbers of persons coming to Christ which has increased the percentage of broken persons asking for care and counsel. In fact, according to <u>Christianity Today</u>, the "rebirth rate" became greater than the "birth rate" during the last century.

	Birth Rate	*Rebirth Rate*
World	60%	126%
Europe	11%	41%
North Am	31%	57%
Oceana	53%	93%
Africa	114%	207%
Latin Am	76%	233%
Asia	67%	376%

The overall trend is indisputable. Biblical faith is spreading to the ends of the earth as never before in history. Among the examples of the amazing progress of the gospel are the growing number of non-Western missionaries and the church in China that has grown from 1 million to 80 million in the 60 years since World War II. At the beginning of the 20th century, some 80% of the world's Christians lived in Europe and the United States. At the beginning of the 21st century, some 60% live in non-western countries with 43% in Africa and Latin America.

Love Attracts Hurting People

Why is the church growing so rapidly at this time? There are many reasons but one factor is having a great impact on missions around the world. The dramatic increase in churches that have adopted kindness, love and care has brought millions to faith in Christ. This approach to evangelism establishes the church as a place of comfort and sensitivity that contributes to the numbers of people looking for nurture, care and counsel. If we advertise our church as a "hosspital for sinners" we must not be shocked at the many wounded who show up in our emergency room door.

 Secondly, the cell church movement contributes both to the increase in successful evangelism and the church as a place of healing. Over 700 United Kingdom churches are presently transitioning to the cell structure. These congregations have also adopted the Alpha program and Servant Evangelism to minister to the unchurched. This results in many new Christians from dysfunctional families, broken hearts, addictive habits and painful relationships. Thankfully, the cell structure provides a place of confidentiality, safety and acceptance. However, few cell leaders or pastors are able to counsel these new members. The combination of broken babes along with open, loving, accepting groups demands well-trained leaders. Otherwise, the group loses its balance; spirals into a place of dysfunction and the members remain in pain.

Without skilled assistance, broken people become stuck in their problems making their condition worse. Sometimes our care engenders dependency for few leaders know how to bring people to wholeness. They can *comfort the afflicted* but do not know how to *afflict the comfortable*. Both are required to motivate Seekers to leave the rut of pain. We need both kindness and confrontation in a healing ministry. Love and acceptance are wonderful but inadequate to the total task of restoration. Likewise, confrontation alone sounds good to some leaders but leaves their flock frustrated because it is uncaring and ineffective. Pharisaism can never replace speaking the truth in love.

In this book you will learn how to offer both hope *and* change for Humpty Dumpty. We do not want Humpty to stay mired in the clay of hopeless pain, dysfunctional despair or continuous complaints. Leaving people in chronic dependency is not loving or truthful. Leaders need ways to motivate the unmotivated to be motivated. The Helper cannot force anyone to change, but we can certainly increase the Seeker's desire to live a healthy life.

Offering Hope

And Change

Campus Aflame

What happens when Humpty and Mrs. Dumpty's come to Christ and fill the church? We faced this situation in the early 1970's at the University of Cincinnati. The Sweeten's house church near the campus served the first waves of boomers who came to Christ out of promiscuity, alcohol, drugs, violence and rebellion. Almost all of our new "members" were refugees from a society bursting at the seams with destructive habits.

The old ways of "dipping and dropping them", (baptism without discipleship) no longer worked so we had to devise a whole new way of "doing church". Ours was the first generation of *seeker sensitive* ministries. Students with long hair and beards met in homes, sang Bible choruses, studied the word, took communion and witnessed to their friends. They slept on our couches and grazed through our refrigerator. We provided the love they desperately wanted and the structure so desperately needed. We prayed for deliverance from drugs, healing from sexual abuse and wisdom for students facing exams.

Local churches slammed their doors at the sight of these smelly, unkempt rebels so we learned to accommodate ourselves to the new cultural preferences. The converts were baptized in the Ohio River and the Lord filled our house with the prodigals from a thousand homes. The revival began and we were on the cutting edge of a move of God.

A New Reformation

We were forced during the Jesus Movement to equip young men and women to minister to each other because there were few clergy willing to be involved with us. The conviction that the Lord was doing something new grew within us and we saw God work powerfully through ordinary people. Later, in 1983, the Lord told Gary that the campus revival was simply one small part of His global plan. The word went something like this:

> *I am pouring out my Spirit on the church in a new reformation. In the first reformation I took my Word out of the hands of a few and gave it to all my people. In this reformation I will take my Works out of the hands of the few and give it to all my people.*

We believe that this Reformation will be as revolutionary and important as the one led by Tyndale, Luther and Calvin. However, it will only be successful when churches develop ways to both know the word of God and do the works of God in power and love. Then believers will be able to carry out the twin commands of Jesus to "*Go into all the world and make disciples"* (Matt. 28:19), and "*Heal the broken hearted and set the captives free"* (Luke 4:18). The failure of the church is a failure of equipping.

The New Reformation has been developing since the Sixties. Most of the growth in global new births has been the direct result of the life and witness of dedicated laymen and lay women. This New Reformation was a precursor to the revolution in computer networks and the internet for it is based almost completely on developing formal and informal networks among business travelers, churches, para-church organizations, small groups and new apostolic missionary movements. A cell of committed Christians can change the world.

Most congregations in Singapore and Taiwan send short-term and long-term missionaries overseas. They also have dynamic small group ministries in their local communities. The cell group movement multiplies like a computer network and cannot be snuffed out by governments or formal church structures. The New Reformation is changing the world through ordinary people who have an extraordinary God. They minister at home, work and abroad. This is what happens when believers know the word and do the works.

A New Rhyme for the New Reformation

The original Humpty Dumpty rhyme leaves us with a sense of hopelessness and frustration. That is exactly the emotions many feel about the high number of broken people in the world and the church. There is so much negative thinking and helpless rhetoric from leaders that we must give our readers faith that the church can be a place of change and hope for Humpty. We have just been through a terrible terrorist attack on the USA and some high profile Christians are lashing out at those most hurting among us. However, we think that it is a time to show how the love and power of God can transforming evil into good.

3

One of our co-teachers in Singapore, Mrs. Tan Lee Lee, wrote a new poem about helping Humpty change. Linda Crank, our illustrator, added her creativity to the rhyme, making it more complete, hopeful and accurate. May this rhyme encourage the church.

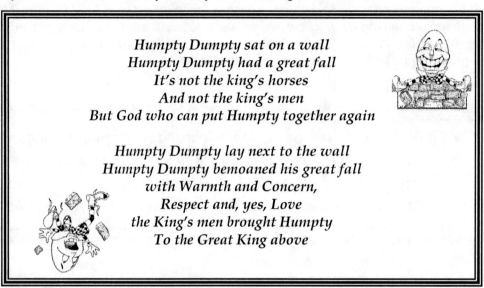

Humpty Dumpty sat on a wall
Humpty Dumpty had a great fall
It's not the king's horses
And not the king's men
But God who can put Humpty together again

Humpty Dumpty lay next to the wall
Humpty Dumpty bemoaned his great fall
with Warmth and Concern,
Respect and, yes, Love
the King's men brought Humpty
To the Great King above

We are not fearful or discouraged about the church. We believe that congregations can become communities of love, truth and power. The New Reformation equips the saints to do the ministry of care, counsel and discipleship. No organization or clinic is as successful as the church in putting Humpty and Mrs. Dumpty back together again. We need not be embarrassed or ashamed about the effectiveness of the church to heal, deliver and restore. It is the only hope for a broken world.

A Healing, Growth Continuum

Pastoral care is a healing-growth continuum. Not everyone has an acute need for healing, but everyone has a need to grow. About 10% of us are born with birth defects that require medical or psychological treatment. However, 100% percent of us are born again with defects in character, knowledge and maturity. Additionally, we also have wounded spirits, minds and emotions from the shock, trauma and abuse of life. Pastoring Humpty always requires discipling and sometimes it requires healing.

A healing ministry focuses on repairing pain, dysfunction, wounds, hurts and compulsions. We need to be counseled, healed or delivered from problems. *Growth*, however, emphasizes that we are immature, naïve, unaware and unlearned about God and the Christian life. The answer is to be trained, equipped or discipled by a spiritual advisor. Humpty needs healing *and* discipling, mending *and* molding, treatment *and* teaching.

Pastors need to differentiate between the depth of a person's dysfunction and his level of maturity. This will keep us from being overly focused on problem people to the neglect of equipping the healthier members. The first priority is to equip the saints to do the work of ministry. To over emphasize healing, and neglect equipping with the Word and works leads to immature members and a spiral of crisis management. The final result is neglect of hurting members for there is no one well enough to minister to the sick. The strong must bear with the failings of the weak. As Jesus asked in Luke 6:39, *Can the blind lead the blind?* The answer is a resounding, NO!

Type A and Type B Church Members

We classify members as Type A and B from a definition used by cell churches. *Type A* members do not have problems that cause serious interruptions in work, family or church life. They will sometimes have conflicts, emotional struggles and concerns but rarely seek out special ongoing counseling. Instead, they receive enough support and prayer at small group meetings or Sunday school classes. These members are strong enough to their receive their pastoral care through friends, worship, tapes and books. They account for about 70 to 80% of a congregation and should be the focus of training and leadership development.

Type A members have been divided into two levels to differentiate the very mature from the persons not yet at maximum strength in mind and spirit. *Level 1* members are most wanted in leadership. They are exemplary in mental, emotional and relational health but make up only 10% of the congregation. To equip believers to this level of maturity is our goal.

Level 2 members have few life interrupting problems but lack maturity in Word and works. They may range in maturity from quite healthy to teetering on the brink of a serious crisis. Like a man who is overweight with high blood pressure, there is no heart problems yet, but additional stress can bring one on. Approximately 60 to 70% of the church is in this functional group. From this group will come most of our learners.

Type B members all have some level of life interrupting problems. *Level 3* folk experience family disputes, behavioral problems, mild depression, light anxieties, or bad habits that disrupt daily living. Paraprofessionals, recovery and support groups and classes are appropriate for ministry for this 10 to 20% of the congregation. In churches with strong evangelistic and counseling programs the number will be greater.

Level 4 members are those who have not improved with lay care, counsel and prayer and their life interrupting issues are getting worse. Depression, anxiety, marital conflicts, abuse issues, addictions, and eating disorders are worsening. This 8 to 10% of the congregation will need professional counseling as well as support from lay care givers.

Level 5 is for the very few 2 to 5% whose problems require residential treatment with medical assistance. The issues include suicidal ideas, violence, life-threatening addictions, and psychotic mental illness. Teen Challenge is an example of residential treatment.

The original estimates of percentages within each grouping came from our 30 years of counseling plus estimates in books and journals. However, a recent research paper suggests that the percentage of needy Type B. people has risen over the past forty years. In 1957, 19% of respondents said they had faced a nervous breakdown. This is similar to the 20% for those in *Type B* categories above. However, in 1999 this group had grown to 27% indicating about a 10% increase. The chart below reflects the new research.

<table>
<tr><td colspan="3" align="center">**Type A and Type B Members**</td></tr>
<tr><td>A-1</td><td>10%</td><td>Leaders, strong and mature, receive help through worship, small groups, classes, tapes and books.</td></tr>
<tr><td>A-2</td><td>60%</td><td>The majority of people in the church, who need to grow into maturity in the Word and works of God. They experience few major disruptions in daily life.</td></tr>
<tr><td>B-3</td><td>20-30%</td><td>Issues, pains and conflicts disrupt the normal living. Paraprofessional helpers, recovery, support groups, groups and personal counseling are needed.</td></tr>
<tr><td>B-4</td><td>8-10%</td><td>Depression, anxiety, marital conflicts, parenting issues, ADD/ADHD, abuse, addictions, eating disorders. Need professional help and/or medication.</td></tr>
<tr><td>B-5</td><td>2-5%</td><td>Psychosis, suicidal, destructive -- requires residential treatment with medical assistance.</td></tr>
</table>

Type A members must be equipped to provide care and counsel for their *Type B* colleagues. Only then will the church be able to adequately minister to the flock of God. Paraprofessionals can counsel all *Level 3* and many of those in *Level 4*. A wholistic ministry provides access to all five levels of care by actively equipping Paraprofessional Helpers for *Level 3* ministry and referring *Level 4 and 5* members to competent Professionals.

Lifeskills for Care and Counsel

The Lifeskills training is the most effective way to equip Paraprofessionals for ministry to each other. In fact, we used Lifeskills as treatment in the Lifeway Hospital Unit for *Level 5* residents along Professional counsel and medication. Lifeskills taught them how to minister to each other. Since the laity had learned and applied counseling skills at church, we concluded that hospital patients could also minister to one another so we followed the same healing principles as the church with great success.

However, we do not recommend that congregations focus on *Levels 4 and 5* by hiring professional counselors. This approach takes so much time, energy and money that 70-80% of the members will be neglected. Instead, develop a list of trusted therapists to whom you can refer *Level 4 and 5 members*.

We intentionally include *Level 3* people in Lifeskills classes. The term, *equip* means to mend as well as to mold into shape. All classes and groups should be layered with both *Type A* and *Type B* folks. By providing Lifeskills classes for everyone we greatly advanced the wholeness of the congregation and reduced the need for Professional counselors.

Four Levels of Learning and Skill Development

Learners do not instantly understand and implement new knowledge and new skills. It takes time, practice and repetition to integrate new information into one's life. This is doubly true for process skills. Caring effectiveness relies upon doing the skills and processes rather than just memorizing new information. The four stages of learning a skill are summarized below.

- *Unconsciously Incompetent:* I do not know what I do not know. (I know nothing about fishing or think I need to know anything.)
- *Consciously Incompetent:* I discover what I do not know and what I need to know, but I cannot do it. (I hear how complex catching a fish can be.)
- *Consciously Competent:* I must think about the skill, since it does not come naturally and habitually. (I fish on my own with the manual open.)
- *Unconsciously Competent:* I naturally and intuitively bait the hook, cast the rod and pull in the fish with no thought about the theories. (I do not have to think about how to fish.)

Practice Makes Permanent

Whatever we practice will become a part of us. After each new lesson you will be able to discuss the lecture, practice new skills and move ever so slowly toward *Unconscious Competence* one step at a time. The acrostic DREAMS covers all the factors that go into learning a new skill and will remind you of what it takes to become a care giver.

D *idactic* is the lecture, reading part of learning. This is effective for getting principles and basic information across but ineffective for learning skills or motivating people to change. Think about what is required to teach a person to fly. *Didactic* lectures will cover the theories of flight, the principles of aerodynamics, the data about thrust and weight as well as weather information and so forth. These are crucial to become a good pilot.

R *eflection* Once we hear the principles, we need time to think how they may be applied and consider what aspects we need to review. Students need time to internalize new ideas. Then the principle becomes part of us. A new pilot thinks through what it will mean to fly.

E   *xperience* makes a skill permanent and moves us toward *Unconscious Competence*. You need a safe, fun place to practice new skills. You will join in role-plays, fish bowls and funny dramas. Pilots practice on the ground in what is called a Link Trainer where he/she takes off and lands in safety. One can electronically crash the plane many times without injury.

A   *ccountability* allows us to evaluate progress and discover if we are learning the skill. A pilot practices his skills electronically to gauge whether or not he can do the real thing in a real airplane.

M   *odeling* is a powerful source of growth. It is one of the best ways to learn how to do something different. You need to see good models and compare them with bad models. We will show you how to be an effective Helper. New pilots watch films and live presentations of good piloting techniques.

S   *pirituality* Prayer, scripture and worship are critical to Christian learning. The Holy Spirit is the Counselor and we are but His aides. He has been sent to lead us into all truth. This is a major difference between secular and Christian Helping. Humanists depend upon themselves but we depend upon God. They must know all, do all and tell all. We depend upon the Holy Spirit to know, do and tell. Every wise pilot will ask God for guidance, protection and wisdom.

> ### *If God is only your co-pilot, change seats!*

Life Scan Summary

Many pastors are overwhelmed by the increase of broken people attending their churches. Humpty is arriving at their doors in droves. There is nothing wrong with this trend. It is simply the result of revival in the world, an increase in the number of churches who reach out in love, and the fact that many people are staying stuck with their problems. Hope and Change for Humpty Dumpty provides the principles and processes for you to meet the needs of equipping your people to care for each other. It is a process that pastors or counselors can learn and pass on to the entire congregation.

TIPS for Life

Personal Reflection and Practice

- Reflect on the people in your church or small group and consider the percentages we have suggested.
- Do you agree or disagree with our estimates?
- Does your church minister to folk in all the different levels?
- How does it do that?
- What are the equipping programs in your congregation?
- Do the teachers practice DREAMS?
- What factors have encouraged you to grow in Christ or receive His healing?

Two

Humpty Dumpty
had a Great Fall

1

The Church as a Healing Community

_____

From him the whole body, joined and held together by every supporting ligament
grows and builds itself up in love, as each part does its work. Ephesians 4:16

Only the masses of simple, humble people and their growing
Spiritual power will be able to convert the atheists.
Feodor Dostoyevsky, The Brothers Karamazov

During the summer of 1969, Gary had an epiphany that proved to be the foundation for his life's work and ministry. God spoke to him in a way that changed him at the time and has continued to reverberate throughout his career. It was not a ram caught in a bush as Abraham experienced, but two agnostic psychologists who caught his attention and through whom God chose to call him to life of *Equipping the saints to do the work of ministry in the care and cure of souls.* For three weeks, he participated in a workshop with two famous psychologists, O. Hobart Mowrer and Carl Rogers. Their comments struck Gary with great force and shaped his career forever.

The early Christian church was the most powerful healing community that the world has ever known.
- O.H. Mowrer

First, professional counseling is no more effective than that done by friends and lay leaders such as teachers, pastors and professors. Second, the current rate of psychological problems among young people will make it financially and logistically impossible for professionals in the future; most counseling will be done by trained lay paraprofessionals.
- Carl Rogers

Despite the fact that Gary had a graduate degree in counseling, these ideas were new, inspiring and enlightening. Two of the more influential, unbelieving psychologists of all time sparked Gary on a life-long career of training Christians in the art and skills of soul care. He was led by the Lord to develop a creative alternative to the traditional counseling model to make the church into a healing family.

The power of a caring community is awesome. Healthy groups affect their members positively. Research clearly and consistently indicates that attendance at religious services correlates with healthier physical, mental and emotional lives. This includes all churches regardless of their theology. People who go to church on a regular basis experience reduced heart disease, alcohol/drug abuse and hypertension. The most potent weapon for preventing crime, premature death and social problems is found on Sunday mornings.

The Bible and Healing

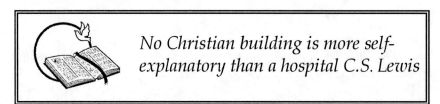

No Christian building is more self-explanatory than a hospital C.S. Lewis

It is common to look backward to the Greek philosophers of Hippocrates and Galen for the roots of modern medical compassion. To do so ignores Jesus Christ, the person most responsible for shaping the attitudes and actions of compassion and healing. Almost every charitable hospital, orphanage and mission of mercy that exists in the world today arose from Judeo-Christian thought. It is Jesus the Jew, not the Galen the Greek, who has more than any other figure in history bequeathed the healing arts to the modern world. The worldview of scripture has influenced every advanced medical system regardless of the current religious views of physicians.

Jesus did more than anyone to alert the world to the importance of mental, emotional, physical and spiritual health. No other great teacher left such a legacy. Not Confucius, Buddha, Mohammed or any lesser figure was known as "The Great Physician." His work is usually divided into the three parts: preaching, teaching and healing. However, even the teaching and preaching often focused on health and healing.

- About one fifth of the four gospels are devoted to His healing ministry. Some 727 of the 3,779 verses relate to the healing of physical, mental, emotional and spiritual problems in 41 different accounts of healing.
- The Holy Spirit anointed Jesus to heal and deliver. Luke 4:18
- Jesus sent the disciples out to continue the ministry of healing. See Mark 6:7-13, Matthew 10:5-10, 28:18-20, Luke 9:1-6, 10:1-10, Book of Acts, James 5:13-21.

Healing *comes from the old English word* hal *and means, wholeness or holiness. The Hebrew word,* shalom*, that is usually translated as* peace *means wholeness of the entire person. Jesus uses several different words to describe health and wholeness, including,* blessedness *"markarios",* life *"zoe" and* wholeness *"hygeis". Even the term used for* salvation *"sozo" is interchangeable with healing of the body and soul. The church is a salvation community that includes body, soul and family. It also has a spiritual dimension. Jesus said that the most important commandment was to:*

Love the Lord your God with all your heart, with all your soul, with all your mind. This is the first and greatest commandment, and the second is like it: Love your neighbor as yourself. All the Law and the Prophets hang on these two commandments. **Matthew 22:36-40**

The care and cure of souls is at least a three-way relationship that includes two persons and God. There is no other way to be whole and holy. The early church was a powerful community of wholeness because the believers cared for each other. Healing did not depend upon a specialized counselor. Jesus' commands to continue the ministry of teaching, preaching and healing were followed by the early church for many years.

Healing and radically changed lives provided strong arguments for an evangelical theology by confronting Gnosticism, the major error of the early church. It also gave opportunity for evangelism and showed God's love in action. Pagans killed sickly children but the church members took them in to their homes. Pastors in the early church complained that so many people were using oil from the church lamps for healing prayers with anointing that their energy costs were soaring. Wouldn't you love a problem like that?

The Marks of a Healing Community

We are committed to the necessity of equipping and releasing the gifts of all the people into a *supernaturally natural* environment of healing and growth. We have personally seen several churches develop communities of love, power and truth so we know it can be done. Lay members with gifts of helps, healing, teaching, administration and encouragement were equipped for ministries of care, prayer and counsel. The whole of each congregation grew to be greater than the sum of the parts and it *Built itself up in love.* Eph 4:16

> *He who knows the calamity of a man and does not free him of it commits a great sin.*
> -The Shepherd of Hermes

There are two aspects of a healing community. The first is called *grace and truth to outsiders* and the second, *healing flow for insiders*. Both point to the importance of our attitudes and behavior toward people in pain. An attitude of grace and truth toward all persons outside the group is the first essential. In Alcoholics Anonymous, it is the attitude of the *sober* members toward those who have not yet reached or even sought sobriety. In the church, it is the attitude of the *saints* toward sinners, the *insiders'* view of those outside the fold; it is the *counselor's* view of those unable to help themselves that offers grace to the people most in need of it. Healing congregations do not hoard their grace but lavish it on the world.

When those who have been touched by God's grace extend it to those outside, the fellowship is prepared to care and cure. When those who have been personally loved with an everlasting love, show the same kind of acceptance to the undeserving, there is movement toward becoming a source of health. When sinners are accepted, as they are, warts, struggles and failures intact, we can see a family that will heal the broken hearted and set the captives free. This is the *grace-applied* part of a healing community.

There is a second and important aspect of *entering the fellowship*. Along with an attitude that accepts people with grace is an expectation that the wounded, sinful, powerless person will not stay that way. A good hospital accepts the sickest and most hopeless patients but is never satisfied to leave them that way. Its health care team has a better way. The doctors, nurses, aides and leaders are fully committed to wellness but accomplish it by taking in the sick and dying. If they succeed only in acceptance but fail as healers their promises are empty lies.

The same is true for the church. Acceptance is essential but not enough. Many loving congregations fail to fully restore those who come. Love alone does bring some healing. However, when we add His truth and power the healing is greater and lasts longer. A church is different from a club that requires standards of wealth, dress, and status to join. While attending the Master's Golf Tournament in 1999, we found that entry to some of the venues was open to only a few who wore specially colored badges. Only the well connected were welcome. Scripture expressly prohibits that in church for to make such distinctions violates the law of love as described in James 2:12.

On the other hand, we are not to be so naive as to believe that all who come to our fellowship are without weaknesses, sins, problems and immaturity. St. Paul makes it plain that spiritual leaders are to *restore those who are caught up in trespasses and sins* Gal 6:14 and *equip those who are immature.* Eph 4:11-25 For the church to refuse to mend the broken and restore sinners would be like physicians and nurses who refuse medicine to the sick or teachers who withhold knowledge from unlearned students. The most natural act of the church is equipping the saints who are not "saints".

The other major dimension is releasing God's *healing flow in the congregation.* The care and cure of souls that comes from simply being with other ordinary Christians can hardly be overemphasized. Pastors and leaders need to train the laity to interact with health. Then the whole body, with its varied gifts, talents, skills, and experiences, gives strength, power, and love to each member. This alone brings about healing and growth for God designed the church to work as a body that mends itself.

 From him the whole body, joined and held together by every supporting ligament, grows and builds itself up in love, as each part does its work. Eph. 4:16

In a healthy fellowship, broken members will become part of the healing flow. Every leader was formerly a broken, immature member. This is one difference between Lifeskills and the medical model. Valerie ministers to Nancy at one meeting and Nancy ministers to Valerie at the next. Good care and counsel do not come from filling a role based on credentials, education and position. These vital church functions occur most effectively by allowing the Spirit of God to flow through us to others. Pastors need the prayer, advice and wisdom of members; and members need the teaching and leadership of pastors.

> *Brothers, think of what you were when you were called. Not many of you were wise by human standards; not many were influential; not many were of noble birth. But God chose the foolish things of the world to shame the wise; God chose the weak things of the world to shame the strong. I Cor 1:26-31*

May, a visitor to our city, called the Teleios Center for an appointment. She was assigned to Leah, a veteran Listener. Leah asked one of the new Helpers, Danielle, to assist her in ministry. After a few weeks, Leah went on vacation, leaving the newly minted Helper, Danielle, to minister alone. Danielle listened carefully and discovered that May was holding on to old resentments toward her mother. At the right time, Danielle asked May if she would forgive her mother, but she refused.

After more conversation, it became apparent that May was not a born-again believer so Danielle shared the gospel. A week after May accepted Christ as her Savior she was willing to release her mother with a prayer of forgiveness. The combination of Danielle's love, salvation and releasing her mother led to a dramatic reduction in May's depression and improvement in her family relationships. In a few weeks she stopped taking anti-depressant medication, reconciled with a brother and decided to renew her marriage vows.

The emotional destruction that comes from broken relationships cannot be repaired without establishing safe places with loving human contact. Every child is born fearing rejection. May's dysfunctional family left her with deep scars of abandonment. The fruit of the Spirit, released through the church community, brought substantial healing and restoration to her wounded soul. Then, when she trusted Leah and Danielle, they applied the truth of salvation and the power of prayer to bring about restoration. A little later, Leah returned and led May through a series on inner healing prayers to root out the rejections from the past.

A study at McLean Hospital of Harvard University points out that abusive and neglectful parents actually cause brain damage in their children. "A child's interaction with the environment causes connections to form between brain cells. These connections are pruned during puberty and adulthood. So whatever a child experiences, for good or bad, helps determine how his brain is wired." This brain damage has long-lasting effects.

> ***Death and Life are in the Power of the Tongue.***
>
> **Proverbs 18:21**

However, the situation is not hopeless. Positive interactions can heal the damage caused by childhood trauma and abuse. "Positive parental support and sometimes psychotherapy can help normalize brain function. Many people actually flourish despite childhood trauma" for youngsters "move on and get past it. Something, someone, somehow, an extended family, a church group or whatever has touched them and helped them continue on in a normal way." God's love is a healing balm for body and soul. A loving fellowship of prayer and God's word can restore brain functioning in adults from abusive backgrounds.

There are three Greek terms for truth and each one reveals a different aspect of God's plan. The truth convicts us, heals us and delivers us. The word of God touches hearts and reveals the hidden things of the Spirit. Additionally, the truths gained from scientific research on brings new insights, guidance and shows us how God brings healing.

- *Logos* is used to indicate the doctrine from *word*s of scripture and the word made flesh in the incarnation of Jesus. *In the beginning was the word and the word was with God and the word was God.* John 1:1
- *Aletheia* means *unveiled reality.* Jesus took the veil off reality so we can see how things really are. Before His coming, the truth was veiled. *If you hold to my teachings, you are truly my disciples. Then you will know the truth, and the truth will set you free.* John 8:32.
- *Cosmos* indicates the created order. Many scientists engage in research as a direct result of their commitment to God as personal creator. *Since the creation of the world God's invisible qualities-His eternal power and divine nature have been made known to them and is clear from what they have seen.* Romans 1:20

Learning from the cosmos is controversial among some believers, but we see no contradiction between the truth of scripture and the facts derived from His creation. We are thankful for the research about heart disease for angioplasty saved Gary's life. We are also thankful for the truth about medications that help relieve the depression of millions.

> *Psychology, can be instructive…even atheists can be good observers of God's creation revealed in humanity. To deny psychological insights is to deny common grace and natural revelation.* True Spirituality, *Francis Schaeffer*

Gail Andrews struggled with depression for twenty years. She came from a well-educated family but her low energy, sad feelings and lack of motivation kept her from achieving much in life. At her husband's insistence, she came to Lifeway Counseling. After several sessions, we recommended three actions. First, take a class on Renewed Christian Thinking to learn how to rehabilitate her mind. Second, see our psychiatrist who can proscribe anti-depressant medication. Third, continue to see the Lifeway therapist.

After a month of individual counseling, extra classes of Renewed Christian Thinking and a daily dose of Prozac, Gail emerged from her darkened cave into a world of light. The changes were remarkable. A year later, however, the clouds of depression returned and she could not understand why when she returned to see us. We asked what had changed. "I was feeling so good that I quit my medication and stopped practicing RCT." When Gail practiced the truth of God's word combined with the truth from nature, she made progress. However, when she stopped applying both truths, relapse was inevitable. She thought she had "lost her healing" but she had simply forgotten the path to healthy living.

> *Rhema* means that God reveals His truth to us in a super-natural manner through a word of wisdom or word of knowledge. God's insights about the Seeker's heart and His guidance about what steps to take for healing inner wounds is essential. With a word from the Spirit, our wisdom is joined with the mind of the Maker and an intervention can be implemented with confidence.

Early in Steve's ministry, a young woman came to him for help with her depression. After several sessions, her condition worsened and Steve was mystified about what to do. During prayer at the end of a particularly difficult meeting, Steve was led to pray for the young woman's time in the womb. She began to weep and after some time, the depression seemed to miraculously lift. At the next appointment, she was bright eyed and chipper. The Holy Spirit showed Steve how to pray through a *rhema* about her early years in the womb. The woman later discovered that her mother had attempted an abortion at three months. Steve, of course, had no human way to know this fact but God knows all things and can reveal significant information to us in a *rhema*.

Power Encounters

Almost all of us think of the gifts and power of God when we hear about the healing community but that is only one way to think about healing interventions. The first book Gary wrote, called Breaking Free from The Past, was on the subject of inner healing and spiritual warfare. It was based upon the premise that every memory, good or bad is locked in our emotional memory bank from the cradle to the grave. Second, that the memories associated with shock, trauma, abuse and neglect wound the spirit and cause future events to become distorted. Those distortions had led the young lady to adopt an attitude of rejection leading to anxiety, depression, fear and the development of habitual shame.

The young woman needed the power and truth of God to set her free. After receiving the *rhema*, Steve prayed that Jesus would enter her heart and set her free from the pain of the past. In this instance, a simple prayer unlocked the door to healthy living. However, in most cases,

Seekers must also take time renew their mind with God's truth for several weeks or months before the depression lifts.

Equipping the Church

The release of God's healing gifts to all church members is essential to developing a healing community. When everyone, not just the paid staff, walks in joyful acceptance of their call and ministry, all the parts of the body function in harmony. One of the best ways to accomplish this goal is by developing small groups. When we put the truth, fruit and gifts together in a lively small group environment, the presence of God and His life changing direction will become evident. Good groups magnify the healing flow of Christ.

How do we empower, equip and enable our churches and cells to be healing communities? How do we prepare them to operate with *grace and truth* toward outsiders with the *healing flow of* gifts *in the community*? Is it enough to set up a counseling clinic in the church and simply hire an expert therapist? Should we allow Alcoholics Anonymous to establish its program in our facilities? Although each of these can be a part of a healing community they are not enough. Special programs are never enough to convert the community into a place of healing.

By trying to fix a few broken people, we do little to bring maturity to the whole family. In fact, a dysfunctional church makes it difficult for the individual members to improve. The congregation is much more powerful than any individual. Additionally, if an expert counselor were to work with every hurting member it would do little to impact the majority of the members. By focusing on *Type B* members, the larger group is left out.

The milieu is a powerful source of life or death, so we need to intentionally insure that life is the congregation's primary product. For example, the persons who most influenced the patients in our psychiatric hospital unit were the other patients. They spent all day and all night together. Next were the orderlies, cleaning staff and nurse aids. The professional nurses, counselors and doctors have less contact with the patients showing once again that the *Context* is critically important to growth.

If a moderately distressed patient arrived on our unit, and the other residents were very ill, the new patient could get worse rather than better. The power of the group can hardly be overestimated. Knowing the importance of the *Context* or milieu, we used the same Lifeskills process developed at church to create a therapeutic community among the patients and staff. The residents, counselors and nurses all learned to relate with Lifeskills. The patients ministered life to each other in the evenings and on the weekends as well as in the daily group meetings. The positive environment benefited staff as well as the patients. In fact, some residents became congregational leaders and teach the Lifeskills classes.

Susan came to the Lifeway Unit depressed and suicidal. She was the victim of abuse that left her confused, sexually active and seeking to deaden her pain with alcohol. After a few days of rebelling against the system, she discovered that we were different from every other program she had ever tried, and she began to trust the therapists and residents. Later, Susan said that she appreciated the therapists but her friends in the unit were the key to healing. They listened, helped her face her bitterness, and led her through <u>Renewed Christian Thinking</u>. Now Susan is a highly successful social worker in private practice where she uses listening skills, <u>RCT</u> and <u>Breaking Free From the Past</u> to minister life to clients much like she was in the past.

Broken persons will move toward maturity in a healthy congregation. This is similar to the process of osmosis. Healing can be a gradual, often unconscious process of assimilation or absorption similar to learning a language in a new culture. Health or sickness is transferred from the majority to individual members. Our task is to raise the level of congregational health as well as specifically minister to the *Type B* members. After equipping the leaders to minister life to the majority, we must also equip Paraprofessionals to counsel those who are addicted, depressed, anxious, or reactive.

Recent research with seminary students was designed see how they responded to people in trouble. Some were chosen because they came to seminary with a strong desire to help the poor and needy. Others were chosen at random. Some were asked to prepare a sermon on the topic "The Good Samaritan" and others could choose any topic on which to speak. Some were told that they had to rush over to the church to deliver the sermon while others were informed that there was no hurry. All were faced with a sick man by the road.

As they walked to the church, which group stopped to help the groaning man on the ground? The students who had a drive to minister to the needy? Or those immersed in the story of the Good Samaritan? Or, did that make any difference? Only one factor was found to be significant: whether or not the students were in a hurry to get to the church to preach.

The difference was in the *Context* not the *Content*. The unhurried students stopped more often to help the groaning man. Those in a hurry to preach about the Good Samaritan did not act like one. The environment was more influential than words. Jesus noted that we ought not pray as the pagans who thought God impersonal. They think they must pray constantly in order to get their gods' attention. Jesus said to pray simply and directly as a way of showing our faith in a living God. Pagans turn prayer wheels for hours but the Lord's prayer lasts but a few seconds. A church filled with attitudes of love will produce members who care but a climate that portrays God as distant, hard of hearing and impersonal will produce angry, distant non-listeners, who treat others with irritation and sinners with rage.

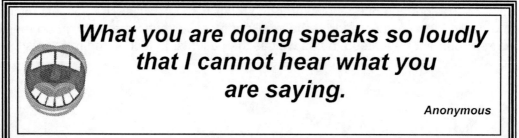

An Equipping System for the Church

We are passionate about teaching Lifeskills to everyone and develop a *Context* of love. We also like to establish specialized helping ministries for the care and cure of souls. To do this, we have identified seven levels of training: Prevention, Personal Growth, Peer Support, Professional Entry, Clinical, and Expert.

The first three, Prevention, Personal Growth and Peer Support, focus on equipping the entire congregation with first aid processes for the soul and spirit.

- ***Primary prevention***-proactive efforts to reduce emotional and behavioral deficits or disorders or maintain healthy functioning; and
- ***Secondary prevention***-early identification, diagnosis, and treatment of deficits to avert more serious breakdown or establish healthy functioning.

For either kind of preventive effort, the audience can be classified into one of two key strategies: *raising protective factors* and *lowering risk factors*. Protective factors add to the chances that people's lives will improve over time and lowering risk factors target specific issues and predictable problems.

An important dimension of healing churches is the development of special classes for couples preparing for marriage. Gary recruited a lay Helper who was finishing her master's degree in counseling to design the ministry as her thesis. It accomplished both primary and secondary interventions by preparing for the transition into marriage. It also provided resolution of conflict over differences like financial decisions, parenting styles, and cultural expectations and prepared the couples to resist relationship deterioration in life crises such as a serious illness or a job change. It also gave them social support for self-esteem and practical aid.

A very interesting class was designed by Gary for families facing teenagers. Adolescence is not a disease nor do we require counseling for it. However, parents need to be prepared to rear kids who are facing their issues of growing up, leaving home, dating, preparing for college and developing new peer relationships. Parents and their children met for discussions, teaching and support.

Both of us sponsored classes on parenting, listening, problem solving, conflict management, renewed thinking and prayer therapy/inner healing. Hundreds grew personally and became spontaneous Peer Helpers. The Bethel Bible teachers attended listening and small group dynamics classes and it changed their teaching approach. They moved from lecturing on facts into developing communities of care with biblical facts and a biblical lifestyle. Several of these teachers went on to become Professional counselors.

In this way we equipped the *Type A members* for Prevention, Personal Growth and Peer Helping. *Type B* members also attended the classes where they received healing, reducing the need for individual counseling. Several became lay Helpers who taught the classes and served as Listeners in the Teleios Ministry, becoming a self-replicating cycle of health and maturity.

Lay Training Process

Paraprofessionals work alongside and under a professional's direction. The selection criteria are: (1) A passion for caring (2) Enough knowledge to tell others about the principles (3) A willingness to receive specialized training (4) Gifts of teaching, helps or leadership (5) Teachable, available and dependable (6) A good character and reputation (7) Can submit to authority and supervision. Our five stages of training are:

1. We teach, you learn
2. We teach, you observe/support other students
3. We teach, you assist
4. You teach, we assist
5. You teach, others assist

After training, graduates are able to carry on alone as teachers and lay Helpers. The pastoral staff's counseling load was dramatically lowered after two years of equipping and opening the Teleios Center. They normally spent 12 to 15 hours each week in counseling. However, their load was reduced to zero. Additionally, the following ministries drew heavily from our graduates:

- A monthly healing service
- Small group leaders
- Support/Recovery groups
- Pastoring the sick and homebound
- Deacons and Community Ministries
- Marriage and Family ministries
- The Teleios Counseling Ministry

Many Lifeskills graduates found that their newly acquired skills were in demand at work, school and in the community. One of our Trustees says that learning to listen saved his job. The pressure on companies to integrate minorities and women into the workplace put a premium on caring colleagues. Men who failed to relate harmoniously were warned and then released. Brad took the listening class after receiving a warning from his boss and discovered that it was exactly what he needed to survive and thrive.

 Life Scan Summary

The church is the *most powerful healing community that the world has ever known.* The church grows and reproduces in a continuous cycle of life when the right nutrients of truth, love and power exist together. A healing community has *grace and truth for outsiders* and *healing flow for insiders.* It welcomes the broken hearted, the wounded, the forgotten and lonely but challenges members to live out the truth on the journey of transformation. Healing comes from love encounters, truth encounters, and power encounters. We can raise the level and functioning of the church by developing a systematic, sequential, and systemic approach of training everyone in Lifeskills.

TIPS for Life

Personal Reflection and Practice

- Recall a time when you spiritually grew or experienced healing.
- What was most helpful?
- How did you realize growth or healing had occurred?
- How did it affect your relationship with others?
- How did it affect your relationship with God?
- What was it like to adjust to the changes from the growth or healing?
- What did you learn from the experience?

3

Four Essentials of Effective Helping

And now these three remain: faith, hope and love. But the greatest of these is love.
1 Corinthians 13:13

Resolve to be a master of change rather than a victim
of change. - Brian Tracy

Many find the account of Woody Allen's counseling disgusting. They are appalled by the idea that a person can spend 30 years in psychotherapy and still rationalize away his bizarre, immoral and abusive behavior. In spite of great investments in time, money, and effort, Mr. Allen is apparently no better off after all those years of therapy. It is easy to conclude from this case that counseling is a futile activity.

This stereotype is not true. People usually do get better when they see counselors, lay or professional. In fact, research on counseling effectiveness consistently points out that the majority of people who seek help for their problems do improve. Woody is an abnormal example instead of a poster boy for successful treatment. Most Seekers make positive changes when talking through their problems and exploring solutions with a Helper. This is encouraging for it means that our desire to be useful change agents is founded in reality. We can help Humpty and Mrs. Dumpty get their act together.

Keep it Short, Easy and Relatable (KISSER)

Thankfully, research has also uncovered the aspects that contribute most to achieving successful change. Four separate factors are essential to fostering a person's growth, and healing. They are *Content, Confidence, Caring Interaction, and Context*. This is true whether we are working with Type A or Type B church members. In order to be a successful change agent, we need to master each of these four factors.

The first factor that contributes to a positive outcome is the *Content* of the Helper's conversations. This includes his theoretical convictions, expertise and skill at using a specific technique. For example, a physician must learn how to do differentiate one disease from another in order to prescribe the best drug to heal patient's disease.

Thousands of men and women pursue graduate degrees in counseling, social work, psychology and psychiatry. They amass great stores of knowledge about the 600 hundred plus counseling theories that have been created in the last 30 years. The preponderance of graduate school curricula is focused on teaching the students a specific model with a specific *Content*. This approach is based on the medical model theory that mental and emotional disorders can be treated in the same way that we treat a physical disease. *Content* covers the didactic theories about the causes and cures of behavioral problems as well as the ideas about what to do to solve those problems.

Content is also the preferred curriculum in many paraprofessional programs. We are urged to read books and attend seminars on the theories of Christian Counseling. The shelves of Christian bookstores groan with titles on setting boundaries, inner healing, deliverance, child discipline, finding your significance, divorce recovery and Multiple Personality Disorder. Unfortunately, they are contradictory and translate poorly into action, leaving paraprofessionals confused and befuddled. However, the right *Content* does contribute to good outcomes if applied in the right ways.

> *All effort is in the last analysis sustained by the faith that it is worth making.*
>
> **Ordway Tweed**

A second factor is the Seeker's *Confidence* that the Helper and the helping process will be beneficial to him. The Seeker needs to have hope that he can get better. To simply talk about our problems can be comforting but *Confidence* in the Helper is key to change. Without it, he/she may drop out of the process or fail to follow through on essential action steps.

The Bible calls this hope and faith. God is always with us to transform our pain and give us comfort. At first we may not see how the Lord is working when we have a problem. Through prayer and love the Seeker can begin to trust God and the Helper for a new beginning. Hope is an emotional and spiritual sense that we can succeed. People who persevere in the face of pain, problems, and pressures usually have hope.

Faith is a conviction that God is with us in our troubles. It is often expressed in an active prayer life. There are few atheists in the foxholes of emotional pain, and we need to encourage faith through our own prayer life and biblical focus. Wise Helpers look for ways to tap into the Seeker's hope, faith and trust that God will use the counseling process to help him/her move on in life.

The third factor is the *Caring Interaction* between the Helper and Seeker. Counseling is a *cooperative relationship between two people.* Christian counsel includes God in the relationship. Over 40 years of research on counseling outcomes concludes that the *quality* of the relationship is critical to growth and healing. The core skills needed to bring results are being genuine, respectful, empathetic, and warm (GREW). Mastery of the GREW skills is essential not only for care and counsel but for all effective ministry.

Gary's 1975 doctoral dissertation integrated research on the core skills and evangelical theology. Out of this work came the Teleios Ministry, several books on training lay and professional Helpers, the establishment of Lifeway Counseling Centers and the Lifeway inpatient hospital. The original materials were called <u>Apples of Gold</u> based on the truth that, *Words properly spoken are like apples of gold in a tray of silver.* Proverbs 25:11 Humpty's restoration depends upon having pastors and friends who relate to him with the GREW attitudes and skills.

The final factor is the person's *Context* or the *Climate* away from the Helping relationship. Spontaneous events, supportive people and answers to prayer influence how a Seeker responds to our influence. The motivation to change may come from unplanned events such as illness, pregnancy, death, job changes, radio programs, sermons, books, or relational interactions. We call it SOS for *Support Outside Sessions* and it can be either an ill or a kind wind.

ontent
onfidence
aring
ontext

Within *Context* are also the personal strengths, resources, and resiliency of the Seeker. These traits strongly affect the course and outcome of any change process. All of us have attempted to motivate people who were unwilling to act because their friends might be upset. Parents who wish their teenagers would resist peer pressure know this concept well. Recognizing and utilizing the strengths of the Seeker's support system and motivational factors can make the difference between staying stuck at *Considering Change* or moving on to make a *Commitment* to change.

Unfortunately, many Seekers are not aware of all their resources or underutilize their strengths and this will inevitably increase the duration of their problem. A positive outcome is dependent upon Seeker self-awareness and self-motivation. Wise Helpers uncover the person's strengths and put them to work.

The family, social network, work environment and religious support systems are all positive influencers. Worship services as well as support, fellowship, and recovery groups are key parts of a wholistic system of care. Over 70% of Americans say their whole life is built on religion. In fact, research clearly reveals that family stability, hope and attendance at worship services are the most important factors in the prevention of alcoholism, drug abuse and suicide. Additionally, we know that depression and heart attacks are negatively correlated with church attendance.

To neglect the Seeker's *Context* is tantamount to counseling malpractice. Dramatic changes sometimes occur in chronic situations after a person hears a sermon, experiences a positive family event or encounters the Lord. The Helper has no influence over these blessings yet should listen for and build upon them to affirm the Seeker's growth.

A woman recently called the Lifeway Counseling Center to get help for overcoming childhood abuse. During the first meeting Debbie listened while Sharon poured out her anguish and shame. At the end, Sharon said, "I feel so much better, you have really been helpful." What was the major factor used by Debbie? Was it *Content, Caring Relationship, Seeker Confidence* or *Context*?

During the second meeting, Sharon said, "I am not sure that I can ever get over this pain. Have you ever seen people like me get better?" Debbie replied, "Yes, but it may take some time. Every person in your shoes can experience substantial healing through counseling. I see it all the time." What factor was Debbie supporting here?

Sharon mentioned that her pastor severely condemned women who had been abused. Debbie listened, clarified the situation and asked if Sharon would like to join a Christian support group for abused women. Which factor is the focus of this interaction?

Finally, Debbie asked Sharon to name times when she was able to rise above her abuse. She also prayed for Sharon's inner healing and gave her a copy of, Renewed Christian Thinking. They spent one session discussing how Sharon could renew her mind according to the scripture. What factor is emphasized here?

> *Making the simple complicated is commonplace; making the simple, awesomely simple, that's creativity.*
>
> **Charles Mingus**

These four factors cover all the essential elements of a caring relationship. They are real whether we are helping as a friend, family member, mentor, pastor, boss, paraprofessional or professional counselor. The four factors are the foundation stones and support structure around which efficient and effective influence occurs.

The Professional's Surprise

In graduate school and preparation to be clinical therapists, neither of us ever heard of these four factors. Instead, we focused on mastering the one factor of *Content.* Interestingly, the researchers also estimated the influence of each factor. Even though all are four are important, some are more powerful than others. Try to guess which factor has the greatest percentage on finding a solution. (A solution equals 100% success.)

1. *Content* of the counselor. (School knowledge.) ___%
2. *Client Confidence*. (I have faith that he/she can help me.) ___%
3. *Caring Relationship of Client and Counselor*. (As seen by the Client.) ___%
4. *Context of the Client's life*. (Motivational level and supportive people.) ___%

If one seeks assistance for depression the counsel will vary dramatically according to the Helper he chooses. A person with a medical model might say, "All you need to do is take this medicine." This is based on *Content* and depends upon the ability of the Helper to diagnose and treat the depressive illness. The Seeker, his family, church, friends and motivation are not important. The Helper is active and the Seeker is expected to be passive.

A second counselor with a medical model may say, "I will tell you how to renew your mind. When you think correctly the depression will go away." Others with a *Content* model believe that inner healing, deliverance or Neuro-Linguistic Programming (NLP) will do the trick. These approaches depend almost totally upon the Helper's knowledge and expertise. He is the hero and the Seeker is dependent upon his ability to pray, teach or prescribe.

Some counselors will do little more than build a solid relationship with the Seeker because they think that *Caring Relationship* can unilaterally heal the wounded heart and remove the depression. Medicine or other interventions are not needed. "Just love people and they will change. "All they need is someone to love and accept them."

A few people see problems as having little to do with the Helper's skills or interventions and certainly not his caring love. They say the Seeker should make all the changes herself. It is up to the depressed person to have the motivation and necessary to get better. This is the view that the *Context* factor is all that matters. "If you will get out of bed and go to work everything will be fine." Loving relationships, medicine, renewed thinking or prayer for healing are not necessary. Still others point to peer group, family dysfunction and the presence of the media as making victims of the Seeker.

Some believers place their emphasis on faith and hope. "Only believe and you will be healed," is their cry. A pastor with this view once visited a member who was in the Lifeway hospital. "If," he said, "you had enough faith you would leave the hospital now and be healed." She resisted his manipulative urgings and stayed to receive substantial healing. The faith movement has rightly emphasized the power of our belief but it sometimes comes across as a panacea rather than reality. Thankfully, God's power, grace and mercy are always available whether we have faith or not. Sometimes we must have faith for a Seeker.

Balance is the Key

"But," you ask, "which of these counselors is the most effective? Is one superior to another." The answer is simple. All four factors are important to successful growth. However, some factors are more influential than others. You, like we, may find the research surprising. Have you already made your own estimates?

Researchers have discovered that *Content* contributes about 15% of the movement toward a 100% *solution*. Despite our love of teaching a great deal of *Content*, it is not the most important part of healing and growth. Although most seminars, books and teachings focus on Didactic or intellectual thinking, it accounts for a very small portion of the change process. Paraprofessionals are usually encouraged by this revelation because it further confirms that they can be effective Helpers. A formal, graduate school education is not as important as they thought. Oh, what a relief it is to see what really works in life.

> *The physician must be prepared not only to do what is right himself but also to make the patient, the attendants and externals cooperate.*
> **Hippocrates**

We know it will work in practice but are not sure it will work in theory. Roy Underhill

Another 15% is provided by the Seeker's *Confidence*. His hope, faith and positive expectation will improve his situation as much as all the Helper's techniques and knowledge. A pill is only as effective as the Seeker's belief in it. Anything that destroys *Confidence* reduces the possibility of finding an effective solution. This shows how important it is for physicians to learn and use all four factors.

You probably already guessed that *Caring Interactions* add greatly to the progress of growth. The Bible has once again been proven to be right about the things that are important. In I Corinthians 13, the Apostle Paul compares many things to love and all of them come up short. For example, the beautiful speech of tongues or angels does not compare with love, nor do prophetic words or a deep knowledge of biblical and psychological theories. A counselor's faith or charitable gifts haven't the positive effect of loving relationships. Paul's view is supported by the research that shows *Caring* adding some 30% to the process of finding a lasting solution for any problem.

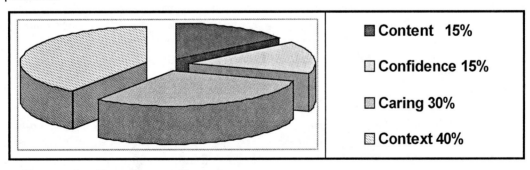

■ Content 15%	
□ Confidence 15%	
▨ Caring 30%	
▩ Context 40%	

Factors that Contribute to Change

Helpers need to relate with love in a practical way. In our view, the active use of Lifeskills is an outward manifestation of the fruit of the Spirit. When we integrate all the Lifeskills into Helping and adapt them to the Seeker's situation, good things happen in both persons. If the alliance between us is good, the Seeker will probably grow. Without the fruit, however, relationships suffer and progress is more likely to break down.

Context

Truth separated from Experience will always remain in doubt.

GRS

If you have been adding, you know that *Context* is the factor having the greatest bearing upon positive changes. Effective change agents help Seekers put the *Context* to work. We understand and respect the people, systems and events that promote good and bad decisions and helps us influence their responses to up-building influences.

While attending a seminar in Chicago, Gary spoke with a therapist who resisted the notion that pastors could have an important role with his clients. "The pastors may not agree with my treatment," he said, "so I do not want them to know what I am doing. I try to keep them out of the client's life and my practice. They are not psychologically trained and do not understand my profession. I try to keep these people away from church and from religion. That is their biggest problem." Gary pointed out that such an attitude was self-defeating, harmful to the Seekers and doomed to failure.

Pastors are critically important to the ongoing welfare of his clients, but he was ignorant of the fact. It is arrogant and disrespectful to take such a stand, yet it is common. However, we did not point that out to this therapist who assumed that his expertise alone was enough to heal hurting hearts. Instead, we noted that the client spends more time at church than with the counselor so it is impossible to prevent the church's influence.

While clients may spend about an hour each week with a counselor, the other 167 hours are spent with friends, family and coworkers. Religious clients spend two to ten hours each week in worship, study and group meetings. It would be foolish to ignore such an important source of assistance and medicine for the soul.

The *Context* also has to do with a Seeker's level of motivation, personality and temperament. As the old saying goes: *You can lead a horse to water but you cannot make him drink.* To that we add, *You can lead a man to truth but you cannot make him think.* The conviction of the Seeker is very important to the change process. Whether we are trying to encourage a diet, a new language, smoking cessation or healing of depression, we go take many small steps on the way to success. By tuning into and accommodating ourselves to the Seeker's ways of thinking, motivational level, and personality we can increase our influence.

In years past, we relied on inner healing experts like John and Paula Sandford to tell us what to do and when to do it. Perhaps this is one reason so many fell back into trouble after they had been "miraculously healed and delivered." Relapse was so prevalent that we said that people had, "lost their healing." After so many failures, we finally learned not to rush in quickly with inner healing prayer or deliverance. Now we spend more time assessing the four factors and getting the client's agreement before we pray. As a result, we see few instances of people losing their healing or having dramatic relapses.

It is important to understand what a person does during the 167 hours he is not with us. We discuss his friends, work mates, family members and church colleagues. Are they encouraging growth and healing or do they pull the client down to their level of dysfunction? One man said would quit drinking if it did not mean losing all his friends. His drinking was not only the result of internal wounds. It was also related to the need for social connections. To motivate him to stop drinking we also helped him find new friends.

At a seminar on child rearing in Scandinavia, we were asked to consult with a pastor who was frustrated with the behavior of his youngest child. After listening for about thirty minutes, we discerned that the boy was extremely sensitive to noise, light and rapid movement. The parents were unaware that the way our brains are wired can make a dramatic difference in learning, obedience and behavior reactions. They had been expecting the child to act exactly as his big brothers had and were angry with his "rebellious" behavior. However, the boy was not rebellious but overly sensitive. He didn't need punishment but peace and quiet. Knowing how he was built enabled his parents to provide better ways for the child to mature in peace.

Researchers from Brown University wrote an article in the New England Journal of Medicine saying that even the most powerful new medications are not effective when used alone. Depression and anxiety are the most common behavioral problems in America. There is essentially no difference in outcomes between talk therapy and medication therapy when used separately. However, effectiveness jumps when used simultaneously. (Peggy Eastman, February 2001 AARP Bulletin)

- Anti-depressant & anti-anxiety drugs alone elicited a 55% positive outcome
- Talk therapy alone elicited a 52% positive outcome
- Drugs and talk together elicited an 85% positive outcome

There was a 30% increase in effectiveness when a combination of only two factors was used. They did not even analyze *Context*, the factor that has the greatest influence. Many studies show the power of church attendance, community involvement, prayer, support groups, recovery groups and other positive peer systems. The Brown research again shows that all four factors are important to growth and healing.

Steps to Change

Although Alcoholics Anonymous and other steps groups long ago concluded that healing comes "One day at a time one step at a time," recent research sheds new insight about the stages of growth. For twenty years a group investigated how people intentionally change. They studied men and women who had successfully modified unwanted habits without outside assistance and compared them with folk who changed with counseling. It gave special attention to those who overcame addiction to alcohol, nicotine, and food.

After a great deal of head scratching and thinking, the scientists concluded that there are actually six steps in the process of change. This means that knowing the stage at which a person finds himself is an excellent predictor of what the Helper ought to do to get a positive outcome. The provide us with a map outlining a Seeker's motivational level at any point in time, and implies how we can best encourage them to continue to change. We are also able to minister to a slowly changing Seeker without getting frustrated or discouraged.

People are not necessarily rebellious or in denial when they are at one of the early stages. Motivation is not a static trait but a dynamic process that is the product of the four factors. *All people are motivated but not necessarily motivated at the same level or to do the same things as the Helper.* The success of our advice, biblical intervention, confrontation or prayer will vary greatly according to the person's motivational stage.

**There is a Tide in the affairs of men,
which, taken at the flood, leads on to Fortune:
Omitted, all the voyage of their life is bound and in Miseries. –
*William Shakespeare***

The Six Stages of Change

The motivational level of the Seeker is of critical importance to how much progress we can make in our helping relationship. It is vital, therefore, that we understand his motivational state and respond effectively. Prochaska and DiClemente developed one of the most practical and helpful insights on how to understand and respond to a Seeker's motivation. According to them, all of us go through six stages as we move toward finding solutions to life's problems. They are: *Pre-Conviction, Conviction, Considering Change, Change Commitment, Continuing to Change and Completion of the process.*

The first stage is *Pre-Conviction.* At this time a person does not believe she has a problem. She may feel coerced by others to talk with us or she may ask for help to please a family member, employer or the court system. Despite coming to us, she is not personally motivated to change even in a crisis. The Seeker may temporarily modify her behavior during a crisis but as soon as the pressure is off she will return to her old form. For instance, a smoker who attends a stop smoking class because of her doctor's advice might say, "As far as I know, I don't have a problem with smoking. I don't really need to change."

> *It isn't that they can't see the solution. It is that they can't see the problem. G. K. Chesterton*

Conviction sets in when we become personally aware of a problem. The light goes on inside the smoker's head and she senses the need to change. She contemplates the fact that reduced consumption could be a good thing. She begins to wrestle with the pros and cons of possible solutions. The emphasis is on *thinking about change* rather than *Commitment*. The smoker is on a seesaw rocking back and forth from change to staying the same. She may say, "I have a problem and I really should work on it. I've been thinking about changing that bad habit."

Later the smoker will move to the place where she believes that change is actually going to happen. This is the very important *Considering Stage* where she may even experiment with small changes to see how it feels to smoke fewer cigarettes each day. She will also figure out what will or will not work as she moves up the stages of change.

Researchers originally left this stage out by assuming people went directly from *Conviction to Commitment*. After closer analysis, they realized the importance of the processes that take place in the *Considering Stage*. Before moving on to *Commitment to Change*, we need time to live with the implications and discomfort that it will demand. Taking a radical step forward is not easy and we need to carefully consider what it will cost. She will say, "Oh yes, I definitely am going to quit and soon. I'm getting ready but there is a lot to do before hand."

When the Seeker reaches a firm commitment and activates her plan, she is entering *The Commitment to Change*. It is marked by strong, visible, overt, actions like throwing the cigarettes away and buying a medical patch. Others notice and talk about it. However, *Commitment* can be stressful for all concerned. Maybe this is why Jesus respectfully asked the paralytic man at the pool of Bethesda if he wanted to be healed. Being healed is costly if one has had the comfort of victim status. People may say, "I am working hard. Anyone can talk about change, but I am actually doing it."

Gary finally quit smoking after trying hundreds of times. After each meal he automatically reached for a smoke. While drinking coffee or in the middle of a deep conversation he felt anxious without a cigarette. To quit this dirty and disgusting habit, many other behaviors had to change in addition to puffing on a cigarette. Finally, a break through came when his daughter was born, and he saw the danger of prematurely ending his life. This *Context* factor was enough for him to discard the cigarettes and never smoke again.

The next step, *Continuing to Change,* is when the Seeker consolidates her gains and maintains the new habit. Maintenance requires constant learning about the new lifestyle. Since there is temptation to relapse, we need to help her develop a relapse prevention plan to keep her from falling back into one of the earlier stages. If a relapse does occur it is easy to become discouraged and hopeless. We must be ready to encourage a disheartened Seeker to get up on the horse and ride again.

Relapses are normal and do not mean that the person will not continue the changes begun. In fact, we can learn valuable insights from the events that led up to the relapse and assist the Seeker by asking good questions, evaluating what helped and what hindered the progress and what to avoid the next time. Healing is stressful and only step by step practice over a long period of time reverses old habits and develops new ones.

Completed Closure occurs when she has 100% confidence that she can maintain her new behavior. She has no temptation to smoke and relapses are very rare. At this point, the new behavior itself has become a positive habit that is difficult to break. This is our goal and we can rejoice. Learning a new habit is like learning any new skill. It takes perseverance, hope, faith, support and practice, practice, practice. In Chapter One we laid out the phases of mastering a new learning and *Closure* is the place where we are unconsciously acting on a new habit pattern.

> *Small things done with Love can change the World.* Mother Teresa

Life Scan Summary

One lesson to take away from this chapter is the importance of understanding and accommodating ourselves to the Seeker's situation. If one is stuck at *Pre-Conviction* we are much more likely to see him find a solution we patiently listen to his feelings until he moves to *Conviction*. This will result in greater change than if we push him to make a *Commitment* before he is ready. Those who take only one step forward in the early stages are twice as likely to realize *Closure* than if they do not move at all.

The four factors and the six stages are interrelated. When one is not yet willing to commit, we can relax, pray and look for ways to help him find motivating people. Our expertise accounts for only 15% of the change and it encourages us to pray more and talk less. Putting the whole puzzle together gives us peace. After suffering a slight heart attack a friend of ours remained unconvinced that exercise was needed. Rather than urge him to go to the gym, we patiently waited and listened to his side of the story, praying that he would gain insight and wisdom. He was finally *Convicted* and before long *Considered Change*. We knew he would not go all the way to the *Change Commitment* in one fell swoop.

Sometimes a *Pre-Convicted* person will gain insights through a self-test. Lifeway Counseling Centers provides self-assessment checklists to churches so they can be filled out in private. A person picks one off a rack and takes it home to read to see if the checks add up to a potential problem. It may open him up to *Conviction* or *Considering Change*. The person moves toward *Commitment* without any direct assistance. Hope is essential to convincing *Pre-Convicted* persons to seek assistance. Robert Spitzer, M.D., recently proved that homosexuals are able to change their same sex attractions and behavior. This is a tremendous step forward in the battle to provide healing for this group of suffering people. It challenges the myth that sexual preference is immutable and offers hope to millions who want to be free. His simple research study has the potential to touch millions of *Pre-Convicted* homosexuals with the truth so we now must move them toward to the *Considering Change stage* by prayer, love and hope for healing.

TIPS for Life

Personal Reflection and Practice

Change is inevitable. It is something we do on a daily basis. What <u>small</u> change would you like to make to improve your life? Below is an example of a Lifeway checklist to help you consider any changes that may benefit you.

- What is the best and worst that could happen if you make this change?
- Who will the change impact most?
- How will it affect family, fellow workers, children and church members?
- What do I need to do before making the change?
- Who can help me with this change, and how?
- What will be the cost of not making the change?
- How will I make this change work in my life?
- How long will the journey take? In your mind walk through the stages.
- How long will you take for each stage? How will it proceed?
- How will you know the change has occurred?
- How will you acknowledge your successful changes?

4

A Road Map for Helping

Do nothing that will not edify or build up. Ephesians 4:29

We travel to several countries to teach and equip the church each year, and the challenges of each trip are varied and exciting. As any ambassador on foreign soil, we need maps and tour books so we do not get lost. It is easy to become disoriented, confused about directions, and distracted by the sights and sounds in the new surroundings. The customs, languages and traditions of each country are different, so the possibility of misunderstandings and errors are great.

In some places, the language is similar enough to English to get a bus or cab. However, in Taiwan and Russia the alphabet is so different that there is no English comparison and confusion is common. A taxi ride from the airport to a flat in St. Petersburg took Gary two hours because the driver could not find the address that was written in English. Counseling is similar to visiting a foreign country for Helpers must master all the cross-cultural communications challenges between them and the Seeker. Lifeskills' is designed to teach Helpers how to communicate in the culture, language and customs of the different Seekers.

Lifeskills follows a simple road map to help you navigate the new terrain of care and counsel. The guidebook provides a clear process of navigation among the twists and turns in this new, unfamiliar territory. Each encounter has its own language, customs and taboos, much of which is difficult to understand. Our map will enable you to gauge the progress of a Seeker's cooperation and recognize when you are lost, violating some obscure custom or getting into dangerous territory.

- It lays out a plan for each stage of the journey.
- It indicates the signposts to look for.
- It reveals the mile markers along the journey.
- It warns of dangerous curves and slippery roads.
- It gives hints about what do if you get stuck or lost.
- It tells you how to ask for directions.
- It offers simple ways to get back on the road.

Why Do We Need a Map?

Despite the fact that most parents are not experts in child rearing, they do need to understand how their children's needs vary at different stages. There are simply too many factors to remember every detail about a child's development, nutrition, illnesses, cures and rules of good discipline. However, we can learn the most important aspects of child rearing at each stage of his/her development. A child of three works on learning letters, colors and shapes, not philosophy. A child of ten needs speaking, listening, reading, writing and spelling skills rather than training on how to write a novel. A teenager is preparing to launch out in life as an independent young man or woman not preparing for retirement.

In the same manner, new believers are counting the cost of following Christ rather than learning to be pastoral leaders. A mature believer needs to look at her gifts and integrate church life with work and home. A wise Helper knows how to gauge the needs, desires and motivational levels of a Seeker at each stage of his/her growth and maturity. Otherwise, we will be like parents who expect their three-year-old child to understand and care for them. Wise leaders support Seekers at each particular growth level and resist advocating acts too advanced for the person to do in real life.

The Lifeskills Road Map is designed to help us assess the Seeker's level of motivation and maturity so we can maximize our influence at each stage of the growth/healing process. Is the Seeker at the beginning of the change process, the middle, or near the end? Are we cooperatively working to teach the alphabet, sentence structure or a graduate school research paper? The Helper's approach, involvement, suggestions and goals will be different for each person since no two people are at the same place with God.

Helping is not for the benefit of the Helper but for the Seeker. Preaching is for the listener not for the preacher. Group life is for the cell member not the leader. Servant leaders must learn how to lay down personal priorities, plans and ideas to fit the needs of the one seeking ministry. Mature servant leaders are experts at discerning the Seeker's needs. After discernment comes a wise intervention of grace and truth, leaving the result to the Holy Spirit. Our techniques are not infallible nor are they designed to put us in control of the outcome. In fact, they should lead us to more dependency on God, not us.

> *Helping is not for the benefit of the Helper but for the Seeker.*

Timing and Helpful Actions

Timing and accurate, effective input are the two most important parts of choosing an effective *Content* intervention. Doing the right thing at the right time in the right way is our goal. Perhaps the most common complaint we hear from trainees is frustration about Seekers who tell them the same stories again and again. "How do we get the Seeker to move on? We are unable to get people unstuck from that one issue." The answer is not easy but it is simple. When a Helper with the discernment of the Holy Spirit, lovingly responds to the Seeker's true needs, at the right time in the right way, we are more likely to discover the Lord's solution. The power of the message is directly related to the peace of the messenger; and the peace of the messenger is directly related to resting in Christ.

Christian Interventions in Pastoral Care and Counseling

Helpers have many possible interventions to choose from in ministry. We can pray for healing, confront sin, give advice, quote scripture, ask questions, listen, argue or cast out demons. However, deciding *when* to act is as important as *what* to choose as an action. Sometimes people suggest the same answer to every problem. Every so often, an old intervention with a new name comes along and many join the cause because the testimonies of proponents sound so good. For example, prayer therapy or inner healing has many names and new practitioners arise every so

> **Doing the Right thing at the Wrong time is as futile as doing the Wrong thing at the right time.**

often. In each incarnation, we hear that patient care with warm, loving listening and wise counsel is no longer needed. All we have to do is ask Jesus to heal the broken heart and bring truth to the lies. Then the Seeker will be completely restored.

Although God heals wounded hearts and delivers us from Satan, we know of very few people who have been immediately delivered from immaturity and bad habits. Discipleship, in addition to prayer and spiritual warfare, is the rule. We are familiar with most Christian counseling models. No matter what method you prefer, it can be integrated into a more comprehensive model of healing and discipleship. Lifeskills will expand the number of tools in your toolbox and teach you the right time and right way to use each of them.

If the only tool we have is a hammer,
every problem will look like a nail. Anon

Remember that there are three categories or tools of biblical interventions: *The Tool of Truth, the Tool of Love and the Tool of Power.* It is easy to quote scriptural truth but to quote the *right* scripture at the *right* time in the *right* way and get the *right* results is not so easy. It is easy to pray, to advise, to confront and to conduct spiritual warfare. However, it is not so easy to confront, pray, deliver or give advice in the *right* way at the *right* time. Wise Helpers know how and when to use each tool to get the best results. All tools are not equally effective at all times. The following table illustrates this situation.

The Wrong Thing at The Wrong Time	*The Wrong Thing* at The Right Time
The Right Thing at The Wrong Time	**The Right Thing** *at* **The Right Time**

There are four options facing us each time we minister. The wrong thing at the wrong time is the worst of all worlds. For example, sharing the gospel is a good thing, but witnessing to an unbeliever, at the wrong time can be harmful. We prefer to say the right things about salvation at the right time and see the person pray to receive Christ. The effectiveness of the intervention is multiplied when timing and ministry intersect perfectly.

We became enamored with the Tool of Power during the Jesus Movement and we used those techniques often for healing of memories and spiritual warfare. We knew that Jesus could enter a painful memory and eradicate its negative dimensions in body, soul and spirit. We also saw Jesus clean out invading spirits time after time. This intervention was a great source of healing and we looked for any opportunity to "use it" on our walking wounded. We laid hands on people at any time of night or day because we were eager to see God's power at work.

Unfortunately, we got ahead of the Lord and often saw ineffective results. In fact, the Lord told us to stop practicing spiritual warfare until we better understood how the process and timing of power intersected most effectively with the Tools of Truth and Love. After several months of study, we changed our timing and saw a dramatic increase in positive outcomes. We had been using the right intervention but at the wrong time. After we changed the process, hurting people improved more rapidly and experienced fewer relapses. Jesus warned His followers about the dangers of rushing into deliverance prayer too quickly.

> When an evil spirit comes out of a man, it goes through arid places seeking rest and does not find it. Then it says, 'I will return to the house I left.' When it arrives, it finds the house unoccupied, swept clean and put in order. Then it goes and takes with it seven other spirits more wicked than itself, and they go in and live there. In addition, the final condition of that man is worse than the first.
> Matt 12:43-45

Three Stages of the Helping Road Map

The map is based on the assumption that Helping is a cooperative relationship between a Helper, Seeker and God. Helpers are trying to understand the heart of another human and the heart of God. Only then will we discover God's solutions to their problems. Our road map is called *The VCR of Cooperative Relationships* for it has three highway markers with the signs, *V, C,* and *R.* Each marker alerts us to the motivational level of the Seeker and what our most effective cooperative response is at that point. A Seeker at the *Pre-Conviction* stage requires a different interaction than one who is *Committed to change.* How can we judge what is needed at each stage?

> *When he, the Spirit of truth, comes, he will guide you into*
> *all truth. He will not speak on his own; he will speak*
> *only what he hears,*
> *and he will tell you what is yet to come. He will bring*
> *glory to me by taking from what is mine and making it*
> *known to you. John 16:7-14*

The Holy Spirit is the true Counselor. He convicts us of sin, calls us to repentance, and shows us how to proceed. We must take care not to become impatient and attempt to do His work for Him. We cannot be the Holy Spirit for anyone, not even ourselves. Medical doctors understand that they can only place the bones together so God can do the healing. Although we want to be *like* Jesus we *are* not fully open to the Spirit. We are not omniscient.

Jesus had tremendous discernment about people's motivation. He knew when to accept and when to confront; when to touch and when to pray without touching; when to visit the sick and when to delay His visits; when to have compassion on the multitudes and when to leave them behind. We too need the gift of discernment to carry out a healing ministry. We can strengthen discernment through study and practice, but only the Holy Spirit can understand the heart of another person. The VCR Model Road Map is designed to help us in the discernment process.

- It helps us relax and trust God.
- It allows us to assess the Seeker's level of motivation.
- It simplifies the six stages of change.
- It shows us when an intervention will be most influential.

- It reminds us how to avoid mistakes that can block progress.
- It helps us focus on the four factors of influence.
- It guides us in timing, prayer focus, homework and interventions.
- It allows us to gauge our progress from one session to another.

The VCR Road Map stages of cooperation are simple and easy to remember.

The Visitor-Host Stage

V
- Seekers are uninterested in change
- Helpers are good Hosts

The Complainant-Listener Stage

C
- Seeker admits problems
- Sees others as responsible for solutions.
- Helpers listen, clarify and get specific

The Ready for Change-Solution Focused Stage

R
- Seeker desire to change themselves
- Seeker will work hard on goals
- Helper cooperates with goals

Stage One: Visitor-Host Relationship

We call the person who sees no personal problems a *Visitor* because he/she is willing to *Visit* with us but is not willing to discuss problems or concerns. This is the same as the *Pre-Conviction Stage.* Our task at this point is to be a good *Host* and build a relationship of love and trust. No interventions other than silent prayers will be attempted.

This is true whether we are interacting with a person who does not know Christ, a problem drinker, a rebellious teen, or a blatant sinner. The person is a *Visitor* if we think he should change but he does not admit having a problem. Sometimes *Visitors* speak with Helpers because a friend, family member or law enforcement agency tells them to. At other times, we come to see a person's needs as a pastor, cell leader or friend. Many is the time when we receive a complaint about one member from another member. Those being complained about are truly *Visitors* and we must be good *Hosts* when we see them.

The Helper-Seeker relationship is a dance in which each partner plays a part. Each hears the music, but not necessarily the same tune and each follows the music he hears. A wise Helper will tune in to hear the music from the Seeker's point of view. A Host *cooperates with the dance style of the Seeker. He accommodates himself to the preferences, ideas and interests of the* Visitor *even if they seem strange. A* Host *who tries to force his culture and tastes upon a* Visitor *will very likely be rejected.*

In the *Visitor-Host Stage*, Seekers:

- Admit no problem to be solved.
- Do not complain about any issue.
- Do not seek a solution.
- Have no desire to change.
- Are not open to discussing problems.
- Are not open to probing questions.
- Are usually meeting with us for their own reasons.

Scripture warns us against judging people on how they look, what they do and how they speak. At the first stage of a *Cooperative Relationship*, take great care not to judge a person's character. Jumping to conclusions about their need to change can temporarily block the Holy Spirit's ability to guide them into His plan. Paul offers guidelines on how to think about being a good Host.

*One man considers one day more sacred than another
does; another man considers every day alike. Each one should be
fully convinced in his own mind. He who regards one day as
special, does so to the Lord. He who eats meat, eats
to the Lord, for he gives thanks to God; and he
who abstains, does so to the Lord and gives thanks to God.
Why do you judge your brother? Or why do you look down
on your brother? Therefore, let us stop passing judgment on
one another. Instead, make up your mind not to put any stumbling
block or obstacle in your brother's way. Rom 14: 5,6,12*

Here is the application of love for the good of the Kingdom. "Let's face it," says the apostle Paul, "we who are in the family of God have many different views about religious rituals. Some of us are sticklers for celebrating feast days while others think feasts are foolish. However, as long as they are celebrating God's goodness it makes no difference so not judge one another because it could make the brother stumble and fall." The strong person knows that meat sacrificed to idols means nothing, yet others think they should not touch it. Paul says, accommodate to the weaker person's point of view. The principle is plain: *The strong should bear with the failings of the weak.*

Effective Helpers are to be strong believers who can look beyond the Seeker's behavior and apply mercy and grace to his needs. Mercy points to the removal of true guilt. Grace bestows a person with blessings he/she does not deserve. Since none of us deserve either mercy or grace, we must rely on the kindness of God to bring change. *It is the kindness of God that leads to repentance. Romans 2:4* We must be taught how to pass on the kindness of God. Parents, pastors and parishioners find judgement easier than compassion; the Law easier to preach than mercy; punishment more fun than forgiveness and karma easier to explain than grace. Only with the Spirit of God can we develop the patience and wisdom needed to deal with difficult people, especially those who are rebels.

*Brothers, if someone is caught in a trespass, you who are spiritual should restore him gently.
But watch yourself, or you also may be empted. Galatians 6:1*

Even intentional rebels should be treated with love and tender mercy. The Helper of sinners needs to be *spiritual* which clearly means that only a very mature believer can handle a trespasser. The job of restoration must be done gently for restoring rebels is a risky business. Paul says to be careful lest we are tempted when we minister to rebels. For some, the temptation is harsh judgments. But for others, it is the opposite desire to avoid any confrontation by being too soft on sin. The strong must bear with the failings of the weak rebel and look for an opportunity to kindly and gently bring them to face the Savior.

> *Pain is not necessarily therapeutic, especially if it is the result of clumsy execution or a callous attitude. GRS*

To deal gently with rebels is to see to it that their guilt and shame are removed with maximum effectiveness and minimum pain. Pain is not necessarily therapeutic, especially if it is the result of clumsy execution or a callous attitude. However, when we are mature in the fruit of the Spirit, surgery of the soul can be accomplished with the compassion of Mother Teresa and the courage of Florence Nightingale. The cancer of true moral guilt and the heart disease of shame must be removed lest it kill the patient from the inside out.

Applying Scripture to Visitors

Effective Helpers are good *Host or Hostess* by responding to *Visitors* with love. Here we need to the fruit of patience.

- Welcome the person with warm hospitality.
- Attend to their needs and wants.
- Focus on their interests.
- Use simple listening skills with warmth and door openers.
- Ask general questions of concern and interest.
- Refuse to mention what others have said.
- Refuse to preach, confront or judge.
- Engage in small talk.
- Pray silently for the Holy Spirit's guidance.
- Offer to meet again.

Trust, confidence and openness with every *Visitor* is our goal. People share heart issues only with those who develop an environment of safety. It is embarrassing to share failures and weaknesses with anyone, let alone a person we do not trust. However, in a safe environment it is almost impossible not to share one's concerns.

The Complainant-Listener Stage of the Cooperative Relationship

When trust is developed, complaints, grief, pain or resentment will naturally come out in the conversation. Most of the time, we interact with Seekers at the *Complainant Stage,* because trust has been previously developed. We must be prepared to listen patiently to the complaints. In fact, we see complaints as a good indication that he has left the *Visitor Stage.* Progress depends on hearing, understanding and cooperating with the Holy Spirit to resolve the Seeker's concerns.

It is difficult for most of us to listen to complaints for we do not like complainers. In fact, we might be tempted to straighten that person out. We could be tempted tell them how good they have it or focus their attention on God's faithfulness. Unfortunately, that would be an ineffective intervention encouraging Seekers to stay stuck in the *Complainant Stage*. Seekers feel confused, hurt, ashamed and fearful at our rejection or condemnation. The following list identifies the *Complainant Stage*.

- Offers details about his/her problems.
- Sees the solution in others rather than self.
- Is not motivated to change self.
- Is unclear about goals or action steps.
- Is unclear about solutions.
- May be confused, overwhelmed or stressed out.

Effective Helpers respond by bearing with the weak, and;

- Listen carefully.
- Focus on a few key points.
- Respect the person's views without disagreement or argument
- Responds non-judgmentally.
- Asks good questions.
- Becomes concrete.
- Focuses on possibilities.
- Affirms positive actions.
- Shows support.
- Prays for the Seeker's motivation.
- Is a friend to sinners.

It is a mistake to offer a solution at the *Complainant Stage* because it slows down your progress. Patience actually speeds up the discovery of good solutions Seekers return time after time to the same old stories to make sure the Helper really understands the seriousness of his complaints. By prematurely offering advice, solutions, scripture verses or prayer, we imply that his problems are not very important. Interrupting his story before it is finished may cause him to repeat it in excruciating detail to make sure we truly understand.

If Sue tells her story to Joan with a pent up need to share "eight pounds" of complaints, she will not be satisfied until Joan hears all eight pounds. If Joan gets impatient and offers a solution after only listening to five pounds of complaints, Sue will assume that Joan failed to understand the depth of her dilemma and tell the story again and again until she is convinced that she has been heard and understood. When Seekers say, "Yes, but," it usually indicates the we have not really understood the depth of their complaints.

Listening with Love

A *Complainant* is ready to acknowledge that a problem exists but does not see her self as the source of a solution. People struggle with the cost of making the changes necessary to solve the problem. The successful navigation of each stage on the road map of growth is important to the Seeker's ability to maintain the progress once started. As we listen and ask thoughtful questions the factors that support a solution, become clearer. Patient interest in the

Seeker's ideas communicates our compassion and concern. About 85 percent of the influence needed to find a good solution are developed and strengthened during the *Complainant-Listener Stage.*

Good listening helps us gather enough information to assist the Seeker in setting sound goals and making wise interventions. As we listen, the overall picture of a person's life with all its strengths and weaknesses, joys and stresses becomes clear. The completion of the *Complainant-Listener Stage* is indispensable to an assessment of the problem and a good solution depends upon a good assessment.

At first, the person will not reveal the whole story but shares a *presenting problem*. They are testing our ability to handle small concerns before opening the deeper issues. Both Christians and pre-Christians are looking for someone in whom they can trust and we do not develop trust easily.

The V C R Road Map process is as important for evangelistic outreach as it is for guiding Christians. Steve Sjogren, in the books, <u>Servant Evangelism</u> and <u>Servant Warfare</u> develops the philosophy of kindness into a powerful outreach ministry. He has built a large congregation of new believers by focusing on reaching Seekers with acts of kindness.

> *Do nothing that will not edify or build up. Ephesians 4:29*

How long will it take us to move out of the *Complainant Stage*? It is impossible to say with precision, but a skilled Helper can move the conversation along quite rapidly. Sometimes, it lasts one entire session or even more if the Seeker has many different and long-lasting complaints. With the guidance of the Lord, one conversation should complete satisfy most of the complainant's needs. Chronic complainers may need Professional Counseling.

The Ready to Change-Solution Helper Phase

The Ready for Change-Helper Solution Stage is a beautiful thing to experience. It is here that our prayers, hard work and patience pay off. The Seeker is finally at the place where she is Ready to Change and we need to be prepared to help them make the right decisions and take the right actions. It is time for the right thing for now is the right time.

Ready for Change	Focus on Solutions
1. Has become a customer!	1. Listens for goals
2. Is ready for personal change	2. Looks for action-steps
3. Is ready for solutions	3. Listens for good options
4. Is willing to work on self.	4. Supports commitments
5. Is willing to act.	5. Helps find useful actions
6. Needs well formed goals	6. Helps with good goals
7. May need to confess, repent.	7. Can forgive, pray or share scripture

The Helper at this point cooperates in the process of setting goals and moving toward lasting changes. He cooperates with the Seeker to find effective and efficient solutions. The Seeker has the insight and motivation necessary to begin the challenge of change so Helpers need to examine their tool bag and see what intervention the Holy Spirit asks us to apply. Do we pray for healing, call for repentance, set a goal for action or suggest the couple attend a good marriage seminar? We need wisdom from above.

Do unto others as you would have them do unto you. Matt. 7:12

During the *Ready to Change Stage* we may slip back to the *Complainant Stage* to explore other issues or deal with a relapse. A lapse in following through on a commitment or even a relapse to a former problem can be a source of insight and renewed motivation or it may cause overwhelming discouragement. In any event, it allows us to examine issues that have eluded our understanding. Normally a relapse lasts for only a short time and the Seeker will move forward to a new place of strength. It is not usually fatal so keep going.

Step-by-Step Progress

> ### There are two things God rarely does: Everything and Nothing
>
> GRS

There are two things God rarely does and which we want never to assume: *everything and nothing.* What usually happens is *something.* If we put God in the box of everything or nothing and He does something, we will miss His presence in our problems and fail to give Him glory. Far too much disappointment and discouragement comes from idealizing the change process and expecting instant perfection. This attitude is devastating and faith destroying.

We expect God to do something, but not necessarily everything in one step. The either or attitude of everything or nothing causes another problem. It fails to adequately reward and affirm small steps of growth. Discipleship is a series of small steps toward a final goal. If we fail to notice and affirm the small steps forward, the Seeker will not be encouraged to keep going. Discouragement leads to disaster.

Only behavior that is rewarded will survive and thrive. GRS

 ## Life Scan Summary

This process of Helping is similar to a three-stage rocket. No flight can successfully reach the moon if it does not have a firm launching pad. Relating with patience and mercy are essential components of trust that launches a helping relationship. After a period of *Visiting*, Seekers are usually secure enough to share their complaints with a person in whom they have confidence. As we listen to the *Complainant*, the specifics of the problem become clear and the possible solutions arise for both to see.

Listening is the ability to focus on the essentials and ignore the side issues. Red herrings come up often in counseling but we must resist the temptation to follow them. This is the second stage of the rocket ship and its process allows us to make any cooperative corrections to the flight pattern to make sure we land on the moon.

The third stage is the when the booster kicks in and we are both *Ready to Change*. The Seeker has considered the cost and moves toward a solution. The Helper assists the Seeker in setting goals that will bring lasting changes.

Tips for Life

Personal Reflection and Practice

- Are you seeking help for an issue that needs to change?
- Is it a coworker, family member, pastor or counselor?
- How does that person cooperate with God and you?
- What is your response?
- Are there any Visitors that you would like to see change?
- What thoughts and feelings do you have when working with a Visitor?
- Do you know any Complainants?
- How do you respond to detailed description of issues?
- How do you feel when they blame others?
- How do you cope with your emotions?
- What helps you stay patient?

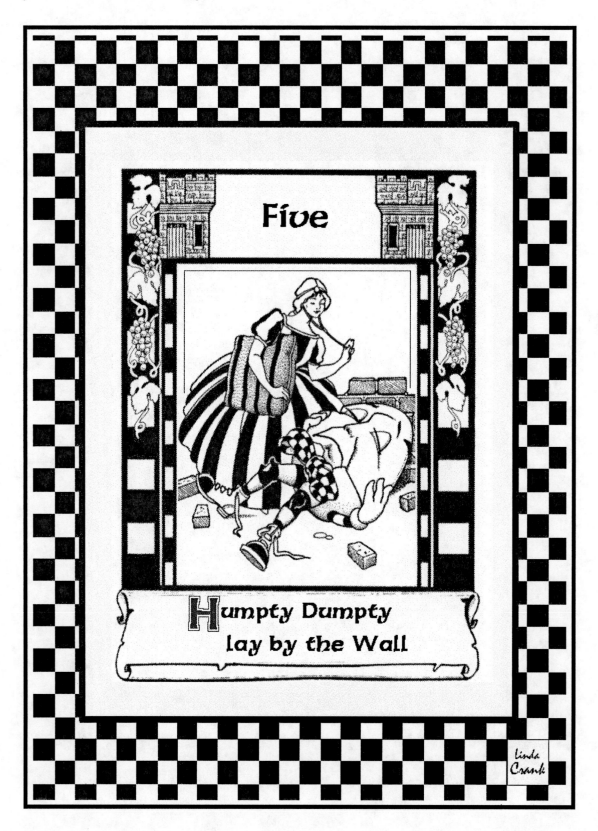

Five

Humpty Dumpty
lay by the Wall

Linda Crank

5

Love Really Works

Do not judge, and you will not be judged. Do not condemn,
and you will not be condemned. Forgive, and you will be forgiven. Give, and it will be given to you. A
good measure, pressed down, shaken together and running over, will be poured into your lap. For with
the measure you use, it will be measured to you. Luke 6:37-38

One of the four factors of effective helping is the Helper's knowledge and techniques. For many years we searched for the Holy Grail of methods and, after much work, developed some interventions that were both biblical and effective. In 1972 we heard about inner healing and eagerly spent many hours of practice and study, making sure we knew how to invite Jesus into the hurts and traumas of the past. Then in 1980 we discovered cognitive therapy and saw how it could be integrated with scripture.

Although we continue to emphasize those essential teachings, the Lord led us to add several insights that make the Lifeskills model a significant improvement over our first series called, Apples of Gold. We are not ready to say that Lifeskills is so different that we should call it oranges instead of apples, but it is certainly apple pie a la mode. Lifeskills are foundational whether one is caring for a *Type A* Helper trainee or a *Type B* Seeker. They provide the relational processes on top of which we add the *Content* or methods of ministry.

Now let's take a quick overview of the skills that are most appropriate at each stage of the VCR process. The acrostic is long but easily remembered: *AS I GREW CALM & SO SMART.* Each letter stands for an important Life skill for ministry.

AS I	**Always Spiritual, Inviting Attitude**
GREW	**Genuine, Respectful, Empathic, Warm**
CALM &	**Concrete, Affirm the good, Look for God at work, Measure progress**
SO SMART	Goals that are: **Seeker Owned, Small, Measurable, Additive, Realistic, Timely**

The Core Conditions

Although all these skills are important, there are some that are foundational to the others. Robert R. Carkhuff, one of the earliest researchers, called the GREW skills "the core conditions of a helping relationship." He said, "When the Helper relates with the core conditions, positive changes will occur." Although this is still true, with the caveat that we now know it is the cooperative relationship between the two persons that is key. Additionally, we have added the Always Spiritual and Invitational aspects for Christians.

A
L
W
A
Y
S

S
P
I
R
I
T
U
.

Jesus promised to send the Holy Spirit to be our Counselor. This sets Christian care apart from all other approaches. Although humanists may be able to relate with care and offer good technical skills, he cannot minister with the truth, fruit and gifts of the Holy Spirit. Only believers have the Spirit that leads us into all truth. We have the Holy Spirit with us in a restaurant, at the park or driving a car. We are *Always Spiritual no matter where we are* so we can rest in the wisdom of the Lord.

We do not need to pray or quote scripture to be spiritual. We do not need to be in a special, holy place to act with righteousness and godly discernment. God can guide our ideas and behavior whether we are acting religious or not. During the Viet Nam protests on the University of Cincinnati campus, Gary heard a woman say that she was going to trash the R.O.T.C. building. He accompanied the police to a dormitory where they arrested a well-known radical and brought her to Gary to identify as the perpetrator. After taking a good look, Gary knew this was not the guilty person.

The woman before him was Joyce Reichman, an activist member of Students for a Democratic Society. The cops had finally gotten an opportunity to arrest a person on their most wanted list and they hated to let her go. They drew Gary aside and suggested that he should identify her as the perpetrator. The pressure to conform to the wishes of the police was great, but Gary was convicted by the Holy Spirit to tell the truth. He refused to be dishonest despite the pressure of his friends and colleagues.

We never know how our behavior will touch another nor how the Spirit will bring someone to God. God chose to witness to this young radical in an unlikely way. Later, when Joyce came to faith, she said it was the integrity of a Christian administrator that shook her core commitment to SDS who was convinced that all people in authority were evil, lying pigs. Because Gary simply acted with integrity, a Jewish agnostic began to think about God.

Joyce did not immediately fall to her knees and profess Jesus because of one Christian act. However, this event did start her on the journey toward a *Commitment to Change*. Joyce was again arrested and Joanna Chernoff, from Beth Messiah Congregation, visited her SDS book table and prayed for her daily. Later, Joyce saw how the SDS treated Gary and knew they were wrong, further challenging her commitment to politics. Finally, she took a job in the office of the well-known ACLU attorney, Allen Brown where she met Elliot Klayman, a new believer in the Messiah. He shared the gospel with Joyce but her *Commitment* came privately and quietly at an obscure church. God conspired to bring this young woman to Himself by planting many spiritual seeds in unlikely places over a long period of time. Who would have thought that He could use corrupt police and a scared Associate Dean to penetrate the darkness of a radical student group? Who would have thought that He could use an ACLU attorney's office as a holy place? Who would have thought that He could use chaos to evangelize? He thought of it. He did it.

Knowing that the Holy Spirit is with us and in us gives us confidence to minister patiently even when we do not know what is happening or what to do. God can reveal His will to us even if we are confused and overwhelmed. Gary simply acted honestly and the Spirit did the rest of the work. He did not share a Bible passage, sing a hymn or use religious terms. Integrity proved to be the key to Joyce's spiritual conviction. Jesus said:

*I am sending you out like sheep among wolves. Therefore,
be as shrewd as snakes and as innocent as doves. Be on your guard
against men; they will hand you over to the local councils and flog you in their synagogues. On
my account you will be brought before governors and kings as witnesses to them and to the
Gentiles. But when they arrest you,
do not worry about what to say or how to say it. At that time you
will be given what to say, for it will not be you speaking,
but the Spirit of your Father speaking through you.* Matt 10:16-20

Jesus sends lambs to bring wolves into the Kingdom. Lambs are weaker, more fragile and more vulnerable than even sheep. The process of evangelization requires that lambs have prudence, meekness, humility and integrity. Lambs must think like a minority group, not like people in charge. The lamb's humble attitude is critical to his success. Arrogant lambs are a contradiction in terms. Lambs accommodate themselves to the people they meet by blessing them, eating with them and asking about their welfare.

Scripture tell us not to be anxious when we are in a difficult situation for the Holy Spirit will guide us from moment to moment. We need His guidance to be prudent when facing down the wolves of sickness, violence and destruction. *Always Spiritual* relies on God's guidance to get us through. Our own understanding is clouded so we need the clarity of the Counselor to lead the way for we only see through a dark glass.

God gives us an *Inviting Attitude*. We do not need to be defensive or anxious when facing unbelievers, people with problems that are over my head or wolves who want to chew us up. Lambs realize that the issues people bring to us are far too complicated to be solved by our own intellect. If we were lions, we would have to be strong, but lambs are weak.

An *Invitational Attitude* welcomes all to the table of fellowship. It is similar to kindness because it bids hurting hearts to come to a place of safety, love and truth. Think how open the Lord was to the Samaritan woman at the well. The disciples were shocked that He spoke with her so easily. He even asked her for water to drink. It was unthinkable for a well-respected Rabbi to relate to a Samaritan or a woman. She was anathema to Jews as a Samaritan who had been married five times and was now living in adultery! Jesus, the radical pastor, openly invited an adulterous woman to chat. He was not anxious about what to say because the Holy Spirit would lead His interactions. We too can relate with confidence for the Counselor is with us and in us.

The Anxious Adverse Advisers

Dr. Rich Walters introduced us to a unique way of teaching about hospitality and *Inviting Attitudes*. He discovered that we could learn about positive human traits by studying their opposites. It is a humorous way to point out our own foibles and tendencies to be inhospitable. We came up with a cast of characters called *Adverse Advisers*. Although these characters really want to be helpful, they leave Seekers confused and anxious rather than peaceful. Each character attempts to help a troubled young man. See if you know anyone who has similar *Adverse Adviser* tendencies.

INVITATIONAL ATTITUDE ♥

Act I

A young man named Joshua went to his father and demanded all his inheritance. The father sadly gave him everything he had coming and Josh took off for the big city with all its thrills. After many months of wine, women and song the lad ran out of money and began to beg for a job. He finally ended up eating and sleeping with the pigs he was hired to tend. This was terrible for his religion forbade contact with swine.

One day, young Josh woke up from a fitful sleep and thought about his situation. He said to himself, "My father's hired hands have it better than this. I will go down to the local congregation and find someone to help me figure out what to do." Off he went to the First Church of What's Happening Now and introduced himself to the secretary. "My name is Josh and I come from a foreign country. I don't have any money for counselors so I'm not sure you can help me or not. I left home several months ago and people who said they were my friends took all my money. I had to get a job so I have been tending pigs and living in the barn. These friends will not give me the time of day now. Can help me get those people to repay all my money? They fooled me and cleaned me out."

The secretary replied, "Certainly, we can help you young man. We have a complete staff of counselors who are here just for such a time as this. Go down the hall and choose one of them. The first door he came to was marked, *The Interrogator.* Josh found that he was eager to understand him and his situation. He asked detailed questions, designed, it seemed, to satisfy his own need for information.

How old are you? How long have you been gone? Where did you grow up? What kind of farm did your father have? Joshua, tell me about your early childhood. Was it happy? What kind of relationship did you have with your father? With your mother? Did you fight often with your family? What did you drink at the bars? Did you do drugs too? Who are your friends? Men, women, or both? How old are they?

After an exhausting hour of interrogation, Josh was confused and frustrated. Not knowing what to do, he decided to try another door and entered to visit with, *The Pharisee*. After a few minutes, Josh learned how he came by that descriptive name. This guy loved to point out all the places where Josh had made mistakes or committed sins. There was no doubt that Josh was to blame for everything that was wrong in his life.

What have you done to deserve such judgment from the Lord? This is probably a sin of past generations and may be due to your own judgments or roots of bitterness. I suggest that you go on a forty-day fast to discover what sin you have committed and spend an intense time in confession before you go home to confess. You will simply take your sin and shame back to the family and bring a curse on them. The heavenly places are reeling at your rebellion, and it may take several generations to purge this from your record.

Hurt and frustrated, Josh next tried *The Prophet* who seemed to know exactly what was going to happen in the future, and it was all bad.

If you think losing friends and money is hard just wait until one of your children dies. We live in such an evil world that no one is safe and the devil is after all of us so beware lest you be unprepared for the worst. Our enemy is everywhere and we cannot rest for a moment. The disaster you have experienced is understandable since you rebelled so badly. The Lord is using this to get you ready for worse things, so cheer up and thank God for His mercy.

Sighing, Josh knocked on *The Historian's* door who seemed to remember just how hard it was when he was a kid and how blessed Josh was to live in this great land.

When I was a boy, my brother left home and had the same experience you did. He was a great brother and my parents were grief stricken for years. I never got over it either. But you young people have plenty of time nowadays to travel around the world and return again because transportation is so easy to find. Did I ever tell you about my trip last year on the Concorde? It was wonderful and I suggest that you try to fly on it as well. When we flew…

Next, Josh visited The Quick Change Artist who was so uncomfortable with her emotions that she tried to make them go away by changing the subject.

So you know about farming do you? I always wanted to be a farmer. Tell me about how you liked the farm back home. Was it a nice farm with cattle, olive trees? Do you think farming would be a good career for me? I need some advice on my career path at this point in my life. Can you help me?

Wondering if he would ever find help, Josh decided to try Dr. Deodorant who tried to dispel his negative feelings with sweet words. He thought he was an encourager, but was actually an enabler who could not stand for others to be uncomfortable.

I am sure that you will find everything A OK back at home. God did this because He wanted you to grow up and know that He cares for you. You cannot depend upon anyone but God so He is calling you to Himself. You are so wonderful and strong that you will be fine. This is but a momentary blip on the radar screen of life. God has it all under control, so cheer up, things could be worse.

Next in line was Miss Bumper Sticker.

Now you know what the Bible says, "Count it all joy when you encounter various trials" because God loves you and has a wonderful plan for your life. Since we live in the last days, he is challenging each of us to learn to live with less. When the enemy comes in like a flood He will raise up a standard to fight for us, because no weapon raised against us shall prosper They meant it for evil but He meant it for good. This world is not my home and we're just passing through, so do not lay up treasures on earth but put them in heaven" because "Jesus is coming soon, whether at nigh or noon."

Josh was shocked to see that the next therapist was called *The Robber,* who acted as though he knew Josh's feelings better than he did. He robbed Josh of the ability to genuinely examine his own thoughts and feelings.

Robber*: Josh, I can see you are very angry with God.*
Josh*: No, I am not blaming God but my friends.*
Robber*: Do not deny what is obvious, Josh. I can hear your bitter anger and resentment. It is impossible for you not to feel anger.*
Josh*: I am upset with my friends who took all my money but I am not angry with God.*
Robber*: You are in denial Josh and you had better wake up to the truth. I am a biblical counselor so I know these things.*

Act II

As Josh knocked on the last door in that long hallway, he met a *Lifeskills* Helper. Unlike the others, he didn't seem to have all the answers but listened to Josh's ideas.

Josh, I don't know if I can help or not. It seems as though you are very upset with everything that has happened to you. Losing all that money and all your friends sure seems unfair and discouraging. Tell me a bit more about what has been going on with you and what you think you need to do now. It sounds like you are in a bad fix right now and need to make some important decisions. We need to spend some time discussing these things before coming up with a solution.

genuine respectful empathic warm genuine respectful empathic warm genuine respectful empathic warm

Consider Joshua's *VCR* stage when he first came to the church. He was upset with people who were his friends because they took his money and then refused to help him out. He did not start off by saying that he had made a mistake. Although that may be obvious to us, it is best for him to come to his own conviction. Josh was in the *Complainant Stage*, blaming his problems on others not himself.

Helpers at the *Complainant Stage* need to Listen Warmly, clarify the root issues and see if a Seeker starts to recognize his own responsibility. He will stop blaming others after a little while if we listen well. At the beginning of the conversation, we open the door and see what comes through it. Before long, Josh may tell the Helper just how remorseful he is to have made such a fool of himself. The fact that he chose to seek simply *Invite* Josh to talk long enough for trust between us to develop. *Adverse Advisers* anxiously get their own feelings mixed up with the

Seeker's problems. They jumped to conclusions about what this young man should do even though they had not fully heard his story. It brought confusion and chaos rather than clarity. They pre-judged Josh giving him their own solutions rather than enabling him to find his own.

> *Do not judge or you too will be judged. For in the same*
> *way you judge others, you will be judged, and with the measurement*
> you use, it will be measured to you. Matthew 7:1

The *Adverse Advisers* reacted with anxious judgments. Anxiety leads to reactivity while peace allows us to respond thoughtfully and calmly. Responding with peaceful *AS I GREW* attitudes and skills allows us to present *good measure poured out into our laps*.

What Do People Really Want?

An accurate assessment of a Seeker's goals will facilitate an effective response. There are a variety of possible Seeker requests and they can change during a conversation. A person may desire *friendly chatter* or *information* while others want *action*. Sometimes we face requests that are *inappropriate* and at other times we are sought out for *counseling*, a release of *angry feelings* or a combination of the things that we call *mixed messages*. Our response depends on the kind of request we get.

Types of Requests   *Appropriate Responses*

1. Request for Information   ⟶   Give the information

Alice: *Where is the nearest coffee shop?*
Pat: *The nearest Starbucks is in Tri-County Mall.*

2. Request for Action   ⟶   Supply the request

Alice: *Do you have a copy of Listening for Heaven's Sake?*
Pat: *Yes, I do. Would you like to borrow it?*

3. Mixed Message Request   ⟶   Clarify the message

Alice: *Do you know of a good book on depression?*
Pat: *I may be able to find one. Tell me more about what you need.*

4. Inappropriate Request   ⟶   Respect the person/Reject the request

Alice: *Can you tell my husband that I worked with you last night even though I didn't?*
Pat: *I am not comfortable with lying. Is there another way I can help?*

5. Anger, Understanding, Counsel   ⟶   Listen, Clarify, Look for solutions

Alice: *My husband is driving me crazy. I just don't know what to do.*
Pat: *Is there any way I can be of assistance?*

Inappropriate Requests

There are times when we are asked to do something that is inappropriate. The range of inappropriate activity can include such things as participating in gossip; engaging in an illegal or immoral activity; doing for another person what he needs to do for himself; or allowing others to violate our boundaries. The appropriate response is difficult but therapeutic. First, accept the person. Second, reject the offensive behavior.

> **Harry**: Dr. Smith, can you loan me $1,000.00?
> **Dr. Smith**: Harry, I really want to help you but I cannot do that. The church does not allow us to loan money to anyone. Perhaps we can discuss other ways of getting the funds you need. We want to help meet your needs but we must maintain appropriate boundaries about financial issues. Our church has a policy that forbids pastors and lay persons from giving money to members or guests. All such requests need to go through appropriate channels.

Another touchy situation for leaders arises we are asked to get into the middle of a dispute. We call this, *being triangled.* Listening to the complaints of one person about another is not triangulation as long as we maintain neutrality and promote reconciliation. However, if we take sides, we are part of the problem rather than part of the solution.

Helpers are always in the middle for that is our role. However, we must never become triangled or we lose the ability to reconcile the other parties. Several years ago, Gary was counseling a couple with marital problems. After a few sessions Gary started to feel sympathy for the wife and irritated with the husband. While praying the Lord convicted him of the error and he apologized at the next session. They said his bias was obvious to them both and appreciated his honesty.

Most unhealthy church conflicts are related to the violation of this principle. Pastors, elders and lay leaders usually do not know how to relate empathically with complainants and still stay peacefully neutral. When listening to someone complain about a brother they take sides emotionally and verbally. The spark of a complaint then becomes a forest fire that easily gets out of control. Peace makers can listen, love both parties and stay neutral.

> *If your brother sins against you, go and show him his fault, just between the two of you. If he listens to you, you have won your brother over. But if he will not listen, take one or two others along, so that 'every matter may be established by the testimony of two or three witnesses. If he refuses to listen to them, tell it to the church; and if he refuses to listen even to the church, treat him as you would a pagan or a tax collector.   Matt 18:15-17 (NIV)*

This is Jesus' way to resolve a conflict when a person thinks he has been offended. The first step is to go privately and resolve the issue. If that works, and it usually does, no more action is necessary. However, should that fail, the Lord says to recruit a couple of neutral counselors to serve as objective referees. They are to listen, discern responsibility and suggest a remedy.

If that step also fails, Jesus instructs us to take the matter to the elders who can sit as a judicial tribunal. If either of the parties refuses to take the elders' recommendations, the penalty is severe. The rebel is to be put him out of the fellowship until he repents.

This is a simple way to stay out of triangles. Complainants ought to talk to each other first. Gossip in the church is toxic to spiritual and emotional health. Jesus has given the church a safety valve for a remedy. Pastor Harry will follow the guidelines established by Jesus to handle a complaining elder.

Peter: Pastor Harry, may I speak with you? An elder in the church is failing in his duties and you must do something. Paul is not rearing his children properly and I am very concerned. His son does not come to Bible study and is rebellious. You must take this to the elder board for discipline. I do not want you to mention my name though.

Harry: Peter, I understand your concern. Elders have a special responsibility to rear their children in the fear and admonition of the Lord. Have you spoken to Paul about this? It would not be appropriate for us to discuss it in the elder board until you have spoken with him personally.

Peter: But Pastor, this is your job. You need to straighten Paul out. I do not want him to be mad at me so I can't speak with him. Maybe I can talk with some other people in the church and they will do something about it.

Harry: I can see that you are really fired up about this Peter, and you want to tell people about it. However, the Bible is clear about our process of dealing with these issues. It is not right to discuss your perceptions and concerns with others before you speak directly with Paul. You must go to him first. So, do not speak with anyone else about this matter.

We suggest that every congregation teach the Matthew 18:15 principles to each new member's class and preach on them each year. Many leaders have not been informed about triangles and too often get pulled into unhealthy conflicts with complaining members. As elders and pastors commit themselves to following the wisdom of Jesus, peace will begin to reign in our churches and destructive conflicts will be reduced.

GENUINE RESPECTFUL EMPATHIC WARM

GOAL
SHARING OPENLY

The Skills and the Road Map

When a person asks us for assistance, counsel and personal ministry we enter into the VCR Cooperative Relationship and need to respond with an interactive relationship of listening. The following chart illustrates the skills that apply at each stage.

Seeker	Helper	Life Skills
Visitor: No problem	Host:	AS I GREW
Complainant: Problems Caused by others	Listens/ Clarifies	AS I GREW CALM
Ready to Change: Self-Responsibility Will take action	Solutions/ Goal setting	AS I GREW CALM & SO SMART

The AS I GREW skills are essential in every stage of a caring relationship. Relating Respectfully and Warm Empathy is the oil that makes the human machinery run with joy. When conflict erupts, triangles pop up and blaming breaks out, we need the peaceful presence of God and the skills of a peacemaker. The fruit of the Spirit is always welcome in a helping relationship.

> *I tried to treat them like me, and some of them weren't.*
> *Bill Russell (basketball coach, about his players)*

Life Scan Summary

The Holy Spirit gives us confidence to have an *Inviting* attitude toward others. Expressing grace and mercy invites others to bring their hurting hearts to a safe place for healing and growth. *Adverse Advisors*, on the other hand, push folk away for they express judgment and inappropriate conclusions.

Most of the time people are not requesting counseling or emotional assistance but want to relate with us for other reasons.

- Friendly Chatter: *How do you like the Olympics this year?*
- Information: *Do you know where the classroom is?*
- Action: *Can you loan me a pencil?*
- A Mixed Message: *Are you still doing marriage counseling?*
- Inappropriate Interactions: *Did I tell you what I heard about the pastor?*
- To Release Anger: *If my boss yells at me one more time I will explode!*
- Care and Counsel: *I am confused about what to do. Can you help me?*

When we are asked to offer care and counsel, we can respond with confidence that God will be with us. The Holy Spirit will provide the peace and insight needed to show others the love of God with skin on it.

While visiting Joe, a friend confined to a state mental hospital, Gary saw the impact of the presence of God on the patients. The orderly escorted him into the recreation room where Joe was sitting and over 100 eyes followed his every move. The fifty adult men in the room stopped talking to stare with wide-eyed interest. Finally, one of them edged over and asked, "Are you Jesus? Are you a holy man?"

The Holy Spirit within Gary had penetrated the fog of mental illness and heavy medication to reveal Jesus as the healer. A mental institution is filled with disease, demons and discouragement. Yet, those in bondage sensed His presence. It was not anything that Gary did or said that touched them. He was a vessel not a magician. Every Christian is anointed for good works and is capable of bringing the presence of God into lives of persons in need.

TIPS for Life

Personal Reflection and Practice

- Analyze your ability to listen. Do you *Actively Listen* or *Actively Interrupt*?
- Do others ever say you are a good listener? Do you enjoy listening or do you get impatient and want to speak?
- Which of the Adverse Advisers do you identify with most closely?
- When you look at the VCR, which stage are you most comfortable with? Least comfortable? Where do you wish to grow?

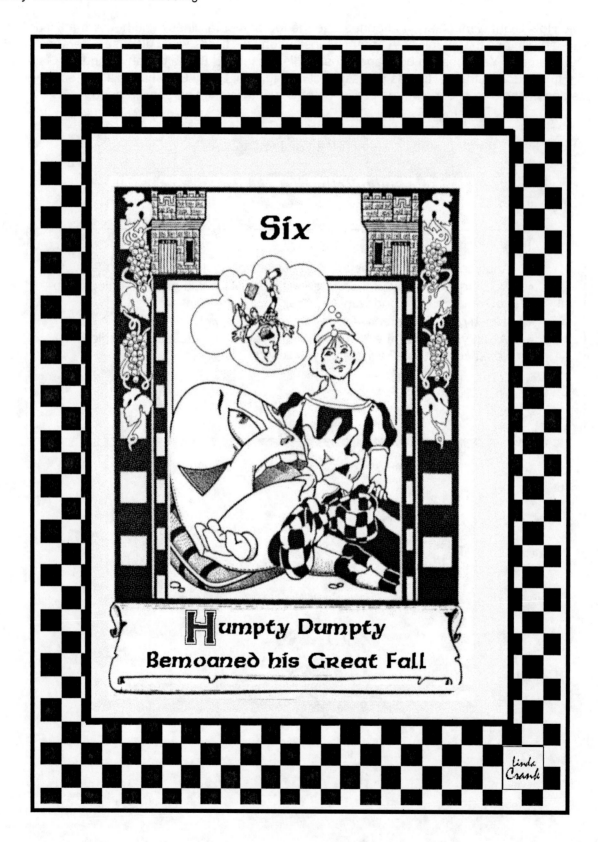

6

Genuine Love that Heals

A blind person cannot guide another blind person can he? Will they
not both fall into a pit? Luke 6:36ff

Trust of the messenger precedes trusting the message. GRS

When President Jimmy Carter invited Anwar Sadat of Egypt and Menachem Begin of Israel, to a summit at Camp David the early discussions went badly. Neither of the two visiting leaders trusted the other so no progress was made. On the last day of the talks, Mr. Carter received Begin in his home for a final conversation. They looked at photographs of their grandchildren and discussed how bleak the future was in light of the difficult Middle East situation.

The men became emotional and nostalgic as they considered the fates of their children and grandchildren. Before long, Mr. Carter called Anwar Sadat to personally share his and Begin's concerns about the future. The negotiations took a completely new turn and the leaders of the two warring nations chose to make peace. As long as the focus was political and impersonal, they could not find a resolution to the severe problems that existed in the Middle East. However, Mr. Carter chose to honestly focus on who the leaders were as persons rather than who they were as leaders and the rest is history. We could call Mr. Carter a *Genuine* person who persuaded Begin and Sadat to put aside their leadership roles and be real people.

Ambassadors for Jesus need excellent people skills or the *fruit of the Spirit* to interact with Seekers from differing cultures. Every interpersonal relationship has cross-cultural aspects. Relationship skills are essential to achieve a positive outcome. We have a desire to see people grow through issues, concerns, inappropriate behavior, sinfulness and rebellion. Being a persuasive change agent in these situations requires wisdom, sensitivity and the Holy Spirit's guidance.

Growing in GREW

The term *GREW* stands for the four core conditions identified in the late 1960's, by Robert R. Carkhuff as being most important factors of effective Helping. More recent research indicates that, although the core conditions are necessary to all effective care and counsel, they make up about 30% of the movement toward a solution. These four attitudes/skills are *Genuineness, Respect, Empathy* and *Warmth*. Although discussed and taught separately they are actually an inseparable package.

Genuineness, the Real Thing

Being a *Genuine* person requires hard work for it requires me to look honestly at my own heart and soul to discern the shadows that lurk within. Genuineness is costly. However, there are also many positive payoffs for us and for our relationships. Honest reflections about life's struggles enable us to better understand and assist others in their journey toward wholeness. When I am honest about my need for cleansing, change and confession I will grow in authentic compassion for others. Genuineness communicates acceptance without license, reality without self-pity, and openness without pride. Being a fake Christian allows us to judge harshly, act pride fully and condemn easily.

Being a Real Person and a Real Helper

James, the pastor of a large congregation in New Mexico, discussed a number of issues about life, ministry and family with his friend Roy. After an hour or so James decided it was safe to seek Roy's wisdom and counsel. Although it was embarrassing, he asked Roy to pray about a deeply personal issue. Suddenly, Roy, who had interacted naturally and easily, became tense, changed his way of talking and took on the *role* of a Helper. It shocked James so much that he changed the subject.

When Roy took the role of Helper he moved from genuine friend to acting like a counselor. In his discomfort, he put on the mask that blocked his ability to be helpful. By trying too hard Roy sabotaged his effectiveness and lost the opportunity to minister to his friend. Roy's lack of self-knowledge kept both men from achieving their goals.

A wise Helper needs self-understanding. The more we understand ourselves and humbly accept our shortcomings, the more we can peacefully assist others as they discover their sins and self-deceits. One of our favorite passages is Luke 6:36 because in it Jesus lays out the process of becoming a Genuine leader.

A blind person cannot guide another blind person can he? Will they not both fall into a pit? A pupil is not above his master. When the pupil is fully trained, he shall be like his teacher.

Why do you so clearly see the speck in your brother's eye but fail to see the log in your own eye. How can you suggest that you take that speck out of the brother's eye yet refuse to notice the log in your eye? You hypocrite, first take that log out of your own eye so you can see clearly to remove the speck from your brother's eye.

It is scary to think that we produce followers like ourselves. Helpers need to examine our own eyes in order to see others clearly. A lack of self-awareness can lead to hypocrisy or wearing a mask of respectability to cover our true intentions and motivations.

Some of us do not want to be *real persons*. As our friend and colleague Larry Chrouch says, "Once we have learned to fake genuineness we have it made in life." Those who do so are called con artists and many end up in leadership positions. Con artists *talk the walk* rather than *walk the talk*. Our Christian witness has been deeply damaged by famous men and women whose actual behavior has failed to match their preaching. When our inner and outer lives are incongruent unbelievers wonder if any Christian is the genuine article. Only lives of integrity will convince the world of God's love and His law.

Steve once had a long conversation with a man who was upset about his working conditions and wanted to get a new job. He was a conservative Christian who complained endlessly about the bad environment that was forced upon him every day by his colleagues. Finally, after an hour of listening, Steve asked, "Tell me, Jay, what bothers you most about that unchristian work place." Without hesitation he said, "Those filthy mouthed, blankety, blank SOBs are always cursing and I can't stand it."

Jay wanted something that he could not live up to himself. He wore a mask of respectability and piety. However, frustration revealed the truth For out of the overflow of the heart the mouth speaks. Matthew 12:34 We, like Jay, are all in the process of growth in righteousness. The Lord used that event to convict Jay to change. He was able to laugh at himself and say, "Maybe I need to do some work on my own filthy mouth before I condemn others." Watch what you say. I will reveal your heart.

Clear-Eyed Perception

Gary once visited a surgeon because of a serious infection. Having an eye examination is an anxiety-provoking event. He wondered if it the procedure would be dangerous or painful. Would it even cause more problems? Gary fearfully looked for a sign of the doctor's credentials, trying to make sure he was qualified. The man looked efficient and dressed like a real doctor with a white coat and appropriate medical instruments. The walls were covered with framed degrees from prestigious medical schools so Gary momentarily relaxed. However, when the doctor took out a long needle and said he was going to open the infected tear ducts Gary again became anxious.

The doctor swiveled the magnifying glass attached to his head and began to examine the swollen ducts while warmly telling Gary what he was doing. Gary immediately started to relax. By the time Dr. Logston said, "Now, Gary, don't blink for a few seconds," he was able to control his eyelids with ease, and the surgeon quickly and expertly inserted the needle into the offending ducts. The relief was instantaneous.

Imagine what would have happened if this surgeon had stumbled into the operating room with bandages covering both eyes. Then, while trying to examine Gary's eyes he mentioned his inability to see well. "My glasses were broken in an accident leaving glass in both eyes." However, I am sure we can operate on you anyway." It would not have been hard to say, "Thanks very much doctor, but I will return when you have had your own eyes healed and are able to clearly see what is wrong with mine."

Jesus was the greatest psychotherapist who ever lived. He knew that our hearts were deceitful with broken places, wounds, unresolved conflicts and hidden issues. He taught us that these issues can bubble to the surface and block our understanding others. When Mrs. Jones discusses her abusive father it might push the unresolved "squishy spots" that are left over from the pain in the Helper's life, blocking his ability to accurately understand Mrs. Jones. The term *projection* is used to psychologically describe the phenomenon that Jesus called, *logs in the eyes*. Both indicate that something from one heart is incorrectly projected onto another.

For example, Mrs. Jones may say that she was deeply wounded by her father's abandonment. An immature Helper may overly identify with her because of his own father's abandonment. If he also *projected* his feelings on Mrs. Jones he might mistake his pain for hers. Projection keeps the Helper from listening rationally and objectively. Being out of touch his heart means that he cannot effectively minister to Mrs. Jones.

If the Helper is angry with his neglectful father he may try to persuade Mrs. Jones that she should feel the way he does. Perhaps she has an opposite or different response all together. She may have developed unique strengths because she had no father to lean on. Or, she may have already become reconciled with her dad. We cannot assume how any other person will respond to a situation for we are all unique.

Becoming Real

> ### How can you draw close to God if you are far from your own self?
>
> **St. Augustine**

The first stage of **Genuineness** *is self-knowledge. We get to know ourselves by thinking carefully about our thoughts and feelings and how they interact in different situations.*

By understanding ourselves, we are less likely to mistakenly project our personal feelings on others.

- I will explore my thoughts and feelings.
- I know my thoughts and feelings.
- I can name my thoughts and feelings.
- I can acknowledge my thoughts and feelings.
- I can discuss my thoughts and feelings
- I know the difference between my thoughts and feelings and the thoughts and feelings of other people, including my family.

The process of self-awareness requires us to know the difference between a thought and a feeling, a skill about which many are confused. Some have developed a habit of saying *feel* when we really mean *think*. Your mother says, "I *feel* you should study." This is obviously a thought not a feeling for she believes her child needs to study. Parents may *feel* frustrated or anxious that their child is not studying. They may be angry or depressed with his failures. These are feeling words that describe emotional responses to the son's lack of studying.

Circle T if the following sentence is expressing a thought and F if it is a feeling.

> T-F I feel like asking my wife out to dinner.
> T-F I feel happy.
> T-F I feel as though you should not do that.
> T-F I feel like you do not like me.
> T-F I feel angry because the teacher will not listen.
> T-F I feel like my wife is beautiful.
> T-F I feel attracted to my wife.
> T-F I feel like she should repent of her sins.

If we finish a sentence with anything other than a feeling word such as mad, sad, glad, fear, guilt or joy, it is a thought not a feeling. Saying, "I feel that_____" when we more accurately mean, "I think that_____" fails to communicate our intentions. It is appropriate to say, "I feel sad about losing my dog" or "I feel frustrated about waiting in line' because these comments reveal our emotional state. However, to say, "I feel like you do not love me" is actually a belief. The thought will lead to feelings of hurt, anger or disappointment.

Danish psychologist Kirsten Callesen has been teaching these materials to Christians in Nepal. It has been quite a challenge because they traditionally had only six words to describe feelings. Kirsten developed exercises to help them know, name and share their feelings. The Nepalese believers were transformed by being openly Genuine for the first time in their lives. After seeing the benefits of emotional expression, several became angry about the lack of prior education in the church. One woman asked rhetorically, "Why has no one ever taught this before?" Kirsten said, "How do you feel about not being taught this before?" The elderly saint finally said, "I am angry." So Kirsten said, "What do you want to do?" The lady vigorously stamped her foot to show her anger. She was learning how to be Emotionally Intelligent as a woman of sixty plus years.

We find the same need for emotional education in the United States, Europe and Asia. We have too often neglected our spiritual and emotional development. The importance of developing a child's Intelligence Quotient (IQ) is well known but fewer understand that Emotional Intelligence, (EIQ), is central to success in marriage, family life and business. In the emerging international market place, EIQ is considered much more important to than IQ. Daniel Goleman wrote a brilliant book called <u>Emotional Intelligence</u> that we strongly recommend. Genuineness is an essential component of EIQ.

Research on the long-term success of high school and college graduates shows that honor roll students often did not fare as well in real life as B and C students. At a 2001 speech to Yale graduates, George W. Bush commented wryly that his election proved that a C student could become the President of the United States. Although some criticized him for affirming C students, he was correct. In fact, successful people in politics, business, industry and family life have always excelled in human relationships, not simply facts or abstract theory. Mr. Bush is famous for his interpersonal charisma, friendly interactions and warmth. He is genuine about who he is and never tries to put on airs. The future belongs to those who can relate successfully with people of all ages, all cultures and all religions.

How can I really know God or understand others if I do not know myself? How can I truly listen to my colleagues at work and understand their feelings and the thoughts that produce those feelings if I do not have personal insights about my own emotional state? Develop your EQ by find a friend to help you find your logs and blind spots. Take the Myers-Briggs Temperament Test or a gifts checklist to get a better idea about your preferences and passions. Decide to become a genuine *human being* not simply a *human doing.*

The Nepalese could not be *Genuine* because any sign of disagreement was seen as rebellion. Many of us came from homes where the only acceptable feelings were those prescribed by parents. Places of safety where we can express ourselves without fear of suppression or punishment is the only remedy to past repression. Those who grew up in houses that said, no talking, no feeling, no thinking, no asking questions, cannot know freedom in Christ without understanding and acknowledging themselves. It is never too late to have a happy childhood. However, we must let the little child within come out and play.

MAD, SAD, GLAD

One way to grow is by asking ourselves when we experienced the feelings of mad, sad or glad. Think of recent events when you felt these emotions.

I felt mad when_____ happened.
I felt sad when_____happened.
I felt glad when_____ happened.
I felt guilty when _____ happened.
I felt joyful when_____happened.

Emotions do not simply rise out of the air and grab us. They are indicators of the state of our heart and mind. What thoughts caused you to become angry? What thoughts caused you to be sad? Why did you feel so glad at a particular point in time? By analyzing personal experiences and thoughts, we can develop a deeper understanding of our own hearts and choose whether we wish to change or not. Thoughts trigger feelings and some of us have very sensitive trigger fingers due to wounded spirits.

Counsel yourself by remembering an incident in which you experienced strong emotions. Ask yourself the following questions.

- What did I want in this situation?

- What did I think about the situation?

- What did I feel about the situation?

- When has it been safe to share my real thoughts and feelings?
  How does this affect me? Did I feel anxious or free?

- Where is it unsafe for me to share honestly? How does it affect me?

Application

Knowing our identity in Christ empowers us to express our real thoughts and feelings. Speaking honestly and forthrightly about ideas and concerns, wishes and wants is essential to healthy living. Dysfunctional families and churches punish members who think, feel or speak freely. The unspoken rules from our past may continue to be logs needing removal. Was the home of your youth open to everyone's ideas and feelings? Were you rewarded or punished when you stated an opinion or responded to events with tears, anger or frustration? Are you still living with these unspoken rules now that you are an adult? Would you like to change the rules?

Think of a person whom you want to help. Review the relationship and analyze how you feel during the interaction. Are you sometimes mad, sad, glad, fearful, guilty, shameful, hopeless or excited? Does your emotional state affect the ways you try to help the person? Are you able to be objective or do you project your feelings on them or take their feelings?

 ## You're O.K., Humpty Dumpty

Self-acceptance is essential to being Genuine. Shameful, self-hating ideas about our identity, our thoughts and our feelings will inevitably block self-awareness and stifle honest expression. We can fool others about our true thoughts and feelings but we cannot so easily fool ourselves. Gary had a life changing experience when an honored professor introduced him to a colleague. "Gary, he said, "is a country boy trying to make it in the big city." He and the other professor laughed but Gary felt humiliated.

He had said exactly what Gary feared about himself. The mask had failed to cover up those country origins. Like Job, that which he feared most had come upon him. Later, the professor apologized and said that he was not aware of how he had come across. However, the real issue was not the professor's words but Gary's extreme sensitivity. Later, Gary asked himself, "Why did I allow such a minor comment upset me?" The introspective process led Gary to a deeper level of self-understanding about his shame filled thoughts. He also made a decision to renew his mind according to the scripture.

Gary can now take off masks more easily because he discovered *who* he is in Christ. He has more confidence because he knows *to whom* he belongs. He has learned to accept *who* God made him to be, even if He is not finished with the final product. Now he can even admit that he is a country boy in the big city. He has made great progress toward being *Genuine*. He confronted his shame-based beliefs and replaced the lies with the truth.

On further reflection, Gary discovered that the culture in which he was reared put a premium on masking true thoughts and feelings as a way of seeming to be humble and pious. For example, it was a rule in his family to deny any personal preferences lest others think you demanding or selfish. This led to valiant but futile attempts to read the minds of others and then guess what they really wanted because few people were honest. In fact, many stated the opposite of their true desires. Listen to the following conversation between Gary, his mother and his wife.

Gary: Mother, where do you want to go for your birthday meal?
Mother: It doesn't make any difference. I will be happy to go anywhere *you* want.
Gary: Well, it's your day so choose and we will be happy to take you there.
Mother: I don't know. Anywhere is fine with me.
Gary: (Thinks): Oh no! She is going to put the responsibility on me. I am supposed to intuitively know where she wants to go.) I have an idea. We can go to a buffet where they have a lot of choices and you can get what you want.
Mother: That is fine. Whatever *you* want is okay with me.
Gary: (After getting the food, Gary anxiously awaits Mother's verdict.) Well, what do you think? Is the buffet okay, Mother?

Mother: Oh, its fine, I guess. There is nothing here that I can eat. I am on a strict diet and I just can't find anything I am supposed to have.

Gary: But Mother, I asked you if this was all right and you said it was.

Mother: I knew you wanted to come here so I agreed so you would be happy.

(Later, Mother told Gary's wife that she had cooked all week so they could have dinner at home and not go out at all. When asked why she did not say that, she replied, "I did not want to stop you from going out to a restaurant.")

In this instance, and many more like it, no one was *Genuine*. The cultural rules demanded that all the participants play the game of *cover up* and *mind reading*. Many books focus on the need to manage conflict. We think there is a greater need to manage *false agreements*. Those of us coming from mind reading cultures do not even recognize our logs unless we do some serious personal eye examinations.

Another dimension of *Genuineness* is the difference between *I Statements* and *You Statements*. *Genuine persons* can say *I think, feel, believe or perceive* when referring to their beliefs and feelings. They will use *You think, feel, believe or perceive* when referring to others. For example, Gary's Mother could have said, "I would rather stay home so we could have a quiet family time with all the children and grandchildren. If we go to a restaurant we can't do that." This is the essence of an *I Statement* and it clearly communicates the desires and goals of the speaker. She could have then followed with a *You Statement* such as, "What would *you* prefer to do?"

By using appropriate *I Statements* and *You Statements*, we can more clearly negotiate meals, discover the best compromises, and find agreements that are based on facts not assumptions, hunches, projections or mind reading. Cultures that communicate with hints, hidden meanings, guesses and mind reading end up with generations of bitterness, anger, wrath, misunderstanding and confusion. Speaking with genuineness leads to a peaceful presence and harmonious relationships.

> *If one is estranged from oneself, then one is estranged from others, too.*
> *If one is out of touch with oneself, then one cannot touch others.*
> **Anne Morrow Lindbergh**

Biblical Examples

The congruence of the early church's leadership was one reason they were able to persuade so many to come to the Messiah. Before Saul became Paul, he was an angry murderer whose rages led to persecution and outbursts against the church and its leaders. He even assisted in the stoning of Steven. After meeting the risen Christ, Saul became a believer and followed Jesus. However, his inner life was still full of anger, conflict and confusion. His wrath was simply transferred from the church to his former friends and colleagues.

Barnabas, counselor to the Apostles, risked life, limb and reputation to introduce Saul to the Jerusalem church leaders. Soon after meeting them, Saul attacked the Jewish authorities, throwing the persecuted church into panic and making life dangerous for all Christians. The leaders decided that Saul needed inner healing so they deported him from Palestine back to his hometown of Tarsus where he stayed for almost a decade. His time away from ministry allowed the Lord to remove the logs from Saul's eyes and heal most of his rage. For ten years God took Saul through a series of intense inner healing sessions. What a process that was.

After planting the first church among the Gentiles in Antioch, Barnabas recruited Saul to be his disciple. Barnabas trained Saul and several other leaders for a year before taking him as his assistant on the first missionary trip. Only then was Saul able to use his talents, training and gifts in ministry. It was at least ten years before Saul genuinely understood himself well enough to travel under Barnabas leadership among the Gentiles. Even then, his wrath burst forth as they planned the second trip. He refused to forgive John Mark for leaving the first trip in mid-flight. He was still unable to completely conquer the anger that was his thorn in the flesh.

> **The internal condition of the messenger is as important as the content of the message.**
> GRS

After much work and many years, Paul matured enough to have a peaceful presence in the midst of extreme stress. For example, when preaching to the Athenians, Paul was able to compliment them on being very religious. Uncharacteristically, he saw the positive possibilities of pagans worship. This change gave Paul many opportunities to share the gospel. In earlier times Paul might have viciously attacked them for worshipping false gods. Saul fought Christians when he was a Jew; he fought Jews when he was a young Christian; and he fought John Mark and Barnabas when he was a young missionary.

Evangelists and missionaries especially need to be *Genuine*. Those whom we are attempting to reach with the good news are rightly critical of hypocrisy. The early church leaders knew that Saul was too immature to witness effectively so they made sure he took care of his own heart before trying to do heart surgery on others. Few unbelievers will buy from a person they think is dishonest. Trust of the messenger precedes trusting the message and the power of the message is directly related to the peace of the messenger.

The internal condition of the messenger is as important as the content of the message. Developing self-awareness, inner peace, trust in God and the ability to communicate will influence Seekers who desire to grow.

> *But the fruit of the Spirit is love, joy, peace, longsuffering, kindness, goodness,*
> *faithfulness, gentleness, self-control. Against such there is no law.*
> *And those who are Christ's have crucified the flesh with its passions*
> *and desires. If we live in the Spirit, let us also walk in the Spirit. Let us not*
> *become conceited, provoking one another, envying one another.*
> Galatians 5:22-26 (NKJ)

God's fruit develops in the heart and expresses itself in relationships. The inner trip must precede the outer journey. Paul instructs us to avoid conceit, aggravating one another and envying of another's lifestyle, all of which are heart conditions. Those who examine, know and cleanse the heart will influence others for the kingdom of God.

 Life Scan Summary

Practicing the skill of genuineness is an important step in becoming an effective Helper. Genuineness requires that we examine our inner life and accept ourselves for who we are in Christ. This work will free us to hear the Seeker's journey without interference and distractions. A Genuine person has a better understanding of others and reaches out to them with increased compassion. The more we understand ourselves and humbly accept our shortcomings without self-condemnation, the more we can assist others in the healing process. To summarize Jesus, Blind guides with blind eyes end up with disciples in ditches.

A favorite singer, of ours, Kenny Thacker wrote a song that Helpers find very insightful. Called, "A Little Help" It points us to the source of all counsel, The Holy Spirit.

> *Perhaps you'd listen to the story of my quest for some assistance*
> *I have traveled this world over trying to get to know me well*
> *I've taken notes at all the seminars with painstaking persistence.*
> *Just to find it wasn't worth it when I finally found myself.*
> *All my money time and effort never changed my situation,*
> *And Lord I nearly went insane trying to heal my inner self.*
> *I bought the books and tapes and videos but expert information*
> *Never worked so I looked upward then I found a little help.*
>
> *A little help from heaven gets you back upon your feet.*
> *A little help from heaven takes the tension off the line.*
> *A little help from heaven tends to make you act real sweet,*
> *A little help from heaven eases off a worried mind.*
> *A little help from heaven pulls you out of trouble fast.*
> *A little help from heaven heals you from a sucker punch;*
> *A little help from heaven makes the things that matter last.*
> *A little help from heaven helps you out a great big bunch.*

TIPS for Life

Personal Reflection and Practice

- *Reflect on the characteristics that you like to share.*

- *What aspects of yourself would you only share with someone you trust a great deal?*

- *In what areas of your life would you like to receive feedback?*

- What would it mean to you to be fully confident in your Christian identity?

- What would you do differently. How would you think and feel differently?

To say the right thing at the right time, keep still most of the time.
John W. Roper

The prime purpose of eloquence is to keep other people from speaking.
Louis Vermeil

God's fruit starts in the heart and expresses itself in relationships. GRS

A wonderful source of inner knowledge and cleansing is intense worship in which the Holy Spirit searches and scours the depths of our mind and heart. When we sing, "Search me oh God," He takes us at our word and seeks out any trace of evil to destroy. We call this the "search warrant prayer" for it gives the Holy Spirit the right to search every aspect of our heart. Thankfully, the oil of grace and mercy allow the surgery of the soul to proceed with gentleness.

Seven

With Warmth and Concern

7

Love with Skin on It

Greet one another with a holy kiss. Romans 16:16

This one thing is clear, throughout every stage and type of interaction with our family, cell group members, co-workers, colleagues, clients or partners, the quality of interpersonal relationships is central. It contributes to good marriages, positive parenting, effective management, quality education, sustained growth and personal healing. Truly, love is the greatest asset and church fellowship is the foundation for giving and receiving it. Without it evangelism falters, growth stops and God weeps.

A Prayer for Persons Joined in Fellowship

> *Help us to help each other, Lord,*
> *Each other's cross to bear,*
> *Let all their friendly aid afford,*
> *and feel each other's care.*
>
> *Help us to build each other up,*
> *our little stock improve,*
> *Increase our Faith, confirm our Hope,*
> *And perfect us in Love.*
>
> *Charles Wesley*

In every era of church history we have seen an emphasis on the power of caring. Most noted church leaders have taught us to, "Love one another" and "Forgive one another as God has forgiven you" Ephesians 4:32. Additionally, the music of the Wesley brothers as well as their preaching, teaching and writings set a high standard for care, counsel and mutual fellowship among the flock of God. In fact, one of John Wesley's most creative and powerful initiatives were the groups he called *classes*. They were places of safety, healing and accountability. Wesley could be called the grandfather of support and recovery groups. The founders of Alcoholics Anonymous adopted many of his principles when the organization was formed.

A client's complaints almost always focus on past or present broken relationships. People suffer with life long pain and trauma from dysfunctional families and relationships gone sour. All humans have suffered rejection, abandonment and disappointment from the people they love. This is why the quality of church care is so important. Healing rarely happens if we react to members' immaturity with insensitivity, frustration or anger. We will see no goal setting, no willingness to repent and no true heart changes without the bridge of a strong, trusting, cooperative bond between us.

 What People Want in a Church

Whenever you ask a person about how they experienced a visit to a new church the answer is always the same. They invariably mention the climate. "The place was so cold that it snowed in the worship service." On the other hand they might indicate that the place was warm and friendly. Some churches can, in fact, be too hot for some visitors who react negatively to hugging. In any event, we all respond to the emotional weather of a gathering and decide whether to return or not based on our preferences.

This is one reason we use a thermometer to judge the right temperature of our interactions. On a scale of zero to ten with zero being freezing cold and ten boiling hot we need to temper our verbal and non-verbal interactions to the Seeker's comfort level. Since their comfort varies we are the ones who have to show the greatest sensitivity. Scripture admonishes us to be aware of others' preferences.

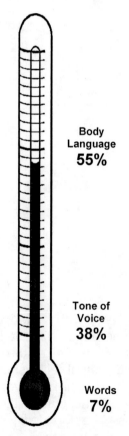

Body Language 55%

Tone of Voice 38%

Words 7%

Factors that Influence Communication

Like one who takes away a garment on a cold day, or like vinegar poured on soda, is one who sings songs to a heavy heart. Prov 25:20

A friend went to visit a man suffering from cancer. She entered the hospital room and said cheerily, "Praise the Lord for this beautiful day." He looked up at her through the fog of medication and replied, "You haven't spent much time in a sick bed have you?" My friend used this experience to grow in awareness of how to minister to a person with a heavy heart.

Dr. Albert Mehrabian's extensive research on the proper temperature of a relationship found that it was even more important than the words we use. He found that the actual words contribute only about 7% of the total message. Our tone of voice is a factor five times more powerful than the best-chosen language for it carries some 38% of the message. Learning to "tone ourselves down" is important to our ministry.

Try this experiment. The next time you see a dog, make a nasty comment in a warm, loving tone of voice. Try something like this. "You ugly old dog. I am going to beat you with a stick." The dog will probably wag her tail and come over for a pat on the head. Despite the *Content* of the words, she senses your love and kindness. You may also try the opposite tack and say loving words in a harsh tone.

Dr. Mehrabian discovered that body language speaks even more powerfully than tone of voice. It was found to contain some 55% of the message. Remember when the small children met Jesus and interacted with Him? His body language and tone of voice drew *children to His side and to His lap. We cannot fool children about our character. Some of the self-appointed disciples tried to shoo the children away as if to say, "The Rabbi is too important to be with youngsters." But Jesus thought differently and challenged their callousness by saying:*

74

Let the little children come unto me for such is the kingdom of God. Mark 10:13

Little children intuitively sensed that Jesus loved them. Body language communicates our inner heart reality. No matter how hard we try to act like a spiritual person, the ways we interact with others betrays the condition of our soul.

The eye is the lamp of the body. If your eyes are good, your whole body will be full of light. But if your eyes are bad, your whole body will be full of darkness. If then the light within you is darkness, how great is that darkness! Matt 6:21-23 (NIV)

If our eyes are full of darkness, evil will grow because no light can enter and illuminate us. Jesus used irony as a teaching method, and Charles Dickens used that mode in his famous story The Christmas Carol.

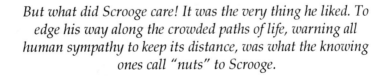

> Oh! But he was a tight-fisted hand at the grindstone, was Scrooge! a squeezing, wrenching grasping, scraping, clutching, covetous old sinner! External heat and cold had little influence on him. No warmth could warm, no cold could chill him. No wind that blew was bitterer than he, no falling snow was more intent upon its purpose, no pelting rain less open to entreaty. Foul weather didn't know where to defeat him. The heaviest rain and snow and hail and sleet could boast of the advantage over him in only one respect, -- they often "came down" handsomely, and Scrooge never did.
>
> Nobody ever stopped him in the street to say, with gladsome looks, "My dear Scrooge, how are you? When will you come to see me?" No beggars implored him to bestow a trifle, no children asked him what it was o'clock, no man or woman ever once in all his life inquired the way to such and such a place, of Scrooge. Even the blind men's dogs appeared to know him; and when they saw him coming on, would tug their owners into doorways and up courts; and then would wag their tails as though they said, "No eye at all is better than an evil eye, dark master!"
>
> But what did Scrooge care! It was the very thing he liked. To edge his way along the crowded paths of life, warning all human sympathy to keep its distance, was what the knowing ones call "nuts" to Scrooge.

Scrooge's *evil eye* revealed the sourness of his soul. How great was his darkness! Scrooge even compares unfavorably with foul weather! No wonder we are told that non-verbals are some 93% of communication. Dickens saves his most important comment for the last. "This was the very thing that Scrooge liked." Non-verbals expressed the deepest longings of a heart, "warning all human sympathy to keep its distance." The dogs preferred the safety of a dark alley to the dangers of a dark soul.

We who minister in the name of the Lord must take great care lest we allow a cold, hardened soul develop within us. Then, like the Pharisees, we would tell others to love God with our words but non-verbally reveal that those words are lies. A well-known preacher told about his own bumpy entry into healing ministry. After many years of preaching without the benefit of a theology or practice of healing, he encountered the Holy Spirit in a new way and sensed a call to travel and speak about wholeness.

During the very first sermon on the topic, he came to the pulpit and, with a voice shaking with anger and his finger pointed accusingly at the congregation shouted, "God loves you and wants you to be healed!" Upon hearing and seeing this display of accusation, a young child said loudly, "Let's get out of here, Grandma. That man is mad at everybody." When the little children come to us do they feel our love or discern our anger. Do little children prefer your company to that of others?

Growing in Love

The preacher in this story was obviously self-disclosing personal foibles in order to make the point the God was still working on the development of his soul. That is a journey worthy of our commitment and support. Unfortunately, many leaders are out of touch with their inner life. Pastors are often people who are concerned with everyone else's spiritual condition when they need to be taking the time to work on their own relationship to God. Jesus offered the following advice for those who would be leaders.

No good tree bears bad fruit, nor does a bad tree bear good fruit. Each tree is recognized by its own fruit. People do not pick figs from thorn bushes, or grapes from briers. The good man brings good things out of the good stored up in his heart, and the evil man brings evil things out of the evil stored up in his heart. For out of the overflow of his heart his mouth speaks. Luke 6:43-45

Non-verbal communication makes up some 93% of our message. Since it arises mostly from the unconscious heart, spiritual surgery of the soul is the only way to improve our relationships. Revisit the chapter on Genuineness to make sure you are developing congruence between the verbal and non-verbal dimensions of your life.

Loving Warmly

Behavior is largely determined by the condition of one's soul. However, once the Holy Spirit has done His work in us, we can speed the growth process by putting into daily practice the truths that God has already imputed to us. The only appropriate response to the Holy Spirit in us is putting on behavior that glorifies the Father. Practice does not make us perfect, but it does make the newly acquired behavior permanent.

The public knowledge and acceptance of caring non-verbals is widespread. We could ask about any group of Christians to give us a list. Imagine that a friend came to you with a courageous but humble request. He had read the Bible and had come to the conclusion that his ability to relate with love to others was impaired. The habits formed during childhood had hardened into a lifestyle of studied coolness and uncaring self-absorption and the Holy Spirit Convicted him of the need to change.

To respond to the request, you sit at a restaurant observing the way he relates with another person. You watch closely and take careful notes on all the ways your friend could improve. Here is a partial list of the things he does during the interaction with a colleague.

- His handshake is perfunctory and cool.
- He averts his eyes from the face of the colleague.
- He occasionally studies his date book.
- He receives a phone call and makes another one.
- He leans backward in the chair.
- He looks at his watch.
- His impassive face shows no expression.
- His questions and statements are abrupt.
- He shows no non-verbal response to his associate's statements.

Most of your friend's non-verbal errors are on the side of the scale we consider inappropriately cool. Our model is like the porridge of the three bears in that it is not too hot and not too cold, but just right. We try to accommodate ourselves to the mental, emotional and physical preferences of the Seeker.

Another of our famous acrostics has been developed to help you remember how to communicate effectively. This one spells, SOLAR TEA and comes from the way that Gary's Grandma Taylor made iced tea in the summer. She set a Mason jar of water and tea bags out in the sun. The warm rays of the sun made the finest, most gentle tea imaginable. Interacting with SOLAR TEA will bring warmth to the lives of hurting people.

What you are doing speaks so loudly that I cannot hear what you say. Anon

Scale of Warmth

0———1——2——3———4———5——6——7———8——9——10

| Cold | Cool | Tepid | Warm | Hot | Blazing |

The letters in SOLAR TEA stands for behavior that will promote health and growth. Think about a person you enjoy being with. More than likely their warmth matches your preferred level of comfort. They probably attend to you in the ways you feel most comfortable. Those whom we deem to be cool, withdrawn or impassive do not impress us as friendly. Overly intense people leave us with an uncomfortable feeling.

Sensitive Space: The space between us needs to carefully chosen. In some cultures, it is appropriate to be quite close to clients but in other cultures, the comfort zone is farther apart. For example, in the United States most of us are comfortable at about an arm's distance. Standing or sitting closer than that seems a bit too hot. Some Americans enjoy hugs and very close interactions but that is not the norm.

On the other hand, more distance between us feels too cool and distant. Some research indicates that male counselors communicate a lack of interest when they sit behind a desk. Many pastors sit in front of their desks to communicate a welcoming attitude. The climate that is created by our personal space may say more about our theology than the content of our sermons.

S

O

L

A

R

Open: A posture of openness indicates a welcoming attitude while closed arms and crossed legs may send a message of anxiety. A closed posture is not *invitational*. We often see newly minted counseling graduates withdraw into an uptight posture with a clipboard clutched tightly to their chest and eyes squinted in fear. A new counselor may say he was anxious because, "I kept wondering what I was going to do and say. I was also scared that they would ask me something I could not answer or have a problem that was over my head." Practice an open posture by intentionally taking deep breaths, smiling and establishing rapport through small talk. After a few times it will become a natural part of ministry.

Lean forward: When one is interested in what another person is saying, he leans toward them to hear and focus better on what they are saying. He does not want to miss a single syllable or non-verbal gesture. The people to whom we minister have the right to expect our intense interest so we make it a practice to lean toward them.

Appropriate Eyes: Psalm 139 says that we are fearfully and wonderfully made. God gave us the ability to see others' emotional state as well as communicate emotions through our eyes. Gary's son Timothy tried to communicate with his dad one day on the way to school but Gary failed to establish good eye contact. In frustration, Timothy grabbed his dad's chin and turned his head around so their eyes could fully meet. The little child taught his father about the importance of eyeball-to-eyeball communication.

Looks can be hard or soft, cruel or loving, anxious or peaceful. We can tell how a person is feeling even from a great distance. It is best if we look at the Seeker in a soft, but casual manner rather than with a piercing gaze that penetrates his skull. In fact, it is usually best not to look directly into the person's eyes but at the bridge of his nose. Looks that cause others to become uncomfortable are to be avoided. This includes staring, gazing with disapproval or looking bored.

Jesus had a visage that drew people to follow Him. The wounded, sinful, financially poor, disregarded, unsavory and abused came running to Him for help. Only a man with kindness shining from his eyes could have accomplished such a feat. The eyes of Jesus must have been the opposite of those in Scrooge before he repented. The story of Scrooge's salvation inspires us to realize how God can change us from a cold and uncaring hermit into a warm and loving uncle.

Relaxed: Our posture and body language tend to be contagious. People who speak about difficult issues will normally relax if we indicate we relate to them with peace. Anxiety is toxic to Christian ministry. Fear can only be overcome with faith. Another term for *relaxed* is *peaceful presence.* Our peaceful presence communicates trust in God and encourages others to grow in hope and faith. A friend who works as an ambulance nurse says that going to an accident scene with peace is critical to the patient's well being. The emergency personnel are trained to exit the ambulance in a calm, collected manner and walk, not run, to the injured parties.

By adjusting ourselves to the energy level of others, we communicate genuine interest. If the person is excited and I sit smiling placidly, nodding my head, the Seeker could interpret this as disinterest or condescension. If, on the other hand, I match the Seeker's energy level as much as possible, she will sense that I care about her. Scripture exhorts us to mourn with those who mourn and rejoice with those who rejoice. By entering into the person's frame of reference we can more easily understand her situation.

Touch: The 2000 presidential elections in the United States indicate just how important it is to relate with warmth. Vice President Gore was thought to be the stiffest, coldest person in American politics. He changed that perception with one act. During his acceptance speech at the Democratic Convention, Mr. Gore grasped his wife and gave her a long, passionate kiss. His approval rate immediately jumped and he was seen in a brand new light. The media suddenly found him to be a warm person, caring and compassionate. What changed so many minds? How was he able to persuade voters that he had become so different? It took only one kiss.

Not to be outdone, George W. Bush came up with a plan to combat Mr. Gore's lead in the polls. He went on the television show of one of the most popular women in the world, Oprah Winfrey. In front of millions of viewers, Mr. Bush kissed and embraced her. Boldly bussing a famous African-American woman electrified the public. He showed what we call, *non-possessive touch.*

His brotherly kiss and hug communicated warmth, caring and an emotional greeting without any demand or interest in control. In this hypersensitive era of sexual harassment, the difference between a non-verbal home run and one that is a triple play can be found in the term, non-possessive. Had Mr. Bush grabbed Oprah harshly or passionately, his polls would have plunged.

Women are especially sensitive to anything that smacks of control. Yet caring touch is essential to our emotional life. Residents of retirement homes live, on average, seven or eight years longer than those who stay alone. Community or koinonia means going the same way and is important to our health and welfare.

Dr. James Lynch saw the positive results of non-possessive touch at John Hopkins University Hospital. Comatose patients on respirators had dramatically positive changes in heart rate, breathing and brain wave activity when gently touched physically and verbally by a nurse. Dr. Lynch was deeply moved by how easy it is to minister life to very sick patients.

However, he also observed how damaging, uncaring interactions were to the same patients. When doctors on their official rounds spoke about the patients in clinical, non-caring tones all the signs of anxiety immediately showed on the monitors. Despite the fact that the patients were unconscious, the power of both caring and non-caring relationships on their physical health was obvious when measured by clinical machines.

Death and life are in the power of the tongue. Proverbs 18:21

The well-known family therapist, Virginia Satir, was a genius in building relationships. One of her most famous sayings summarizes the importance of non-possessive touch.

> *We need four hugs daily to exist emotionally.*
> *We need eight hugs daily to maintain our health.*
> *We need twelve hugs daily to grow as persons.*

The Bible places a greater emphasis on warmth than even Ms. Satir. St. Paul writes in Romans 16:16 to *Greet one another with a holy kiss.* Perhaps Ms. Satir under estimated the need for hugs, and we actually need sixteen holy hugs and holy kisses each day to remain spiritually and relationally healthy. Holy hugs and kisses prevent diseases, keep us calm, make us smile, lessen stress and help us relax. All for free.

Environment points us to the conditions of the office or meeting area. The environment should make people feel safe. Many of us grew up in unsafe relationships and are super sensitive to anything that feels risky. We need to make sure the conversation is private so no one can overhear confidential information. Also, we must eliminate anything that may distract either of us. The decorations need to be calming and uncluttered. Peaceful colors and comfortable chairs should be chosen.

Small groups need a cozy space without being too cramped. However, the space requirements will vary from country to country. Some cultures thrive in what we Americans would consider cramped conditions. Having wide-open spaces is not as important in Europe and Asia as in Australia or America.

An *Accommodating Attitude* calls us to respect and reflect the person's culture, language, values and expectations. This is one of the most important factors for moving folk toward the *Ready to Change Stage.* As ambassadors of Jesus, we need to discover a solution that will fit and please the values, preferences and priorities of the Seeker.

On his first trip to Asia, a kind student informed Gary that one of his personal habits was offensive to that culture. He was surprised and embarrassed to learn that the way he clapped his hands had an unpleasant connotation to the students. He immediately accommodated himself to their customs and has not repeated his error since that early visit.

This is especially critical when it comes to touch. In Gary's home church, Harvest Fellowship, the congregation values very warm interpersonal relationships. The members hug each other at every opportunity and take a long break after worship as a hug time. However, that is not acceptable to many of our friends in Asia. Some Muslims forbid even male-female handshaking. We do everything possible to accommodate ourselves to those traditions and watch the group carefully for cues to follow. We are guided by the proverb, *When in Rome, do as the Romans do.*

Warm Love Develops Healing Communities

A psychology class experiment shows just how powerful body language can be in shaping others' behavior. A group of six students decided to influence the teaching style of a notoriously dull professor. In the middle of a typical lecture, the students began, on cue, to focus on the professor's words with rapt attention and eager interest by leaning forward in their seats and nodding, showing eye contact and smiling. Within thirty seconds, the teacher became more animated and excited. He paced around the classroom with vigor and offered the students an increased amount of warmth. He smiled, nodded toward the students and laughed. After attending in this manner for a few minutes the students went back to their old ways of slouching and impassive features. The lecturer also returned to his old style, prompting the question, "Who is teaching whom?"

> **People do not care how much you know until they know how much you care.**

Remember that some 30% of influence toward finding a solution to problems comes from the caring interactions of the Helper and Seeker. Even if our Empathy is not the most accurate, *Warm love* can overcome it. Our insight and wisdom may be lacking but *Warm caring love* will show the Seeker that we are trying. We may not be geniuses at solving problems, understanding the scripture or gifted healers whose touch results in instant release, but *warm love* can be even more important. It is no mystery why the apostle Paul said that the greatest is love.

Loving Relationships and Health

Dr. Robert Hatfield of the University of Cincinnati, tells how Dr. Renee Spitz, a famous French physician, set up the most advanced orphanages in the world. He discovered, to his horror, that despite the best medical and nutritional care possible, his children were depressive, sickly and weak. Worn out and defeated, Dr. Spitz took a vacation to the mountains of Mexico where he discovered quite by accident, that the answer to his dilemma was not in technology but in love. During a daily walk Spitz came upon an old building used as an orphanage. The facilities were terrible, the food basic and the staff uneducated and sparse. However, the children were strong and happy. He was stunned and wanted to learn how they were able to produce such thriving children.

 What he found shocked the scientific world and changed the way children's homes are run. Each day, ladies from the local village came to the orphanage to nurture the children. They hugged, rocked them and sang to the kids for an hour. The emotional, physical and mental results were amazing. The children thrived in every way so Dr. Spitz returned to Paris with an appreciation for the power of love.

This research mirrors that of Harry F. Harlow some forty years ago. Dr. Harlow's long-term studies found that monkeys separated from their mothers developed aberrant sexual behavior, violent tendencies and brain lesions. Recent data reveals that the same results are also occurring among abused and neglected children. A child's human interactions causes connections to form between brain cells. These connections are pruned during puberty. Whatever a child experiences, for good or bad, helps determine how his brain is wired. There is a growing body of evidence that there is a history of childhood abuse among adolescents who commit violent crimes."

Unfortunately, brain damaged kids with violent tendencies and sexual deviancy seems to be on the rise in our nation. The only way to repair this damage is to make sure that they get a lot of love from adoptive/foster families and churches. The church has a positive impact on the health of individuals, couples and families. Now, however, it is time to expand the impact. The only hope for at risk children is a great increase in faith-based communities intentionally reaching out to those families in need.

Models for Church Life

With the *AS I GREW* skills, we have practical ways to live out God's love and acceptance. The research now available on the power of faith, hope and love to heal wounded hearts and damaged brains is a tremendous encouragement to those committed to the Great Commandment. Churches need to develop their congregations into communities of warmth. Society has increasingly become focused on high technology with a less emphasis on caring for each other. One church used the following steps.

- A special, high touch worship service with weekly communion. Members came forward for a personal touch and word of encouragement. Anointing with oil, a listening team and healing prayer were also available.
- A Christian education facility staffed by retired *grandparents*. Every child was warmly greeted and hugged as he/she entered the building.
- Lifeskills classes were offered to members every quarter, raising the level of care for the entire congregation.
- Over 125 persons were commissioned to be lay pastors to provide prayer, support, hospital visits and friendship.
- Over 60 persons served as lay counselors for anyone wanting a specialized ministry of care and healing.
- Small groups provided a caring community of support and learning.

This congregation grew in numbers, vitality, depth and outreach. It provided numerous ways for members, friends and visitors to grow through Christian community.

These three remain, faith, hope and love but the greatest is love. I Co 13:13

Process Not a Program

This acrostic is meant to give you some hints about ways to build caring relationships. Simply memorizing the SOLAR TEA acrostic is not actually learning the skills and attitudes necessary to communicate life, health and peace. Start adding more warmth in your daily discipline and see how people respond. The people around you will, no doubt, feel refreshed by your lifestyle of SOLAR TEA.

Life Scan Summary

Science and Scripture agree that nonverbal caring is critical for a person's total development. An attitude of caring love promotes healing and growth. Body language and tone of voice convey ninety-three percent of our messages. Simple ways to express *Warmth* are described by the acrostic SOLAR TEA.

TIPS for Life

Personal Reflection and Practice

- How well do you express warmth? Rate yourself on a scale from 1 to 10. One is aloof, inattentive. Ten is consistent warmth with body language and tone of voice, including the ability to express intense emotions like anger or grief.

1	2	3	4	5	6	7	8	9	10

- How will you know when your warmth improves by one point?
- What would be different about your behavior?
- How would this affect others?
- What would they say is different about you?
- Set a goal to increase your warm interactions with a friend, family member or colleague.
- Keep a journal noting what happens as you work on the goal.
- What feelings do you experience?
- What barriers do you encounter?

Eight

Respect and, yes, Love

8

Tuning in to Others

My dear brothers and sisters please take note of this: Everyone should be quick to listen
and slow to speak. James 1:19

The skill of Active Listening is the rocket ship on which the payload of core conditions ride. We cannot relate with AS I GREW without good listening skills. In fact, the hard work of helping people change is made easier by listening. Some therapists can interview clients with clinical precision and accurate diagnosis but they do not minister life. Our goal is to listen to the heart. The soul that is understood grows in life, health and peace. With one ear tuned to the voice of God and the other to the cries of a hurting heart we offer a refuge for safe exploration.

When pastors call me to help their organizations, they always
ask me to speak; but when they want me to help them, they always ask me to listen. GRS

From the earliest days of research on care and counsel, listening with *Empathy* has been cited as a core helping skill. Listening with empathy is foundational to the success of parents, pastors, secretaries, salesmen and ambassadors as well as therapists. *Empathy* is essential to all human dialogue.

Empathy is the ability to imaginatively and accurately tune in to
the mind and heart of another person
in order understand his thoughts and feelings in a way
that he knows he is understood. GRS

Empathy is often mistaken for *sympathy* or "feeling into the feelings of other people." Empathy is the cognitive ability to accurately understand another person's thoughts and feelings despite the lack of fellow emotion with that person. We can have accurate *Empathy* for a hurting individual even if we cannot relate with the same personal feelings. Otherwise it would be impossible for a man to minister to a mother depressed over her miscarriage.

Sympathy goes farther than accurately understanding the ideas and feelings of others. To sympathize with a depressed woman means we actually experience her emotional state. This is also called compassion and mercy. We can learn the skill of *Empathy* but sympathy is a gift of God that cannot be taught. *Empathy* keeps the focus on the woman so she can gain insight about her problems and their possible solutions. Our goal is to teach you how to relate with accurate *Empathy* whether you have the gift of sympathy or not.

In our past books we indicated that sympathy should be avoided. However, we have come to the conclusion that we were wrong. Martin Synnes, a pastor and theologian in Norway, argued that sympathy is a good scriptural word that ought be preserved. We had thought that sympathy connected too deeply with others' feelings and would tempt us to rescue people from their responsibilities. A further study of the scripture has led us to conclude that sympathy is a godly way of relating even though it is a challenge to manage. In order to make this distinction clear, we have added to the scale of relationships. We now use the following terminology.

0-2   *Callous:* an uncaring disregard for others' thoughts and feelings.
3-4   *Apathy:* a lack interest in others
5-6   *Empathy:* accurate discernment of other's ideas, concerns and feelings
7-8   *Sympathy:* compassion with inner experience similar to another person
9-10   *Enmeshed:* confusing my feelings and ideas with others' ideas and feelings

> *Science may have found a cure for most evils; but it has found no remedy for the worst of them all – the apathy of human beings.*

A callous disregard for others: Some people relate with a cold and hardened attitude toward the concerns of others. During the 20th Century we have seen several political leaders who ruled with brutal callousness. For example, Stalin said, "The death of one person is a tragedy. The death of a million is a statistic." Mao, Pol Pot and Hitler fill the definition of extremely callous leaders.

Callousness is an extreme lack of concern for others. It can lead to unethical and immoral behavior. The extreme of an empathic failure is a *sociopathic personality disorder. A sociopath* can steal food from babies or take the last cent from a destitute retiree without feeling remorse or even understanding their plight.

Apathy is a lack of interest in others. *This may be the greatest problem facing the church. Many of us are simply too tired or too busy to tune in to another person's life. Does the pursuit of success in sports, music, academics and computers take valuable time away from caring for the people around us? We may also have "compassion burn out" from watching so many television disasters and traumas that we feel overwhelmed.*

Empathy is complimentary to the spiritual gift of discernment. Discernment is a gift of the Holy Spirit that enables us to see the truth about the hidden things of the heart. *Empathy* is an observation skill that empowers us to bring clarity to misunderstanding and confusion. Disturbances of the mind need insight from either empathic understanding or discernment. *Empathy* informs us when and how to do the right thing at the right time in the VCR process. It also communicates that we care and is essential to trust and hope. Discernment and empathy together enable us to move toward ministry with sensitivity, clarity, patience and power.

ENMESHED
SYMPATHETIC
EMPATHIC
APATHETIC
CALLOUS

Teaching *Empathy* is one of the chief responsibilities of the church. Lack of human understanding can cripple a family, small group or a congregation. It is not low IQ (Intelligence Quotient) but low EIQ (Emotional Intelligence) that causes so much conflict in today's congregations. Many churches need remedial *Empathy* training.

Sympathy is qualitatively different from *Empathy*. In *sympathy*, we actually share a bit of another person's thoughts and feelings through an inner emotional response to his/her situation. This is also called compassion in scripture. As we respond with compassion we first feel the person's feeling, then we must act accordingly and appropriately to assist them. Both motivate us to minister to others in need.

However, *sympathy* is more challenging for us to regulate appropriately because we can confuse *sympathy* and *enmeshment*. The gift of compassion is not necessary to developing a ministry of helping but it can be a powerful source of motivation. If we only ministered when we felt like it, we would be apathetic most of the time. Only Jesus had perfect compassion and only He managed it well.

> *Therefore, since we have a great high priest who has gone through the heavens, Jesus the Son of God, let us hold firmly to the faith we profess. For we do not have a high priest who is unable to sympathize with our weaknesses, but we have one who has been tempted in every way, just as we are, yet without sin. Let us then approach the throne of grace with confidence, so that we may receive mercy and find grace to help us in our time of need. Hebrews 4:15-16*

Jesus accurately understood the people around Him. He walked among the people and knew their thoughts, feelings and desires. He had amazing discernment and responded to others appropriately. Many biblical characters such as the woman at the well and Zaccheus were touched by His *Empathy*. Because He understood their shattered dreams, they experienced dramatic conversions and decided to walk in a new way. Wise counsel depends upon learning how to discern the longings of the heart.

Jesus was also able to sympathize with the people around Him. He wept over the death of His friend Lazarus. He was able to genuinely and openly share grief even when He knew that the resurrection of Lazarus was soon to occur. Jesus also had compassion for the rich young ruler. Unfortunately, the young man failed to be moved by His mercy.

Since our high priest has been tempted in the same ways as we, He actually experienced our brokenness, sinful state and feelings while on the cross. In Greek, *sumpatheo* means to have a fellow feeling with another person. Compassion drew Him to suffer an agonizing death in order to heal our weakness, pain and guilt. He lived, died and rose again to remove sin and sickness forever. Sympathy adds emotional resolve and energy to our thoughts and provides the intensity necessary to right a wrong. Sympathizers cannot be passive in the face of injustice or pain. They must act with righteous anger and zealous commitment to rescue the perishing and care for the dying.

> *Down in the human heart,*
> *Crushed by the tempter,*
> *Feelings lie buried,*
> *That grace can restore.*
> *Touched by a loving heart*
> *Wakened by kindness*
> *Chords that were broken*
> *Will vibrate once more.*
> Fanny J. Crosby

Compassion includes an emotional response so we can cry with those who cry and laugh with them as well. We take pleasure in their joy and experience discomfort at their pain for *when one member of the body hurts, we all hurt* I Corinthians 12:26. A healing church acts with both empathy and sympathy. Leadership that is apathetic cannot adequately minister to those who need forgiveness, cleansing and healing. Apathetic churches led by uncaring elders take comfort in the fact that they have already been saved. Instead of throwing out the lifeline to those who are drowning they pull up the gangplank to make sure no sick or sinful people get on board.

When we cannot distinguish our feelings from those of another person, it is called *Enmeshment*. Some families make their children into caregivers who become emotional sponges. Some parents exist in a constant pool of anxiety and stress that is absorbed by their children who cannot then develop a sense of personal identity. Like a drop of blue in a bucket of black ink, the child's ideas and emotions are so mixed together with the rest of the tribe that no personal color exists.

The stress of a dysfunctional home leaves some of us with an intuitive sense about the needs of others. We can respond without listening or talking. Our radar is on automatic pilot and we fly according to the emotional state of those around us. Their pain is our pain. Their happiness is our happiness. We become "mind readers" who simply react without thinking about what we are doing. *We* rarely know what *we* feel or what *we* think because *we* are always feeling and thinking for others. Our drive to please and relieve others' pain is the supreme motivation in our lives. We may not be able to tell the difference between our inner life and the inner life of another person.

One Asian leader was shocked when we taught on the need for each believer to discover his gifts, call and passion in life. "I was not even allowed to choose the food I ate," she said. "How can I choose what ministry I enter?" After more listening, we discovered that she simply absorbed the feelings and thoughts of the people around her and assumed their ideas were her ideas.

Many who feel called to a ministry of care are in this boat. We are "co-dependent." Our need to be needed is as great as the alcoholic's need for a drink. Enmeshed leaders will always find those who want someone else to feel for them so the situation goes from bad to worse. Sometimes an apathetic or callous person marries a mate who is co-dependent. It is a perfectly, imperfect match of dysfunction. Each person is looking for the mirror opposite. Once discovered, they stick together like super glue. She wants to feel and do for him and he wants her to own his feeling and relational life.

Enmeshed persons rarely recognize personal feelings because the feelings of others are so overwhelming. This blocks effective ministry for it impedes objective analysis of the facts. One cannot speak the truth in love if he is lost in the subjective feelings of the Seeker. Unfortunately, enmeshment may seem like it is spiritual, caring and compassionate to some persons but it is not.

By learning to be *Genuine* we discover our individual personality. Helpers who are unaware of their inner life get confused about the feelings of others. Enmeshed Helpers try to lower their own anxiety rather than that of the Seeker. They find it difficult or impossible to confront a needy person or say no to their unreasonable requests.

Cartoon: A woman says to her husband,
"How am I feeling today, Fred?"

Enmeshment arises from low self-esteem and poorly defined self-awareness. A mother experiences her son's feelings to the point that she can hardly stand for him to be in discomfort. Her anxiety drives her to interfere with the father's attempts to discipline the child, blocking his emotional growth. Only when she discovers her personal identity in Christ will she be able to allow her son to grow up and his father to be a good parent.

Jesus Models Helping

When Jesus ministered to the woman caught in adultery, He showed both *Empathy* and *sympathy*. The local religious leaders were callous enough to apply the Law without mercy. They had no remorse about stoning her. Jesus, however, understood the woman's plight with accurate *Empathy* and responded with compassion. The *Empathy* of Jesus toward women is amazing. No wonder oppressed females from all over the globe are turning to Him in such large numbers.

Jesus needed great wisdom to minister appropriately in this situation. He first tuned into the men involved to make sure He accurately listened to their concerns. He had empathic understanding of their situation, knowing that, if the woman were an adulterer, one of the accusers had to have personal knowledge of her behavior, making him an accomplice. Otherwise, how would they have known what happened? Jesus perceived their defensiveness and responded wisely. He asked a few "innocent" questions that quickly went to the heart of the situation. His questions were so perceptive that they caused the men to leave the scene.

Jesus: Do you have no more witnesses to condemn you?
Woman: No.
Jesus: Neither do I condemn you. Go and sin no more.

Jesus was not naive. He knew that the woman had "missed the mark." Because He understood her situation, He confronted it with love and mercy. *Empathy* allows us to deal with reality and to choose the right way to intervene. In a few minutes, Jesus had diffused a dangerous situation. The killing was averted, some guilty men repented and a guilty woman was called to change. Who else could accomplish so much in so short a time?

Enmeshment leads us to deny or cover up the difficult facts of a person's life. Empathy empowers us to do the right things in the right way. Jesus was also sympathetic for He showed mercy and forgave the woman's guilt. His merciful feelings led to appropriate merciful actions.

An enmeshed leader might have gotten caught up in the woman's feelings and overlooked her sin and guilt. He could say, "Oh well, everyone is sinning these days. Adultery is happening a lot and we can't really make an example of you." This, however, is not the model Jesus gave us nor will it lead to a clear conscience. He was not trying to get the woman's approval. He was secure enough in His relationship with the Father so He had nothing to prove. This fact liberated him to speak the truth in love. Being enmeshed makes our actions dependent on another's feelings. Wise counselors must have the self-control of a surgeon to lovingly cut out the cancers of sin and guilt.

Alternatively, we might have become enmeshed in the feelings of the accusers and reacted toward the woman with anxiety rather than peaceful wisdom. We might have been tempted to say, "We have to send a message to the community and let them know that adultery is terrible. What will our children think if we let this slide and simply forgive this woman? We all know just how important it is to keep the Ten Commandments in our town. Come on and stone her." Trying to please others will inevitably lead us to deny the inner conscience of the Holy Spirit and may lead us to commit terrible acts against sinners. Personal ministry is not focused on pleasing the crowd. It is rather to live with integrity and courage, reconciling needy people to God.

We must not act out of our own emotional needs but be
free to minister with the compassion of Christ.

Helpers must have their wits about them in order to avoid giving in to either the pressure of the accusers or the desire to please the accused. We must take care not to be swayed by people's feelings or the flock will suffer. This is why it is so important to work on our own inner lives. Jesus noted in Luke 6 that leaders must closely examine and remove the logs from their own eyes prior to doing eye surgery on others. Otherwise we will become blind guides to the sightless and fall into a pit of despair. Spiritual leadership requires peaceful hearts and personal awareness. We must not act out of our emotional needs but be free to minister with the compassion of Christ.

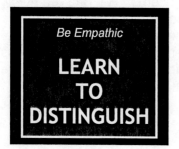

The first step to learning the skill of empathy is distinguishing between thoughts and feelings. Phrases such as "I think, I believe, I want," are indicators of thoughts. Thoughts are beliefs, ideas, concepts and principles. Feelings are the affective dimension of life and are described by words like mad, sad, glad, scared, confused. For instance, "I feel we should be better parents," has no feeling word. The person "thinks" we should be better parents but says "feel." Here are a few more examples:

1. I am <u>anxious</u> about my son. (Feeling)
2. I <u>feel</u> like seeing a movie. (Thought).
3. I screamed in <u>fear</u> when I saw that movie. (Feeling)
4. I <u>think</u> my wife needs to change. (Thought)
5. I <u>feel</u> my wife needs my help. (Thought)
6. I <u>feel</u> that you are a sinner. (Thought)
7. I feel <u>angry</u> about the way he shouted at me. (Feeling)

Listening Styles

There are several ways to listen and all of them can be used with great benefit to develop the skill of Empathy. Reflect on each of the following styles and think about the ones you use most often.

1. Silent attending. Focusing on others with:
   - Quiet attention
   - SOLAR TEA skills

2. Simple verbal attending. Interest shown by:
   - Door openers such as, "I see," or "Uh huh," or "Oh yes."
   - Verbal warmth in the tone of voice.
   - Non-verbal invitations.

3. Active or reflective listening. Focused interest shown by (CROPS)
   - Clarifying confusing or complicated ideas
   - Reflecting
   - Open ended questions
   - Paraphrasing for clarity
   - Summarizing the person's main issues
   - Staying focused on the other person's topic of interest.

4. Comprehensive listening. Perceiving and relating to a person's inner life by concentrating on the conversation and:
   - Connecting ideas, feelings, stories and relationships to clarify the confusion
   - Connecting thoughts with feelings
   - Discovering themes and key points
   - Discerning possible root-causes of the problems
   - Experiencing spiritual discernment
   - Confirming the will of God
   - Listening for the Spirit's guidance
   - Formulating possible solutions

5. Listening with questions:
   - Open-ended questions are designed to allow the person respond as she wants. "How are you feeling about your family?"
   - Closed-ended questions focus on one point. "Did you drive to work today?"
   - Declarative questions are in a statement form. "You seem to feel sad."

- Questions about essential information or a clarification about some fuzzy point. "I am confused. Do you have two children or three?"
- Questions designed to get positive answers. "When are you better?" or "What has the Lord called you to do?"
- Questions designed to measure progress. "On a scale from zero to ten, how are you today as compared to last week?"

Silent Attending, Simple Verbal Attending and occasional Active Listening, are sufficient for most relationships. Advanced Helpers, however, must also master the skills of Comprehensive Listening to discover good solutions. Comprehensive Listening is the most important of all the Helping skills.

Learning to Reflect

There are three steps in developing the skill of active listening. First, identify the Seeker's ideas. Second, identify their feelings. Finally, summarize or paraphrase your understanding of those thoughts and feelings in a tentative statement. For example, someone may say, "I can not wait to see my friends at school. The first step is to identify the thought: *good friends at school.* Next, identify the feelings: *excitement.* Finally, we form a summary statement: *"You are excited about being with your friends at school."*

The Helper is a mirror reflecting back the Seeker's ideas and emotions. The Helper sends back a paraphrased signal to see if he is maintaining accurate contact with CROPS reflections during pauses. *Radar Listening* interacts with the events, beliefs, feelings, and actions described by the Seeker. *Reflection* serves to clarify his understanding of the Seeker, summarizes the main theme of the message and confirms that he accurately understands her perspective. *Active Listening* requires intense commitment and focus.

A simple formula to begin practicing the skill of reflective listening is:

You seem to be feeling_____,
because _____.

This may seem mechanical, at first, but you will soon learn to make it unique and personal by applying your own style and wording. The *key* to reflective listening is making a brief, tentative statement about what you heard the Seeker say.

As with any skill, timing is critical. Reflective listening is helpful when people want to be better understood or better understand their own inner life. It is also effective when clarifying an issue. Certainly it is helpful when a Seeker has a problem to be solved, or is emotionally upset. It can help us cope with and manage our intense feelings. Finally, it is useful when someone asks us to do something that he should do for himself.

Waiting to be interviewed for a job as a wireless operator, a group of applicants paid little attention to the sound of the dots and dashes, which began coming over a loudspeaker. Suddenly one of them rushed into the employer's office. Soon he returned smiling. "I got it!" he exclaimed.

"How did you get ahead of us?" they asked.

"You might have been considered if you hadn't been so busy talking that you didn't hear the manager's coded message which said, 'The man I need must always be on the alert. The first one who interprets this and comes directly into my private office will be hired." L.E. Brown

Perceptions and Facts

We sometimes confuse personal perceptions with facts. Perceptions are personal ideas that can vary from 0 to 100% in accuracy. Facts, however, are statements that can be independently verified. Before jumping to conclusions, make sure your perceptions are closer to 100% than 0% in accuracy.

Look at the following sentence and see if you can figure out whether it is a perception or a fact. "My wife is the most beautiful woman in the world." This statement is true for me so it is my perception of the facts. Since it cannot be independently verified, however, it is not a fact. When we state perceptions, it is always best to claim them as our own unique views of reality by using *I statements*. "I believe that my wife is the most beautiful woman in the world."

On the other hand, facts can be verified by independent means. In "The Emperor's New Clothes," we read how many townspeople chose to believe a perception. Watching a political debate reminds us of how diverse our opinions can be about the same set of facts. Unfortunately, many of the current *politically correct* rules are all about forcing others' perceptions on the world. Politically correct ideas are not based upon facts. Some schools even make their unique perceptions into law. One New York principal outlawed Mother's Day because the adopted son of two gay men had no mother and the celebration of Mother's Day might offend him.

Perceptions Versus Facts

In the following list, mark those statements that are perceptions with a P and those that are facts with an F.

____My wife is five feet two inches tall.
____My grandson is the most beautiful child ever born.
____The Bible says that all have sinned.
____You are a hypocrite.
____My husband never listens to me.
____My husband refused to let me buy a new dress.
____It is a beautiful day.
____It is 98 degrees.
____My golf game was awful.
____My golf score was 101.

Whenever possible use the correct term to describe perceptions and facts. *In my view* is a phrase that reduces anxiety and keeps arguments to a minimum. However, to claim perceptions as facts can quickly turn into a heated debate. When someone says, "God is not going to bless you and that is a fact," our blood begins to boil for we see a human claiming to speak for God. Language is a powerful source of peace or anxiety. Using terms that indicate humility and personal conviction can go a long way toward building a bridge with others.

Comprehensive Listening

> *Great listeners know how to listen musically as well as analytically. President Jimmy Carter relied on "rational discourse" to weigh the pros and cons of various initiatives. He would have people prepare papers, and then he would sift their views in private. Doing it that way enabled him to "listen" to their arguments analytically but not musically. Jimmy Carter did not enjoy being in meetings with people who were posturing, arguing, and haggling. But there's an enormous amount of information in the haggling, ...for it tells us quite a lot about the values, the history, and the personal stakes that people bring to an argument. It's difficult for someone who's lost the last six arguments to say in a policy paper, "I've lost the last six arguments. If I don't win the next one, what am I going to tell my people?"*
>
> *Listening musically enables leaders to get underneath and behind the surface to ask, "What's the real argument that we're having?" And that's a critical question to answer — because, in the absence of an answer to that question, you get superficial buy-in. People go along in a pseudo-consensus, or in a deferential way, but without commitment.*
>
> *Ronald Heifetz. William Taylor, <u>Fast Company</u>, The Leader of the Future; An interview with Ronald Heifetz, June 1999*

Empathy is part of tuning in to both the Seeker and the Holy Spirit. A Christian listens with one ear to the Seeker and with the other ear to the Spirit. We need to heed the call to, "Pray at all times in the Spirit." We can practice dual listening and listening musically by asking God for the gift of discernment while making sure that the Seeker does not have a poor translator and God does not have a blind guide to assist Him counsel. Bad translations lead to bad counsel. We must listen with clean receivers and speak with clear transmitters. Otherwise we can mislead.

> *In the Abrahamic tradition, speech is the medium of divine self-disclosure; therefore, the fundamental stance of the person of faith is to listen. We hear this in the Shema, the great confession recited daily by our Jewish friends. "Hear, O Israel, the Lord our God, the Lord is one" (Deut. 6:4).*

> *The servant of the Lord in Isaiah 50:4, with whom Jesus is identified, proclaims the Lord God morning by morning, as the one who "wakens my ear to listen as those who are taught." Jesus' own fidelity springs from his ability to listen.*

> *The New Testament word upakouo, which we translate as "obey," actually means to "hyper-listen," to listen intently.*

The prologue of the Rule of St. Benedict begins: "Listen carefully and incline the ear of your heart." Frank Griswold, Presiding Bishop of the Episcopal Church in the US

Life Scan Summary

Empathy is: *The ability to imaginatively and accurately tune in to the mind and heart of another person and understand their thoughts and feelings in a way that says to the person that they are being understood.*

Understanding the thoughts and feelings of others is essential for quality relationships. Empathy is different than callousness, apathy, sympathy, and enmeshment. An empathic person communicates an accurate understanding of others' inner and outer life. He is aware of the distinct boundary between his own thoughts and feelings and those of other persons. *Empathy* with discernment allows us to listen with one ear to the Seeker, and the other ear to the Spirit. This dual listening promotes healing and growth for both Seeker and Helper.

Life Tips

Personal Reflection and Practice

- Read the Gospel account of the woman caught in adultery (John 8:1-11). Find a quiet place to be alone and imagine you are there. What is the weather? How does the surrounding landscape look? What do the religious leaders look like? What are they doing? How do they approach Jesus? What is the woman doing as the men talk with Jesus? Put yourself in her place. What do you see and hear from her vantage point? What are your thoughts and feelings? What happens when all the men leave and she is alone with Jesus? How does He speak? What do His tone of voice, face, eyes, and posture communicate? What does he say? How does she respond?

- Recall an incident when someone related to you with callousness. Who was it? What did he/she say and do? What were you hoping the person would do? What feelings do you recall having? What feelings does this recollection evoke in you now? What happened to your relationship after this incident occurred?

Callous	Partially Empathic	Empathy
1---------2---------3---------4---------5---------6---------7---------8---------9---------10		

- On the scale of one to ten, rate yourself as a Helper. What barriers do you need to overcome in order to improve your empathy? With whom are you most likely to be enmeshed? What causes this response?

The goal of our instruction is love, which comes from a pure heart and a good conscience and a sincere faith. 1 Tim 1:5 (NASB)

Nine

The King's Men brought Humpty

9

Respecting The Golden Rule

> *Bear one another's burdens and thus fulfill the law of Christ's love. If anyone thinks he is too good to help another person, he is fooling himself. Let each of us examine our own works and then our reason to feel good about ourselves will be our accomplishments and not the efforts of others. Every person must carry his own load.*
> *Galatians 6:2-5*

*The most important yardstick of your success will be how you treat
other people, your family, friends, and coworkers,
and even strangers you meet along the way.*
Barbara Bush

All the core conditions promote healthy relationships and make it easier to navigate the challenges of the change process. Respect, however, may be the most fundamental. Respect means that we hold others in high esteem. Like God, to whom we show the ultimate esteem, we are called to honor all those created in His image.

> *Then God said, "Let us make man in our image, in our likeness, and let them rule over the fish of the sea and the birds of the air, over the livestock, over all the earth, and over all the creatures that move along the ground." So God created man in his own image, in the image of God he created him; male and female he created them. God saw all that he had made, and it was very good. Gen 1:26-31*

> *The man and his wife were both naked, and they had no shame. Gen 2:25*

These passages are the basis for our identity and inheritance. Adam and Eve were placed in the Garden of Eden to co-rule with God. Just imagine how honored we would be if the president asked you to serve as a cabinet member to help him govern the country. Such a position requires the confidence of the nation, the president and congress. Any sense of shame would hinder your identity, drain the strength of the partnership and weaken your ability to adequately lead. Leadership demands self-confidence.

The term shame means, to lose face for it indicates that we are uncertain about whom we are as humans and what God has in mind for us. Originally, Adam and Eve were naked but able to face each other and God with no fearful confusion. They had confidence in themselves as members of God's forever family. He showed them great respect and elevated them to the status of authority over all other beings. He was confident they had the ability to co-rule with Him.

Shame brings a destructive lack of self-esteem and perplexity about membership in God's family. Adam and Eve related openly to each other and God prior to the fall, but afterwards Shame overcame them. They blamed each other, the devil and God Himself for their own behavior. Being troubled about self, they immediately turned on others in an attempt to hide their face. Shame results in interpersonal destruction and lowered respect for other people.

Looking for Answers

> *Our Respect paves the way for shame-faced Seekers to develop Self-Respect.*

Soul care is a combination of skills, knowledge, art and spirit. Because of our continued struggle with the flesh, we all wrestle with feelings of guilt and shame. Unresolved guilt and shame are experienced as anxiety, fear, defensiveness, self-hatred and depression. These are the feelings that drive people to seek our services. Although secular counselors can bring many wonderful insights to those in distress, only those familiar with scripture can offer full relief to guilty believers.

Our Respect paves the way for shame-faced Seekers to develop self-respect. A lifetime of shame leaves Seekers super sensitive to the behavior of others. Any action that lacks mercy and grace will further add to their sense of rejection.

Suppose a man comes into your meeting wearing a gold ring and fine clothes, and a poor man in shabby clothes also comes in. If you show special attention to the man wearing fine clothes...have you not discriminated among yourselves and become judges with evil thoughts? If you really keep the royal law found in Scripture, "Love your neighbor as yourself," you are doing right. But if you show favoritism, you sin and are convicted by the law as lawbreakers. James 2:2-9

Scripture teaches us to respect all persons equally and not to make distinctions based on how folk look or what they wear. The poor of this passage can be financially destitute but wealthy in spiritual and emotional resources. They are suffering an assault upon their self-respect and need to be accepted as neighbors. James alerts us to our responsibility as leaders.

Who is wise and understanding among you? Let him show it by his good life, by deeds done in the humility that comes from wisdom...the wisdom that comes from heaven is first of all pure, then peace-loving, considerate, submissive, full of mercy and good fruit, impartial and sincere. Peacemakers who sow in peace raise a harvest of righteousness. James 3:13-18

We are to respectfully exhibit heavenly wisdom that brings peace to those who suffer from guilt and shame. As we minister His love the world will be touched.

> *Peace is flowing like a river, Flowing out from you and me*
> *Spreading out into the desert, Setting all the captives free*

Respectful Actions

We see the church as a hospital for wounded and imperfect Christians. It must have a delivery room for those who do not yet believe and an emergency room for all who are wounded by sin. In fact, scripture instructs us on the importance of showing Respect even to those who are in open rebellion.

> *Brothers and sisters, even if a person is caught in some intentional, rebellious trespass, those of you who are spiritually mature should restore them in a spirit of gentleness. However, be careful as you minister and examine yourself lest you also succumb to some temptation.* *Galatians 6:1-5 (Our paraphrase)*

This passage speaks of reconciliation and restoration to rebels: those who intentionally break the commandments of God. It is one thing to help a member who stumbles over the line accidentally but it is quite another to work with a Christian rebel. Can any of us say we welcome this challenge? Paul indicated that it would take a spiritually mature Christian to help a rebel. An immature believer may find himself unable to cope with the challenge.

How is a mature believer supposed to respond to this challenge? We are to *restore the rebellious person in a spirit of gentleness*. A Christian trespasser has a "joint out of place" and needs a gentle doctor to massage it into restoration. We need to bring them back to the fold not inflict more pain.

Even the spiritually mature must take care to guard against two types of temptations. First, those who are driven by mercy may tend to *overlook* the sins of the brother and ignore his trespasses. This will leave him without the benefit of confession, repentance and restoration. Loving confrontation or surgery of the soul is difficult and we may try to avoid it. This is especially true for those who love harmony. However, we fail at the hard work of confession and repentance at the risk of their souls.

> *Dr. Jesus does surgery of the soul that is never painless but always redemptive.*

> *If anyone strays from the truth and you bring him back, you have turned a sinner from his way, and have saved his soul from death, and will cover a multitude of sins.* *James 5:19-20*

We have a God who heals, forgives and delivers souls from the dis-ease of guilt and shame. Far too many Christians are suffering from sickness of the soul because they gave in to the temptation of avoidance. Depression, anxiety, fear, drugs, addictions and generational tragedy could be averted if we took the role of confessor more seriously.

On the other hand, some are tempted to be hard-hitting judges who look for opportunities to rebuke sinful saints. These callous truth tellers see gentleness as soft headed as well as soft hearted. "God will not stand for sin in the camp," they say. Having been in this group for years, we fully recognize its siren song. However, neither scripture nor experience convinces us that judgment will effectively restore a rebel to the Lord or his soul to health. Trespassers will not turn to Christ for relief if leaders act like attack dogs rather than sheep dogs.

> *Come unto me all of you who labor and are heavy burdened and I will give you rest. Take my yoke upon you and learn of me for I am gentle and humble of heart; and you shall find rest for your souls. For my yoke is easy and my load is light. Mt. 11:28-30*

Jesus was gentle and humble. He called weary believers to come to Him for restoration of their souls. Dr. Jesus does surgery of the soul that is never painless but always redemptive. His yoke is not hard but easy. It is not harsh but gentle. He said we should aggressively search for the one lost sheep. After discovery, we cannot imagine that Jesus would beat the rebellious sheep for running away.

Bearing Burdens and Carrying Loads

St. Paul's instructions about the temptations of a restoration leadership are explicit. His principles for ministry are both psychologically insightful and pastorally brilliant. They are as contemporary as the teaching on boundaries and as current as the books on lay ministry. In one paragraph St. Paul establishes some of the most important ministerial processes known to the church.

> *Bear one another's burdens and thus fulfill the law of Christ's love. If anyone thinks he is too good to help another person, he is fooling himself. Let each of us examine our own works and then our reason to feel good about ourselves will be our accomplishments and not the efforts of others. Every person must carry his own load. Gal. 6:2-5*

First, we are to help people whose *burdens* are too heavy for them to carry. Burden, *baros* in Greek, is a problem so large that one cannot carry it alone. This requires that we have empathy for their situation and sympathy to take appropriate action. It is agape love in action. When a person is overwhelmed with a burden too great to bear we can put our shoulder to the wheel and assist them. *Two shoulders make for lighter burdens.* The Good Samaritan saw a man with a burden and helped him lift it.

Second, we are not to be apathetic and think we are too good to be servants. Arrogance indicates that we are deceiving ourselves by failing to apply love to our relationships. The essence of agape love is servanthood.

One of the indisputable lessons of life is that we cannot get or keep anything for ourselves alone unless we also get it for others. J. Richard Sneed

Third, we need to make sure each person carries his own load. Only then can he/she have self-respect. Every person, including a rebel, needs to examine his works and find accomplishments. Responsibility develops self-esteem. Dependency destroys self-respect. A burden is a weight too heavy to carry alone but a load is a personal responsibility that we can, and must carry if we are to care for ourselves. This distinction is important for it can make the difference between success and failure, energetic ministry and burn out and communicating respect or disrespect to Seekers.

> ## *Don't ask of your friends what you yourself can do.*
> **Quintus Ennius**

In the following outline, we humorously model how to violate this scripture and act disrespectfully. Examine the interaction carefully and see how many times the guidelines of St. Paul are violated by Gary.

Steve: Gary, I was hoping I could get you to be my mentor. I need an older man to give me advice, counsel and wisdom.

Gary: I am glad you asked me to help you grow in the Lord. I am an expert at this and know what to do to make you a strong man in the Lord.

Steve: Great. I have been trying to find someone to disciple me but it is hard to find anyone who knows what he is doing.

Gary: You have come to the right place. I know what to do to make you grow. In fact, I will do all the Bible studies for you and run off computer copies; you will not have to do a thing. I can do the Greek and Hebrew word studies and give you all the commentaries as well. It will be easy to grow that way.

Steve: I really want to grow in prayer as well. Can you help me there?

Gary: Oh, yes, indeed. I am a great prayer warrior so all you have to do is tell me your prayer requests, and I will take them to the Lord.

Steve: WOW! That is great. What do I do if I need to hear from God?

Gary: That is no problem. I hear from God regularly. In fact, I have the gift of prophecy. Unfortunately, most of the pastors will not recognize it. Just tell me what you want to know and I will find out from the Lord and tell you what God says ASAP. Anything else you need?

Gary grossly neglects Paul's guidelines in Galatians by taking both Steve's burdens and his loads. When this scripture teaches us to help people carry their burdens, it uses the Greek term *baros* indicating a weight so heavy it cannot be carried alone. On the other hand, when Paul says to encourage those with loads, the Greek term is *phortion*, and means a weight that is light enough to carry alone.

In order to better understand the instructions on burdens and loads we will examine the Golden Rule and differentiate it from spurious counterfeits. We have discovered two additional rules that many of us seem to follow that cause confusion and burn out. We call them, *The Lead Rule* and *The Stone Rule*. These "rules" also weigh us down without adding the value of the Golden Rule.

- The Golden Rule: *Do unto others what you want them to do unto you.*
- The Lead Rule: *Do for others what they need to do for themselves. (Carry loads as well as burdens.)*
- The Stone Rule: *Do for others what only God can do. (Confuse our mission with that of God.)*

The Golden Rule respects God, self and others so it is consistent with the Great Commandment. It is Jesus' law of love and calls us to bear burdens for one another. In the above role-play, Gary failed to heed the wisdom of Jesus. Seekers often need assistance to bear their heavy *burdens*, but sometimes they also want us to also carry their *loads*. If we give in to the temptation to rescue a Seeker from his load, it will almost always lead to his having increased difficulties.

Gary responded with *The Lead Rule* and failed to allow Steve to carry his own load. Gary did not show *respect*. A failure of respect can bring self-condemnation to a Seeker for, as Paul states, when we carry our own loads we have reason to boast in ourselves rather than in our neighbor. The Lead Rule can also result in Helper burnout for we pick up so many loads that we get overwhelmed with all our responsibilities.

Worst of all, Gary failed to show proper Respect for God and implemented *The Stone Rule*. When we act as though we are all knowing *(omniscient),* always available *(omnipresent)*, or all-powerful *(omnipotent),* we are promoting ourselves rather than urging trust in God. By offering to pray for Steve and hear the Lord for him, Gary implied he was God's spokesman. This kind of pride can end in an abuse of spiritual power.

Leaders sometimes attempt to do for others what only God can do. We say, "My door is always open" as though we are *omnipresent*. We may imply that we are *omnipotent;* that we can pray hard enough or long enough for God to answer us according to our will. We imagine that we can "Lead people to Christ" by our manipulative witnessing and forget that only God can save. It borders on *omniscience* to think that our knowledge is enough to change others.

Jesus rebuked Peter sharply when he attempted to block Jesus from following the Father's will. The story is found in Matthew 16:21-23.

> **Jesus**: I must die at the hands of the people.
> **Peter:** No! It cannot be. You must live! (I will rescue you.)
> **Jesus:** Get behind me Satan. Your mind is focused on the flesh not God.

Peter tried to interfere with Jesus' plan by reacting with *mercy of the flesh* rather than the *mercy of God.* He tried to protect Jesus from the pain and trauma of death, but he failed to find out if God was in the plan. He thought it was godly mercy to rescue the Son of God, not understanding that the cross was a load only Jesus could carry. Peter could not lessen Jesus responsibility. Before responding to a burden or a load, make sure you discern the difference between the two and encourage Seeker's to carry the load while helping them lift that which is too heavy to bear.

A Respectful Dialogue

The following interaction between Gary and Steve is written to model appropriate *Respect* along with *Genuineness, Empathy and Warmth.*

> **Steve:** Gary, I hear you are a master discipler and mentor. Can you make me mature in the Lord?

Gary: Well, thanks for the compliment, but I am not a genius at any of this. In fact, I cannot make anyone holy or whole. However, I may be able to assist you in growth if you are willing to work on yourself.

Steve: What do I need to do? Can you teach me to study the Bible and pray?

Gary: I can help you find the right tools to study scripture and we can discover the Lord's word together. However, mentoring is not lecturing on the Bible and prayer. We will study and pray together and see what the Lord says.

Steve: My wife and I are having some conflicts too. Will you talk to her about submitting to me?

Gary: Steve, that is a pretty big request. Why don't we discuss that at a later time? Right now I want to help you examine your own heart.

Respect and Monkey Business

Another aspect of the stone and lead rules arises when one actively tries to give us his load. We call it *taking a monkey* and codependents are very tempted to accept these active, clinging creatures. Some walk around with a veritable monkey zoo on their backs. In the following play, note how Steve tries to get Gary to take his monkey and how Gary resists the temptation. Steve approaches Gary with a request to carry his loads as well as his burdens. He makes it very difficult to say no to his requests. Reflect on how well Gary does in refusing to carry Steve's loads, the *monkey*, while offering to work with him on his burdens.

Steve: Well, Gary it is exciting to get back with my mentor. It is always great to see you because I know I can depend upon you. No one has a mentor like me.

Gary: Gee, thanks Steve. I enjoy it too. How can I help you?

Steve: Well, my wife is not treating me like she should and I think you should talk with her. She really respects your opinions and I am sure she would submit if you told her that it is biblical.

Gary: So you are unhappy with your relationship with Sue and want me to straighten her out. Is that it?

Steve: Yes, she will listen to you. Why don't you come over to my house and see her tomorrow night while I am at the office. You will have enough time to let her know how she should treat me.

Gary: I suppose I can postpone my preparation for teaching and help you out. What is the best time to come over?

Steve: Sue finishes supper about eight, so I will tell her that you will be there a little after that. By the way, my daughter is running in a track meet this Saturday and she needs an adult to be with her. She considers you to be an uncle and I am sure she will appreciate it if you could be there to root for her and her team. I would really like to go but I am playing an important golf game.

Gary: Saturday? But, I am supposed to do a lot of chores around the house then. Can you not find someone else?

Steve: My daughter will not want anyone else to be there but you.

Steve is obviously very good at getting others to take his monkeys. Perhaps you know others like him. How do we deal with Steve? Is it possible to reject the monkey while keeping Steve as a friend? We earlier described the process of dealing with *Inappropriate Request*s and this is a common way that an IR comes to us. We try to accept the person but refuse the request.

The first step is to clearly identify who owns the problem monkey. By listening carefully and clarifying the request we can decide which person is supposed to carry the monkey. We call this, *problem ownership*. Once we know the load's owner, we know who must act to resolve the problem. We clarify problem monkey ownership by asking this question: "Who must live with the consequences?" That person owns the monkey.

Who must live with the results of the conflict between Steve and his wife? It is clear that the problem or load is Steve's because he is in conflict with Sue. Gary has no conflict with Sue so it is not his problem, load or monkey. Gary foolishly took responsibility for talking with her, enlarging its scope to include him. We can only imagine how upset Sue would be if Gary came to her home to preach about how women should relate to their husbands.

If we succumb to the request to take a load, other *monkeys* are added onto the original request and the zoo grows bigger as does the frustration, anxiety and anger. Steve discovered a willing collaborator in his game of manipulation so he pressed Gary into caring for his daughter. What unreasonable request will be next? Monkeys grow into apes!

Problem Ownership Process

There are four different possibilities for handling problems. They are: I own the problem, you own the problem, we own the problem and there is no problem. Once that is clear, we decide what to do to find a solution.

1. I, the Helper, own the problem - I must act on a solution.
2. You, the Seeker, own the problem - You must act on the solution.
3. We, the Helper and Seeker, own the problem - We must act on a solution.
4. No problem! - No action necessary

In some situations, a Seeker will complain about an issue that truly belongs to the Helper. For example, "Pastor, last week I had a hard time hearing you because there was too much noise in the office. Can we meet in a quieter place?" The Pastor must arrange for a better meeting place.

At other times, it can be problem requiring a joint response. "Pastor, my cell group wants to know how we are planning to deal with so many counseling problems in the groups. Can you and I come up with a plan by next month?" A cell leader needs the advice, wisdom and input of the pastor to make any changes in the group structure.

Finally, we may discover that there is no problem. Through Reflective Listening we can sometimes clarify issues to the point where the Seeker and Helper agree that no action is needed. This is the best of all worlds.

Sending the Monkeys Home

The skills of listening, clarifying, and problem ownership empower us to deal effectively with burdens, loads and monkeys. For example, listening with warm concern and clarity is essential to discern problem ownership. Without good listening skills we cannot find the one who must live with the solution. Here are ways to clarify the situation.

- Listen carefully and warmly. Clarify whose problem it is and state that fact.
- Slow down your response to monkeys.
- Understand the VCR stage of the Seeker. Many monkeys are simply part of the *Complaint Stage*. Many Complainants do not really want us to carry their load. All they need is an understanding ear.
- Affirm the Seeker' ability to carry the load. Show *Respect* and confidence in their strengths, abilities and offer hope.
- Be specific about the issue and the responsibility for it.
- Ask one key question: "What do you want me to do?"

Lifeskills with Steve

This round we will try to model appropriate responses to monkeys and practice the Golden Rule. See if you agree with the way Gary handles Steve's monkeys. Write down how you might respond to the same situation.

> **Steve:** Gary, it is wonderful to know that I can call upon such a wise and strong leader to help me.
>
> **Gary:** Thank you Steve. How can I help you?
>
> **Steve:** My wife will not submit to me and I know she would respect you enough to do what you say. Will you talk to her about treating me better?
>
> **Gary:** Tell me some more Steve. You seem pretty frustrated. What is happening and how are you dealing with it?
>
> **Steve:** Just last night I asked her to fix my lunch and she said she did not have time. I was really upset but I didn't say anything.
>
> **Gary:** So you were angry that she did not make your lunch, but you didn't discuss it with her so she doesn't know how you feel.
>
> **Steve:** That's right. She should know better than that. I should not have to tell her. Besides, she will not listen to me but she would listen to you.
>
> **Gary:** It doesn't sound as though you have tried to talk with her about this issue so far. Are there also some other things you are upset about?
>
> **Steve:** Yes, and you need to talk with her about them as well.
>
> **Gary:** It seems to me that it is important for you and Sue to discuss how to resolve your differences. It sounds as though you have a pattern developing between you that could cause trouble later on down the road. Why don't we take a look at that pattern and see if you can figure out a way to change it?

Gary related to Steve with all the *GREW* skills. He asked an open-ended question to get more information about the relationship between Steve and Sue. He also named Steve's feelings to make sure he understood his reactions to the situation and helps Steve understand that Gary was paying attention.

He clarified the fact that Steve was avoiding conflict in not one situation but several. When Gary mentioned that he saw this pattern of avoidance it offers Steve a new insight while keeping the focus squarely on him. Despite Steve's best efforts, Gary refuses to take the monkey of speaking with Steve's wife. Standing firmly and refusing monkeys challenges our love and faith in God as well as our resolve to help others grow.

No issue is more important to Helpers than learning to live by the Golden Rule and avoid monkeys. The sure way to burn out is living by lead and stone rules and accepting monkeys from those who fear self-responsibility. If you want to see others' grow you must decide to stop rewarding and reinforcing dependency on you rather than God. Can you see places where the Lord is calling you to stop carrying monkeys?

Life Scan Summary

The core attitude of *Respect* is key to promoting healthy relationships and navigating the challenges of the VCR. Respect essentially means that we hold others in high esteem. Like God, in whom we have the ultimate esteem and glory, we are also called to bless all those created in His image. All persons have worth regardless of their personal condition. We try to show respect for everyone, even if we strongly disagree with his/her lifestyle. The skill of *problem ownership* is essential to preserve *Respect* in the helping relationship. Respectful Helpers clarify problem ownership and then act appropriately. We do not want to create a dependent relationship with the Seeker.

TIPS for Life

Personal reflection and practice

- When was the last time you took on a monkey?
- What problem or responsibility did you accept?
- How did this occur?
- How did this affect you?
- What were your feelings and thoughts?
- What happened to your relationship with the other person?
- How could you have declined the monkey?
- What will you do differently the next time?
- When was the last time you attempted to give one of your Monkeys to a person who offered you help?
- What happened?
- When are you most vulnerable to carrying loads and practicing the Lead or Stone rule?
- How will you maintain *Respect* in these relationships?

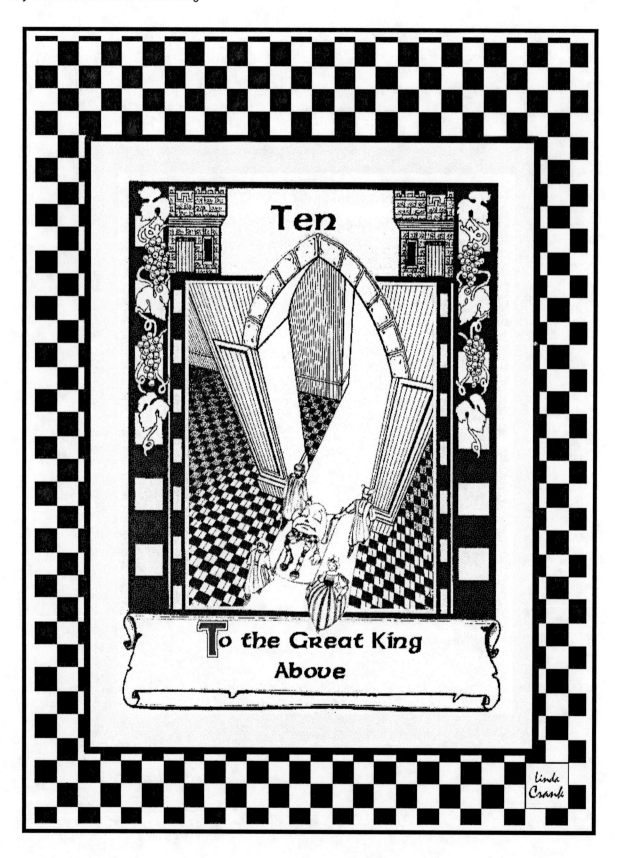

10

How to Host a Visitor

I send you out as lambs among wolves so be shrewd as serpents and as innocent as doves.
Matthew 10:16

Leaders from around the world ask a simple question. "How do we motivate the unmotivated to be motivated?" We have an unconventional answer. First, we recognize that everyone is motivated. Unfortunately, they are not motivated to do what we want them to do. Second, we need to be careful that our attempts to motivate do not backfire and cause the Seeker to do the opposite of what we want her to do. For example, some prevention programs may actually have the opposite of our desired effect.

Research strongly questions the efficacy of drug prevention and Teen Suicide Prevention Programs. The <u>Journal of the American Medical As-sociation</u> reported, "There was little evidence that the programs reduced suicides and suicide attempts." Importantly, the programs reviewed were "intended to raise awareness of teenage suicides by describing the warning signs to young people at risk." Teenagers participating in the study experienced two main effects: (1) they were less likely to recommend the program to peers; and (2) they believed that the programs made kids <u>more</u> likely to kill themselves.

*One is left to wonder why programs based on fear and the identification of pathology continue to be used when other, more effective modes of inter*vention exist—namely skill building approaches. Dr. Scott Miller

This assessment is consistent with most outcome research of the past forty years. We do wish to motivate people to do the right things but we must be careful lest we motivate the unmotivated to be less motivated. Miller goes on to say that "Skill building programs are the most effective ways to prevent suicide and drug use." This is why we teach Lifeskills.

One thing is for certain. We cannot make others change by force or threat. In this era of freedom and democracy, we have seen authoritarian governments fall, dictators shot, and the processes of democracy begun. Autocratic leaders may be accepted in some regions of the world but the spirit of the age is freedom of choice. However, there is no doubt that we can influence others' behavior to be more positive. The renowned management consultant and author, Achik Adizes says that there are three ways to motivate people to change. They are: *authority, power and influence.*

NO

Authority is the ability to unilaterally say *yes* and *no* and others must obey. Not many of us have the sole authority to hire, fire, or give a pay increase. In church or family life, who can say *yes* or *no* to a decision without discussing it with his wife, parents or boss? A small group leader, lay counselor or pastor cannot give permission to buy a product, build a new room or receive a new member without checking with a boss, a board or the congregation. Counselors cannot force a teen to stop rebelling, a man to stop drinking or a wife to submit. We cannot make depression disappear or insomniacs go to sleep. Even if we did have the authority, it is not be wise to make decisions for other persons. Dependency on others delays maturity and stunts Christian growth.

In the language of Adizes, *power* motivates with reward and punishment. In counseling we can reward through affirmation and support or punish with confrontation, rebuke or fear. Both rewards and punishments must be used judiciously lest they lose their effect. Too much affirmation can seem like false praise and destroy the Seeker's trust in our honesty. The Seeker could rely too much on rewards and fail to develop internal motivation.

Nor are we able to punish a Seeker too harshly or too often lest we destroy his trust. Even parents find that they do not have the ability to control a child by *power* alone. In the last analysis the child will grow up and leave home to rebel if he so chooses. Many are the times when a child of religious parents becomes a prodigal and shames the family. Thus, the power has been reversed, for the prodigal now has the ability to punish and reward the parents. An eighty-year-old woman once proclaimed she would never vote for a Democratic candidate because "I will not let my father tell me what to do!" Her father had been a Democrat who attempted to forcefully motivate her to follow his political lead but the strategy backfired and she was still rebelling fifty years after his death.

GOOD BOY!

Influence *is the ability to move people without resorting to either* power *or* authority. *It is our most effective tool in ministry. Influence requires the cooperation and awareness of the Seeker who must believe that our counsel is best for him. A physician once noted that the biggest problem facing the medical profession was not diagnosis of ailments but getting the patient to comply with the treatment plan. Many patients refuse to take their medication, stop smoking, or lose weight. Using influence to achieve* compliance requires the Helper to have mastered and implemented all the life skills.

Wisdom is the ability to use all the resources of *authority, power* and *influence* to move an individual or group toward a goal. It is the Spirit-led ability to know what to do, how to do it and when to do it so maximum results are obtained. The biblical term for a wise Christian is *prudence*. It is often found in accounting where it is essential to ethics and high professional standards. It can be thought of as "careful, thoughtful action".

- A prudent person knows how to regulate relationships and issues to attain the right result. (Use all our resources to accomplish the goal.)
- The opposite of prudence is "senselessness" for such a person is reckless, foolish and lacking common sense about both spiritual and natural things.

> *I send you out as lambs among wolves so be shrewd—prudent—as serpents and as innocent as doves.* Mt. 10:16

What kind of education would prepare you to survive and thrive as a vulnerable lamb among wolves? How would you *prudently* deal with wolves to prevent being shorn and eaten? Jesus did not use this frightening image to keep us from interacting with wolves. To the contrary, we are to lead them to the Lamb of God. This is quite a tall order and requires great skill. We must, like Jesus, grow in wisdom, stature and favor with God and man. The Lifeskills' training process is designed to teach you how to thrive in "Wolf Town."

Scripture praises those who know how to influence wolves without force. Jesus told the Jews how to influence the Romans by using wisdom. His admonitions to "Turn the other cheek," and "Walk the second mile" are part of the strategy for peaceful subversion of the bigger, stronger Romans who were in authority. We Christians, like the First-Century Jews, are a minority. We too must *prudently* use *authority, power* and *influence* to win non-believer's minds, hearts and heads. However, if we act more like wolves than lambs we will lose our godly reputation and the opportunity to witness to the world.

Effective leaders move an organization or person toward reasonable goals. They have the ability to get people with differing agendas and priorities to work together for a common vision and objective. The man who built his house on rock was *prudent.* On the other hand, those who build upon sand are senseless. "The winds will blow, the tides will rise and the house will collapse." Mt 7:24 Those who are building believers into "Oaks of righteousness, a planting of the Lord," (Isaiah 61) also need a plan and a strategy if their work is to endure. It is foolish to build a person's character and lifestyle without a reasonable set of principles and a tested, workable process.

We who desire to help others grow may insanely do the same old things and continually expect different results. A father nearing retirement once asked us to develop a succession plan for the family business. After a few meetings, Steve received a telephone call from Mr. Lee, who opened the conversation by complaining about a recent problem.

> *Insanity is doing the same old things, in the same old ways and expecting different results.*
>
> **Anonymous**

Lee: You are not going to like what I did but I still think it was the best thing to do.

Steve: Tell me what happened.

Lee: My daughter cancelled her plans to bring her family to our home for Easter vacation and it upset my wife and me. (Many details are added for about thirty minutes while Steve listens and clarifies.)

Steve: Tell me how you responded.

Lee: I decided to write her and explain why what she did was unchristian. I wrote her a long letter. Do you want to see it?

Steve: Perhaps later. Has this ever happened before?

Lee: Yes, many times.

Steve: And, what did you do those other times?

Lee: I also wrote a letter explaining why this is an unchristian thing to do.

Steve: Did that change your daughter's behavior?

Lee: No, she never even mentions the letter.

Mr. Lee wanted to help his daughter change yet he had not come up with a workable plan. He attempted the same failing intervention each time the problem was presented. Thus, failure built upon failure leading to frustration and hurt.

Steve: If this has never worked in the past, what makes you think it will work this time?

Lee: Well, I think I wrote a better letter this year. It is longer and has more scripture in it.

Many of us, like Mr. Lee, are caught in a cycle of non-working interventions that reinforce an undesirable pattern. The cycle of conflict around the daughter's visit at Easter had repeated itself annually for almost twenty years and each time he did the same thing but expected different results. The following year Mr. and Mrs. Lee decided not to ask their daughter's family to come to their home during Easter vacation. This change empowered them to break free of the old dysfunctional pattern and develop a new yearly schedule more agreeable to everyone. Mr. Lee made a small change that made a big difference.

We sometimes use the same interventions no matter if they work or not. We foolishly build our counseling or preaching or evangelistic model on our own instincts, habits, preferences and personality, rather than on a pattern that succeeds. When troubles come, the program falls like a house of cards.

Some of us pray for healing while others look for demonic spirits. Others are warriors who confront sin, while still others sympathize. The *Adverse Advisers* insanely act as though change will magically occur with the use of their own preferences rather than finding out what will touch the heart of the Seeker.

A well-designed Helping intervention will have the building materials, the construction site and the actions that will most likely work. Sometimes the blue print calls for listening and sometimes for confrontation; sometimes for warfare and sometimes for nurture; sometimes for inner healing and sometimes for renewing the mind.

At the Visitor Stage we simply want to build trust and Seeker Confidence. We should not get entangled in the Seeker's feelings and problems, nor should we jump to conclusions about what solution will Work. Wisdom waits patiently but interactively for the root issues to emerge. By listening with good questions we can influence the Seeker to move into the next stage and finally toward a solution. Read the following scene and analyze how well Gary does at Hosting a Visitor.

Joseph, a caring cell leader, referred Faye to one of the church's lay Helpers. He saw her sadness and family conflicts and wanted her to get good counsel. Faye agrees to see Gary but is definitely at the Visitor Stage, forcing Gary to be a good Host. See how well he uses the AS I GREW skills.

> *Wisdom never kicks at the iron walls it can't bring down.*
> Olive Schreiner

Case Study for the Visitor-Host Stage

Gary: Hello, Mrs. Green, I am Gary Sweeten with the church's care team. I'm glad we can meet at lunch today.

Faye: *Thank you for taking time to see me. I'm not sure why my cell leader wants me to see you, but I told him that I would do it as a favor to him. Joseph said you were very busy so I shouldn't take too much time.*

Gary: *Thank you for being sensitive to my schedule. However, this is my ministry, and I really love to get to know the members of the church. Please tell me about yourself and your family.*

Faye: *Joseph has probably already told you a lot about me.*

Gary: *I enjoy hearing personally from people rather than getting information second hand, so why don't you fill me in on things.*

(Gary's goal is to establish a sense of safety. Faye has been pressured by her cell leader to come to see him so she may feel embarrassed. We need to work especially hard to build trust and allay the suspicions of anyone referred by another person. Gary indicated that he was happy to see her for this is his ministry.

Faye tested Gary by saying, "Joseph has probably already told you a lot about me." She was fishing to see if Joseph said anything negative. Gary was able to avoid the triangle by saying he wanted to get to know Faye personally rather than through others. Gary thanked Faye for her sensitivity to his schedule. Helpers who affirm a Seeker's positive traits see quicker resolutions to problems.)

> **Faye:** There really is not much to tell you about my family life. We are doing very well since I became a Christian.
> **Gary:** That is good to hear. Tell me more.
> **Faye:** I am married and have four teenage children. My life was pretty bad before I was converted. The Lord is very good.
> **Gary:** Four teens. Wow! You have your hands full.
> **Faye:** Yes, we are very busy. I also work as a manager for Microsoft and my husband is in computer sales for Dell. He travels a lot and is gone from Tuesday until Friday most weeks.
> **Gary:** That is a lot isn't it? How do you manage?
> **Faye:** I love the church and my friends there so I manage by having fellowship with them. Even though my husband is not a Christian, I find it a good place for me, and I get a lot of support and encouragement.
> **Gary:** I see. The church has helped you a great deal even though your husband has not yet come to Christ. Is that right?
> **Faye:** Yes, I appreciate my new friends in the cell group. Things are real good.
> **Gary:** I am happy to hear things are great. What do you find the most helpful?

(Is Faye a Visitor or a Complainant? She is working hard to convince Gary and herself that no problems exist. However, as we look carefully we see some hints of complaints. Gary tries to get more specific on both good and bad dimensions of her life, but allows Faye to go at her own pace. He ends with a semi-closed question designed to help her begin the process of revealing the good, the bad and the ugly. Without a complaint there is no reason to meet. In the following interaction, we will see how Faye hints at problems but reveals her dilemma of not wanting to displease the pastor.)

> **Faye**: Other than the church's busy schedule I enjoy almost everything.
> **Gary**: So, most things are good, even with the busy schedule.
> **Faye:** As Pastor Michael said one time, we do not really have anything to complain about. I'm learning to be a better wife and mother even when my home life is difficult.
> **Gary:** Sounds like growth in the midst of challenges and you do not want to complain.
> **Faye:** I'm learning to trust the Lord when I get worried about what will happen.
> **Gary:** Well, you are learning so much. It sounds as though the Lord is teaching you to trust Him even when you are worried about the future.
> **Faye**: I do not want you to think I am complaining. Pastor Michael said that complaining shows a lack of faith and I certainly need faith to get through all I am facing. Life is not a bed of roses.

(Faye is slowly building enough confidence to be honest. By relating the pastor's statement, Faye reveals her reluctance to share openly. She is fearful of failing to measure up to the church's standards. This is not an unusual belief for new believers.)

Gary: It is good that the church is supportive. However, you seem worried about what the pastor might think of you if you talk about your problems. Is that right?

Faye: I guess so. I am trying so hard to have faith. I don't want the Lord to punish me for a lack of trust. I need Him too much for that.

Gary: So, you're also concerned about the Lord being upset with you?

Faye: Now that you mention it, I am worried about complaining. Is it OK to share our problems or does it indicate a lack of faith in God?

Gary: That is a very good question. In this church, we are free to talk about our concerns so others can better pray. It is not a lack of faith to talk honestly about our struggles. Pastor Michael himself models that for us in team meetings. Just last week he asked for prayer for his family.

Faye: Really? Pastor Michael and the other leaders have problems, too? So you will not think I am a bad Christian if I tell you my concerns?

Gary: No, everyone has problems. The Lord is gracious. He wants us to tell one another about our troubles. The care team is trained to help members look for solutions to the inevitable trials we all face. How can I help you?

Faye: Well, I do have some things to share.

We have attempted to simplify how Visitor-Host Cooperation would work in a perfect world. In real life relationships are not this simple or easy even if they are similar. Gary attempted to empathize when Faye mentioned her fear of God's punishment. He used the term upset to see if he was tracking with her and she agreed that she was worried about whether God approved of discussing our worries.

Gary heard Faye imply she was feeling guilty, fearful and ashamed about her struggles, but he thought it unwise to use those terms in reflective listening. However, he placed this information in the mental file cabinet for later reference. Gary normalized family problems by briefly disclosing the staff's humanity. Although too much self-disclosure is harmful, in small doses it can put the Seeker at ease.

At this point, Faye is a Visitor who:

- Is meeting with us for another reason. Joseph referred her to Gary. Faye may not have asked for assistance until the situation had gotten out of hand. However, Joseph saw Faye's dilemma and urged her to call for assistance.
- Does not openly complain. Faye is not directly asking about how to change. It is up to the Helper to build the trust for Faye to complain. She is already feeling false guilt about not doing everything exactly right and has wrongly projected her anxiety on the pastor.
- Is not interested in looking at solutions because no problem has been admitted. She gives a glowing report about how well she is doing so the Helper may miss her confusion. This is typical for Visitors and tells us to be careful lest they become defensive.
- Is not open to probing questions. Confrontational questions might cause additional false guilt or defensive reactions, making the recovery process more complicated.

Gary attempted to be a good Host by practicing the AS I GREW skills:

A
S
I
G
R
E
W

- Welcoming Faye warmly
- Attending to her needs and wants
- Focusing attention on her interests
- Listening with warmth and door openers
- Asking general questions of concern and interest
- Refusing to mention what others have said (privacy)
- Refusing to preach, confront or judge
- Praying silently for the Holy Spirit's guidance
- *Offering to meet again*

Life Scan Summary

The goal of Christian discipleship is to grow in wisdom, stature and favor with God and other people. Scripture affirms those who plan wisely and who know how to influence others without force. Christians need to be prudent and utilize all available resources of Authority, Power, and Influence to help others change.

The Visitor-Host relationship is a practical application of using relational skills to influence those over whom we have little or no authority and power. The Host must cooperate and accommodate himself to the Visitor. Typically, the Visitor does not think there is a problem. Yet someone has pressured them to seek counsel and care. If the Host responds with excellent AS I GREW skills and invites the Visitor to continue the relationship, enough trust can be forged for the Visitor to air her complaints.

TIPS for Life

Personal Reflection and Practice

Who defers to your authority? With whom do your interact with power? When have you used your influence?

Are you presently Hosting a Visitor? Scale your ability to be a competent Host in this relationship with zero the least hospitable and ten the most gracious.

How well did Gary do as a Host?

- AS attitude 1-2-3-4-5-6-7-8-9-10
- Invitational attitude 1-2-3-4-5-6-7-8-9-10
- Genuineness 1-2-3-4-5-6-7-8-9-10
- Respect 1-2-3-4-5-6-7-8-9-10
- Empathy 1-2-3-4-5-6-7-8-9-10
- Warmth 1-2-3-4-5-6-7-8-9-10
- Open Questions 1-2-3-4-5-6-7-8-9-10
- Privacy 1-2-3-4-5-6-7-8-9-10

11

Learning to be Concrete

And it will be said: "Build up, Build up, prepare the road!
Remove the obstacles out of the way of my people."
Isaiah 57:14

Perhaps you have been wondering how to move Humpty and Mrs. Dumpty to action. Since this is a book for those who wish to be change agents we always have action as a goal. To become change experts we must work diligently on ourselves. By learning the disciplines and skills of relational influence, we can succeed even if we lack a degree in counseling or social work. The act of self-improvement will influence those around us.

You are about to learn how to make the transition from listening to complaints to finding solutions, from empathy for the past to changes for the future. The topics include:

- How to get at the real issues
- How to see the Lord at work in the midst of pain
- How to offer hope to the hopeless
- How to know when to comfort and when to confront
- How to measure growth, change and healing
- How to set good goals

Moving On

The action skills are summarized by CALM for *Concreteness, Affirmation, Looking for Good & God and Measuring progress*. Gary and Faye began to move into this part of the *VCR* road map when she made it clear that her marriage was unhappy. Gary interacted with the AS I GREW skills to build trust and gather all necessary information. Now it is time to transition to the CALM skills.

C *Concreteness* is the skill of focusing on verbal or written specifics with an exact understanding of the most important themes. As the relationship, progresses we ask specialized questions to understand root issues more clearly. Most complaints are non-specific, leaving few clues to a good solution. *Concreteness* makes the general specific, the obscure apparent and the muddled clear and shows us how to move into action.

A *Affirming the Seeker's Assets* Even in the midst of pain and confusion we look for courage, strength, character and positive decisions. *Affirmation* of specific strengths will our build faith, hope and positive expectation. Noting exceptions to problems, blessing small steps forward and asking about assets are the skills you will learn.

L   *Looking for God and Good in the support systems* God's detectives discern where He is at work. They can find good things that are happening away from the counseling sessions and bring them to light for He is always involved in our lives.

M   *Meeting again* The willingness to meet for continued support and influence is a powerful tool for good. Alcoholics Anonymous knows that meeting attendance is essential to growth. Their motto is "Come back. It works if you come back." The same is true for counseling. Our discussions empower Seekers through all six stages of change.

Measuring progress Road maps provide guidance about the direction to a destination but we also need a way to measure how far we have traveled. On an interstate highway, we use the mile markers to gauge how far we have gone as well as how far we have yet to go. This enables us to break the trip down into manageable bites and not be overwhelmed by the distance of the journey. We use the concept of scaling to encourage people as they move toward a solution.

Altering the Inquiry

During the *Visitor* and early part of the *Complainant Stages*, we focus on building trust and opening the doors of the Seeker's heart. We are not concerned about the focus of the complaints, their clarity or moving the conversation in any particular direction of complaints and concerns by asking open-ended questions.

OPEN THE DOOR

- Tell me how things are going.
- I am not sure that I understand. Tell me more.
- Tell me about your relationship with the family.
- What do you like best about the church?
- What brought you in today?
- How might I be of assistance to you?

Declarative questions similarly open doors by asking questions with no question mark. They are useful for reducing defensiveness and resistance because interrogatives may bring up us have painful memories from our failures in school or home.

- So, life is difficult right now.
- It sounds as though you are pretty upset about that.
- I see. You thought the boss was mean to you.
- It appears to me that you were very disappointed about not winning.

Gary said, "Tell me about your family" so Faye could relate her story as she wished. Faye responded defensively with, "Joseph has probably already told you about me." Gary gently noted that, "I prefer to learn about you first hand rather than from someone else." He wanted to cut through her fears and build her confidence. Only then would she be willing to take off her mask. An interrogative might have caused her to lose face.

Being Concrete with Closed-Ended Questions

It is now time to work on questions that are designed to bring specific answers. A well-timed closed-ended question is like a candle in a dark room, revealing truth with clarity. Having too much information is as confusing as having too little. When information is placed into appropriate categories and connected to life events in an understandable pattern it provides us with the steps and power to change. Good closed-end questions make connections and lead us to solutions.

> *A well-timed closed-ended question is like a candle in a dark room, revealing truth with clarity. GRS*

Closed-ended questions demand specific answers. For example, Gary wants to find out from Faye if there is a relationship between her husband's job, his trips abroad and her relationship with the church. He is open-minded about the answer, but curious if such a pattern exists.

> *My strength as a consultant is to be ignorant and ask a few questions.*
>
> **Peter Drucker**

Gary: Faye, did James travel much before you became a Christian?
Faye: I am not sure. Maybe his traveling increased about the same time.
Gary: Think about when you became a believer and when his travel schedule increased. Is there a connection in timing?
Faye: Well, I was converted three years ago and he got the new job right after that. I was lonely and accepted an invitation to attend a cell group. There I accepted Christ.

Most of the issues and problems that bring people counseling are not one-time events but arise from a pattern between two or more people. In this case, Faye was complaining about her husband's travel schedule as well as emphasizing the importance of the church. It is natural for two seemingly disconnected relationships to related. Gary wanted to see if James' travel schedule and her church attendance occurred about the same time and if they influenced each other. His specific question got the information. If the patterns interact he will try to find out how.

> *By being Concrete, we make the general specific, the obscure apparent and the muddled clear. GRS*

Concretely Discovering Expectations

Closed-ended questions are helpful for discovering expectations and we suggest that you do this as soon as possible in your helping conversations. The very first session is usually the best time to find out where the Seeker wants to go.

- What do you want from our time together? (Goal question)
- What brought you here to see me? (Asking for a complaint)
- How can our time together be helpful? (Focus on content)
- What would you like from me? (Expectations of the Helper's role.)

We are sometimes surprised by the answers. Jen, a trainee at the Lifeway Counseling Center was attempting to help Victoria, a 25 year-old woman, to deal with an angry husband. The trainee was upset because the man was abusive and wanted the client to confront him. After thirty frustrating minutes of Jen's advice and Victoria's resistance, Gary, the supervisor, asked Victoria an assessment question.

> **Gary**: Victoria, what do you want from counseling? How can we be most helpful to you right now?
>
> **Victoria**: I want you to help me find a way to spend more time with my husband.
>
> **Gary**: So, all you want is a strategy for keeping him home with you. You do not want us to help develop a plan to confront his abusive behavior. Is that right?
>
> **Victoria**: Yes, that is correct. I want to figure out a way to get him to be with me more. If I confront him he will avoid me even more than he does now.

Jen naturally attempted to influence Victoria to confront her husband but it didn't work. It was futile for Jen to preach, urge or promote confrontation until Victoria saw that it would help her reach her goal. Resistance usually means one of the following things:

- We have not accurately assessed the client's level of motivation
- We have underestimated the cost of the change
- We have attempted the wrong intervention for the right problem
- It is right intervention for the wrong problem
- We have intervened too soon
- We were unclear about our advice

People's goals may surprise us. However, they are usually in a better place to judge than we. However, if the goal is unethical or dangerous we must not go along with it. In most instances, a bad goal is the result of poor planning or irrational thinking. A good, concrete question can be a partial remedy for both problems.

Many leaders assume that it is their duty to carry everyone's monkey. A Singaporean pastor who took our seminars said, "Most of the time, people just want to tell me their story and have my prayer support. They do not want me to actually do anything about the problem for they know I cannot solve it. This knowledge has been very liberating for me." He learned to ask concrete questions and set concrete goals and his people appreciated it.

> *In order to build a house on rock instead of sand we must know the difference between the two.* GRS

Concreteness with Summary Statements

Summary statements boil down the complex information of an open conversation into a simple list. Helping is similar to mining for gold. After cutting through the topsoil, a miner must expertly sift through the most promising rocks and fool's gold to get to the real gold nuggets. Helpers must dig through mounds of complaints, red herrings, and useless rambling and find a few nuggets of important information.

It is impossible to remember everything. In fact, many details are unimportant in finding a solution. However, it is easy to focus on a few reoccurring themes. A summary of key points allows us to keep our eyes on the prize, look for small action-steps and follow-through with the Seeker to measure its effectiveness.

Faye was worried about failing to witness to her husband and not having her family in church. How can Gary find the root issues? What kind of a summary statement could he make to clarify exactly what she needs to do?

Faye: I never seem to be able to get my family to attend church. I just don't know what to do. I have tried everything.

Gary: Faye it seems that you are feeling guilty about the fact that James and the boys are not going to church with you. Is that correct?

Faye: Yes, it is not a good witness. I am sure others notice that my family is not in church and I know God is not pleased with me.

Gary: So you are thinking that the Lord and other people notice when your family is not at church, and they are all upset with you. Is that correct?

Faye: Yes, I suppose I do feel guilty. He is gone so much though, it really hurts that we are not even in church together.

Gary: It seems that James' traveling schedule is one of the most troubling aspects of your marriage. You really got teary eyed when you talked about him being gone.

Faye: Yes, it bothers me that we are apart so much. But his complaining bothers me more than anything.

Gary: Did James complain about the nagging before you became a Christian?

Faye: No, we have always been very busy but he never complained before.

Gary: So, although many things have not changed between the two of you since you met Christ the conflict and complaints have increased.

Faye: Well, on second thought, he complains now about my going to church instead of other things but I suppose the conflict is not new. In fact, he has always complained about something. Maybe that is a key to all this trouble.

Gary: Indeed, this may be a key to understanding your relationship with James. We can discuss it in depth later. Why don't we put a bookmark into our conversation and pick it up next time. I need to go back to work now, but I wonder if we can meet again and continue our talk. Is that possible? (This is the skill of asking for another *Meeting*. It is also shows *Respect* for Faye by asking her permission. It is *Genuine* because Gary is honest about his time constraints.)

Faye: I was hoping you would be willing to talk with me again. Maybe we can meet here at this same place next week. Wednesday is my best day to take a long lunch hour and this place is quiet.

Gary: That is good for me as well. I would like you to do something before we meet. Please look at how your relationship with James has changed over the past year. Examine which of those changes have been positive and which have been negative. I will ask the Lord to give you insights about all these things. It is a good idea for you to tell Joseph what you and I discussed so he can be in prayer as well. (This lets her know that the cell leader will be involved but places the responsibility on Faye to tell him. Gary does not take responsibility for Joseph.)

> **What can be done at any time is never done at all.**

Gary discovered and focused on important issues by using Summary Statements. A concise review can bring healing through insight. Although insight alone is inadequate, a small light can penetrate the gloom to reveal possible action steps. Light at the end of the tunnel will not deliver us from the dilemma of being trapped below ground. However, illumination can provide the hope and faith to keep walking with the assurance of an opening ahead. Gary asked Faye to summarize her relational patterns by assigning some easy homework. This keeps her focused on specific patterns and reduces negative thinking.

Summary statements can also be used to get feedback from the Seeker. A lack of understanding can become apparent by a pointed question and will bring us back to reality.

> **Gary**: So being a Christian is the main problem in your marriage?
> **Faye**: No, I am not saying that at all. It is the best thing that ever happened to me. James is actually glad that I am a Christian because I am not depressed anymore but does not like my nagging him.
> **Gary**: Oh, I see. I misunderstood what you were saying.

Although admitting our misperceptions may be embarrassing, it allows us to develop an accurate understanding of the situation. It also shows the Seeker that we are humans who can admit mistakes and model healthy self-disclosure.

Renewed Christian Thinking and Concreteness

In our book and companion classes called <u>Renewed Christian Thinking</u> we teach a process that makes the scriptural command in Romans 12:2 practical and transferable. Do not be conformed to this world but be transformed by the renewal of your mind, that you may prove what the will of God is, that which is good and acceptable and perfect.

This is a passage we learned in Sunday school but had no idea how to implement until several years ago when Gary, Alice Petersen and Dorothy Geverdt integrated scripture with insights from Cognitive Behavioral Theory. It puts practical feet on the command quoted above and provides churches with a simple, way to equip members with the word of God.

Cognitive theory is based upon the notion that feelings and behavior are the result of our deepest beliefs. Others cannot make us feel bad, mad, sad or guilty. These unwelcome feelings arise from the ways we think. Nor do others cause us to act with vengeance, rancor, pettiness, or spite. They come from within our own mind and others' actions cannot change our heart.

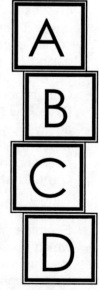

The mind of Christ is developed by understand the four components of emotional/behavioral life. They are the *Activating Events* that stimulate us, the *Belief System* (Ideas, self talk, perceptions and values) that filter those acts, the resulting *Consequential Feelings* such as anger, happiness, and frustration and finally, the *Decisive Behavior* or actions that are the result of my thoughts and feelings. Trying to change my feelings without altering my beliefs will surely end in failure. Blaming others for our feelings is also self-defeating and doomed to create more conflict.

By examining the A B C D's of emotional life and renewing my mind according to the scripture, we are able to more easily deal with destructive feelings and inappropriate behavior. The ABCD process allows us to trace them back to our *Belief Systems* and decide what to do with them with God's help.

Assessing Faye's Thinking, Feeling, Behaving Patterns

An assessment of Faye's conversation will reveal the pattern of her Belief System and how they make her feel/act. Ask yourself the following questions.

- What *Activating Events* does Faye mention as being important?
- What are her *Beliefs* about those *Events*?
- What are her *Consequential Feelings* coming from the *Beliefs*?
- What does she *Decide* to do with these feelings?
- When does she get upset or emotional?
- What does she do when she has these thoughts and feelings?

In the following role-play, Gary listens concretely, using ABCD as a guide. Notice how placing questions in a few simple categories allows Gary to differentiate between actions outside Faye's control and those for which she is responsible. This kind of *Concrete* interaction reveals information we will later use to discover a solution.

Gary: Faye, tell me what you think about when James is traveling?
Faye: I think that he is not as loving as he would be if he were a Christian.
Gary: And how does that thinking make you feel?
Faye: I feel frustrated and upset.
Gary: And your frustrations cause you to do what?
Faye: I start to think about ways to witness to James.
Gary: So, you begin to think about ways to change James. Does witnessing help the situation?
Faye: No. I have not been very successful in that regard.
Gary: When he doesn't change, how do you feel?

The ABCD process unscrambles Faye's jumbled thoughts, allowing Gary and her to understand why she is behaving as she is. If she can clarify her negative thinking, the unhealthy feelings and nagging behaviors will disappear. By clarifying the ABC and D we open her to the Holy Spirit who will bring renewed thinking.

Concreteness on Paper

A wall chart or a sheet of paper points out facts in black and white. Visually oriented folk need to see things in print. Gary used the café placemat to review Faye's concerns.

Gary: Let me see if I fully understand the points you are making, Faye. I will list them on the place mat. Correct me if I am wrong:

1. Your husband is away from home much of the time.
2. You are upset because he is not a loving Christian.
3. It bothers you to attend church alone.
4. You feel guilty that the family is not yet converted.
5. You wish you were not so lonely.

Did I get all of the issues you have brought up? Is there anything that is incorrect?

Faye: I think the most important point is number one or perhaps number five. I suppose they really go together. Maybe we need to think about what I can do to help myself because there are some things I cannot change or even influence.

Gary: So, one and five are the most important of all the items and you want to see what you can do about them. Would you like to add anything?

Faye: No, I think you covered almost everything. I need to think about how to deal with the most important issues. Can we discuss them now?

Seekers leave almost every session with a page or two of notes, diagrams and lists. When items are in black and white they make a more long-lasting impression than if we simply discuss them. The tables in one of our favorite restaurants are covered with sheets of white paper that serve as a writing surface to be taken home after lunch.

Concreteness through Action

In the family class, we relive a family's relationship patterns through role-plays, charts and the dolls. Students concretely discern repeating, dysfunctional interactions. These classroom exercises make plain the normally invisible family configurations. That which has been obscure and complex becomes concrete and simple.

Gary asked Faye to direct a drama showing how her closeness with church affected her emotional distance to James. She can demonstrate the emotional changes by using chairs to represent significant relationships.

Gary: Faye, let one chair represent James and the other God. It seems that as you drew closer to God, James drew closer to his job. Then, your relationship with him became more distant and conflicted. Is that a correct? (Gary leads Faye away from the chair representing James toward the chair representing God.)

Faye: I never thought about it before but it does seem to be that way. Wait a minute! He actually changed jobs and began to travel before I was saved. After that I was lonely so friends invited me to a cell meeting where I found the Lord.

Gary: So, he changed his relational pattern with you first and then you got involved in the church. (Gary moves the chair representing James indicating that James moved away from Faye first. He then guides Faye to the chair representing God.)

Faye: Yes, I can even feel the changes right now as you move the chairs and me. But now he complains about my being gone too much. Maybe we both moved away from each other about the same time.

Seekers are often able to find solutions after a role-play or other action. Faye's insights about James will allow her think differently and feel better as well as plan new and healthier family processes. The chairs provided Concrete that clarified her confusion.

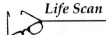

Life Scan

Without the ability to be focused and specific it will be very difficult to get to the root of the problem, making a good solution almost impossible to find. Yes, we may be able to give Faye advice but we will fail to truly understand her dilemma. So much material comes up from the Seeker's heart and life that, we can get overwhelmed when there is no clarity about what is wrong and what a solution might produce. We cannot find solutions for every symptom a Seeker describes.

TIPS for Life

Personal Reflection and Practice

- Rate yourself on the skill of *Concreteness* using a scale of one to ten. Does *Concreteness* come naturally to you?

1   2   3   4   5   6   7   8   9   10

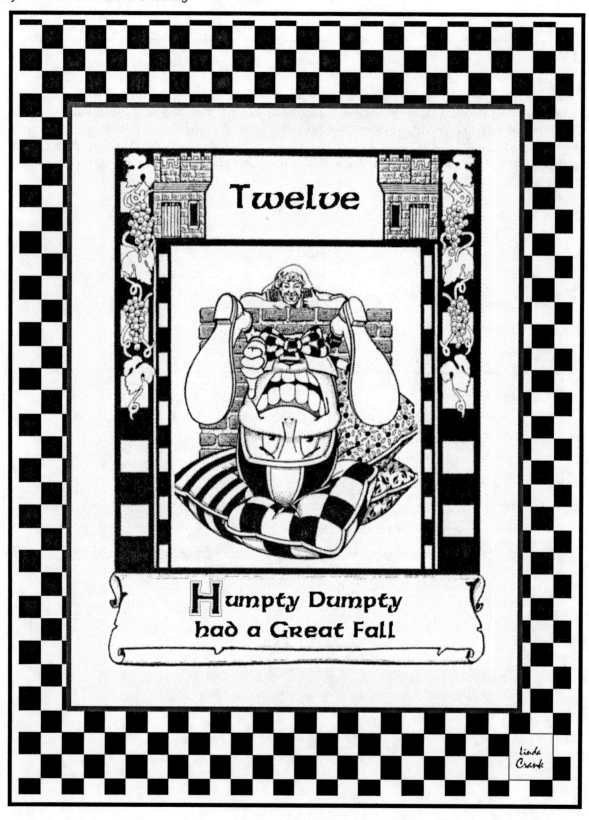

Twelve

Humpty Dumpty
had a Great Fall

12

Moving to Action with Affirmation

Finally, brothers, whatever is true, whatever is noble, whatever is right, whatever is pure, whatever is lovely, whatever is admirable-if anything is excellent or praiseworthy-think about such things. Philippians 4:8

> *There is so much good in the worst of us and so much bad in the best of us, that it's rather hard to tell which of us ought to reform the rest of us.* Alain-Fournier

People can get so mired down in past problems that the future is fuzzy. The clients who come to counseling want relief now! Unfortunately, they don't have any idea about what life will look like when their problems are solved. Most think only about making the pain go away rather than how to live after the pain is gone. This can be problematic because pain actually becomes more acute in counseling. Carrying old emotional baggage and irrational thoughts causes a nagging sense of anxiety. It lies there so long that it becomes a normal, low-level irritant. However, as the defenses and irrational thought patterns are removed, root causes are exposed and chronic pain becomes acute discomfort.

Chronic pain is devastating, toxic and debilitating. Like a toothache, it indicates a deeper problem that will not heal itself. Unfortunately, inner healing is sometimes viewed in the same way as a trip to the dentist. We will do almost anything to avoid a high-speed drill or the searching light of the Holy Spirit. This is why surgery of the soul requires the anesthesia of *Genuineness, Respect, Empathy and Warmth.*

Affirmation

The secular world has little reason for faith, hope and positive expectancy. When troubles come, it seems like bad luck or fate. Christians, however, can always look for the hand of God in their affairs. No matter how difficult life has been, we know that *All things work together for good for those who love God. Romans 8:28*

Because of our faith in the goodness and love of God, we are Asset Based rather than Scarcity or Sickness Based in our approach to care and counseling. Far too often we have been lured into thinking like hopeless pagans who must appease the gods in order for healing to occur. Some even lapse into New Age karma and wonder if bad works have overcome their good works, dooming them to a life of sickness and pain.

As members of the forever family we know that God loves us and has a wonderful plan for our lives. God even sent His own son to redeem us while we were His enemies, for "It is not by works of righteousness that we have done but according to His mercy that He saved us." During times of crisis we may begin to look for personal reasons for our troubles.

An Asset Based approach looks for good things and for God at work in the Seeker's life. God is always available and is always at work in us, even when we are not aware of it. His mysterious ways do not mean He is absent and this philosophy leads us to seek ways to *Affirm* the Seeker's strengths. Asset Based Counseling rests on the assumption that God calls His people to hope and healing. We look for positive signs rather than negative; hope rather than hopelessness; strengths rather than weaknesses.

It is, however, important to genuinely esteem the person before making a compli-mentary statement. Too often we fail to respect the strength and hard work it takes to live with an unfaithful spouse, a troubled child or a chronic illness. Helpers need to empathize with the resiliency of a Seeker beset by crises. To see only weaknesses and fail to affirm their strengths will bring discouragement. Adultery, addiction, grief, job loss or other crises cannot be solved by positive claims or lists of strengths but the person in the middle of such problems will certainly be encouraged to face life with more energy and hope.

A Helper with a "sickness philosophy" looks for problems and then treats them with his superior wisdom, insight and knowledge. The Helper is seen as the hero and the Seeker too weak and ignorant to help himself. The Counselor must "treat" the patient because he has no idea how to treat himself. This is a common philosophy in graduate school, books and seminars on how to do better counseling.

We believe, however, that the Seeker is the real hero. He is the expert who knows himself better than anyone else. He has tried many solutions and knows what will work and what will not. He knows what he can pull off and what he will not be motivated to accomplish. We are consultants who are privileged to cooperate in the healing, growth process. Only God heals and is *The Counselor* who can lead us into all truth and inspire the Seeker with insights, ideas and solutions.

We have a passion for God's answers and His plan for our lives. Even in the midst of struggles, we know that *All things are possible with God.* We have counseled thousands of people with addictions, compulsions, dependencies, sinful habits and serious mental problems. We can say with confidence that substantial healing is possible for all. No problem is so strong that hope is gone. Not everyone changes immediately or completely but substantial healing and growth are part of God's plan.

Therefore encourage one another. I Thessalonians 4:18

How do we implement this approach into our ministry? First, we add action to talk; model grace rather than discuss grace; act mercifully rather than teach mercy; show God's love rather than define His love; look for God at work rather than lecture about trust. We are agents of grace, convinced that it is caught more than taught. When grace pervades our attitude it will invade our relationships. We look for willing hearts not just heart problems. We intentionally seek to find God and good already at work in the person's life so we can affirm it in concrete and practical ways. In our experience, it is not too hard to do once we have made the commitment to be on the lookout for good and God.

> **When grace pervades our attitudes it will invade our relationships.**

Dr. David Jeremiah describes it as inspiring others with renewed courage, renewed spirit or renewed hope. "An encourager is one who puts courage into the faint hearted...one who makes a very ordinary man or woman cope gallantly with a perilous and dangerous situation." In John 14, Jesus said, "I will send another Counselor to be with you forever." The first Counselor sent another Person to be with us forever.

Christians who know *The Counselor* well are good encouragers of hope and strength. The name Barnabas' comes from the Greek *parakletos* and means an encourager. A powerful leader, he also related to those around him with the tender fruit of the Spirit. In Acts 14:12 he handled a very difficult situation with great skill. The Gentiles wanted to worship Barnabas and Paul calling him Zeus and his trainee Hermes. Although Paul was no shrinking violet, they assumed Barnabas was Zeus, the most powerful of all the Roman gods and Paul was simply his spokesman.

Barnabas was also compassionate, tender and patient, especially with those who sinned. His character traits were so strong that they caused the Apostles to change his name from Joseph to "son of encouragement." Barnabas exemplified I Cor 13:4-7.

> *Love is patient, love is kind. It does not envy, it does not boast, it is not proud. It is not rude, it is not self-seeking, it is not easily angered, it keeps no record of wrongs. Love does not delight in evil but rejoices with the truth. It always protects, always trusts, always hopes, always perseveres.*

In Philippians 4, Paul instructs us how to minister like Barnabas. He says are to think about things that are true, honorable, right, pure, lovely, of good report, excellent and worthy of praise. The following strategies will help you implement these attitudes and focus on giving good reports and find things that are worthy of praise. Even when there is chaos, we expect to find assets in the Seeker's life because scripture calls us to look.

> *When one door of happiness closes, another opens; often we look so long at the closed door that we do not see the one door that has opened for us.* Helen Keller

Questions Designed to Offer Grace, Affirmation and Encouragement

One of the ways to refocus the helping process from the painful past to a hopeful future is to ask good questions. There are several different types of questions that are consistent with an Asset Based philosophy. The first is called, a *miracle question* developed by the Brief Therapy Center in Milwaukee, Wisconsin. It has proven to be a wonderful insight. Like all techniques, it must be used with discrimination and sensitivity. Miracle questions focus on solutions rather than problems.

- If, during your sleep tonight, the Lord answered your prayers about this problem, what would be different when you woke up?
- How will you know when the problem is solved?

Miracle questions encourage the Seeker to consider the future. They sometimes can short circuit the *Complainant* process, empowering the person for the *Ready to Change Stage*. We need to think creatively about solutions. Sometimes a miracle question will accomplish that goal but in other instances the Seeker will blink, scratch her head and ignore the question. This probably means that the time was not right so do not give up. Try again at another time.

Another benefit occurs among those who have already begun to see God at work. Many of us experience but do not recognize a miracle. Like the children of Israel, we may murmur so much that we miss the manna. If we miss the manna, we may miss His personal presence. If we miss His presence, we may miss His perfect plan. Give the client an opportunity to reflect upon the goodness of God by seeing if the solution has already begun to appear. We frequently hear about wonderful miracles that have already started.

By re-framing an issue or asking a positive question, we allow our minds to be renewed to see His goodness. Instead of saying, "How badly do you feel that God has not answered your prayers," we ask, "How will you know when your prayers are answered?" Instead of reinforcing negatives try probing for the positive. Interestingly, after asking such a question we sometimes hear that God is already at work and the complaints turn into praises. If there is no positive answer you do not need to be concerned. You have not slipped backward but simply did not move forward in finding a solution.

This process also allows us to consider how God has provided in the past. We can look for areas that God is acting in our behalf and consider what life will be like in the future, after the solution is implemented. Miracle questions sometimes reveal that a partial or hidden solution is already emerging. This revelation sometimes comes as a surprise to the Seeker. In the midst of pain and problems we may not feel God's presence, even when He is with us. The miracle question places a seed of faith in a Seeker's heart that can open hope for tomorrow and blossom into reality by the next meeting.

Coping Questions

Most people actually cope with the pain, trauma and difficulties of life with enormous courage. Despite this perseverance and fortitude, they may be embarrassed about having problems or think that their coping skills are poor. We let people know how special and courageous they are to build faith and hope.

Questions or statements that focus on how well one is coping with troubles can be enormously encouraging. Simply ask:

- How are you able to cope with this situation?
- How do you get through the days and weeks of such pain?
- Where do you get the strength to survive in the midst of these troubles?
- I am surprised that things are not worse than they are.
- You must have a great deal of faith to cope with these problems.
- What other sources of support have kept you going during your struggle?

By asking questions about endurance, we discover from where they draw their strength. We also try to compliment them on the creative ways they have found to survive. Most of the time we hear about prayer, worship, friends and family.

Gary: Tell me how you manage to endure with so many issues facing you.
Faye: The Lord gives me strength, but it is difficult to make it by myself.
Gary: Are there times when you have felt the presence of the Lord?
Faye: Definitely. In my daily quiet times I get the strength to go to work and do all the things at home.

Gary: it seems that you are managing to keep an even keel despite the stresses and strains of work, rearing a family and living with an absent husband. God must be very near to you.

Faye: I guess so, but never thought about it like this before.

> *The deepest principle of Human Nature is the craving to be appreciated.* *William James*

Finding Exceptions to the Problems

Another way to keep from getting caught-up in the messiness of a Seeker's dilemma is to find exceptions to his/her problems. It is almost impossible to be in trouble all the time. No matter how much alcohol one consumes, an alcoholic cannot always be drunk. He has to stop drinking long enough to eat, sleep, work and play. Become an exceptions detective and find the exceptions to problem patterns. In fact, we sometimes find that the exception is the rule. Look for good works instead of bad; positive motivations rather than negative; successes rather than failures.

Listen to the positive ideas, thoughts and events that are there. Listen for comments about small successes and note them. Search for good reports, hard work, support by others or evidence of strong motivation. Look for anything that offers hope. However, do not make them up on your own. They must be authentic.

We often counsel people with sexual compulsions, dependencies and addictions. Recently we read the story about a therapist who is an "expert" on the subject. He describes a man we will call, Humpty Dumpty, who was addicted to pornography. In desperation, Humpty promised to give $1,000 to charity if he failed to remain free of porn for 90 days. One would think that losing that much money would be a strong motivator to stay away from porn. However, after 87 days of sobriety, the man went into a porn shop and gorged himself on X rated videos.

Before reading on, think about how we would handle such a person. How would you look for ways to encourage him? Would you be able to find exceptions to porn use or would his failure be so great that it would overshadow all else? Will we be problem or solution centered: sickness or health? The expert reveals his approach by writing,

 Since he had 87 days "sober," I decided to give him another chance. If he had gone 87 days he could certainly go 90 days. This time he went only 14 days before he relapsed and had to give his money to a charity.

How would an Asset Based Counselor, have handled that situation differently? Could we have found some things in Humpty Dumpty to *Affirm*? What could we have said to strengthen him? Would you conclude, as did the therapist, that Humpty was hopelessly addicted and could not change? Would you "give him one more chance?"

When the counselor said, "I decided to give him another chance" it indicated who he saw as responsible for healing. In the Asset Based Model, we do not presume to have the power to control anyone or give him or her a new chance to succeed or fail. The Seeker is in control of his destiny and he alone must decide to succeed. This therapist assumes the role of a hero-

133

parent who is in control of the client-child. Such a disrespectful attitude may hinder recovery. Humpty needed encouragement and hope not punishment and hopelessness.

Humpty had gone 87 days without falling. That is not a tragedy; it is a tremendous victory. It is, in fact, a series of at least 87 victories because recovery proceeds one day at a time. It certainly does not indicate hopelessness but great expectation that Humpty can change. He has already shown daily success for almost three months!

We would not describe Humpty as an addict but a man with a bad habit. Going that long without a relapse is a miracle not an indication of moral inadequacy. We would affirm his positive changes and the great amount of work it took. We would not criticize one relapse but celebrate 87 successes. A single failure doesn't mean one should be thrown on the trash heap of life. One relapse is not proof that one is unredeemable but normal.

Third, we would ask some of the following questions:

- How did you manage to stay away from pornography for three months?
- What did you do instead of porn?
- What did you think about that helped you?
- Where did you get the strength?
- From whom did you receive positive support?
- How did you resist temptation so effectively?

We are optimistic. We know that Humpty, with God's help, can change even if he is looking at pornography. He had discovered many creative ways to avoid pornography so we will need to learn those from him. He knows how to stay away from those awful materials, but we do not. We have never had this problem nor have we conquered it. He is the hero. We are novices.

Any person who stays sober for even one day should be commended not condemned. If there were trophies for success we would certainly give one to Humpty for 87 days of sobriety. Should an Oscar ever be developed for overcoming difficult situations, Humpty would get it. When only one day of 88 is a failure the person is batting better than Ted Williams, Pete Rose or Joe DiMaggio. Yet, "experts" find it easy to punish, confront and revile Humpty instead of blessing him.

*Do not let what you cannot do interfere with what
you can do. John Wooden*

Sometimes self-diagnosis is a problem. One woman read a book about Attention Deficit Hyperactive Disorder (ADHD) and became convinced her son had the most serious type described by the author. She sent him to a psychiatrist for twelve months with no success and, out of desperation, came to Lifeway. We discovered that the young man was certainly different than other children. However, his problem was not what she thought. He was gifted, not sick; he was brilliant not demented; he was bored not hyperactive; his trouble making came from excess time not excess chemicals in the brain. He was enrolled in a class for exceptional youth and he did well.

> ## *Small things done with great love will change the world.*
> *Mother Teresa*

Positive Blame

Affirmation is a more powerful source of positive change than negative blame, so we do a lot of positive blaming. (This sounds strange!) When a Seeker reports something good we may show humorous astonishment and doubt that it really happened in order to highlight its significance. We call this, *WOW Counseling*. You too can be a *WOW Counselor* by following these guidelines. Say things like:

- *Come on! That's impossible*. (By feigning disbelief we force the client to repeat his positive changes for he must try to convince us that it happened.)
- *How did you manage to pull that off? Tell me about it again*. (By asking for details and more information we allow the person to hear himself describe the great things he has done.)
- *I just cannot believe you were able to do that*.
- *It is wonderful*.
- *What a blessing! Praise the Lord!*
- *That took courage. WOW!*

The following dialogue illustrates how Gary attempted to positively influence Faye to move on toward the *Ready to Change Stage* with affirmation.

> **Gary**: I am glad that we could meet again, Faye. Tell me what things are better since we last talked.
> **Faye**: Maybe I am sleeping better. A little better any way.
> **Gary**: Great. Sleep is important isn't it? Since we met last week, you have felt more peaceful at night. Is that right?
> **Faye**: *Yes, but my husband is still not at home enough. He travels all the time and when he comes home, he works all the time.*

Gary immediately asked Faye what things were better so she could see that positive changes were already occurring. It also gets the session off to a positive start. About 60% of the time, people can remember a positive event. Gary reinforced and supported her peacefulness but even when they do not think of something good we keep focused on God.

> **Gary**: I was wondering if there were any times when things got better with you and James. Is it always bad or are the patterns sometimes different?
> **Faye**: We usually have a good time together when we are on holiday. Unfortunately that is not very often.
> **Gary**: (Ignoring the complaint) What is different on holidays? Why do you seem to do so much better then? Is it the change in his schedule or your schedule?

Faye: We discussed it on several occasions and he says that I am just too busy with the children and work when we are home. He blames me for it.

Gary: I see. It is good to hear that you have discussed this before. Many couples never talk about their relationship. That's good. (An Asset focused statement)

Faye: Really? Do you think it is OK to talk like that? I was afraid that I was not being submissive if I complained about my feelings. I know that most other couples have a much better relationship than we do. The pastor talks so beautifully about Christian marriage that I thought we were the only ones who had problems.

Gary: Oh. So, you have been feeling guilty about having conflict? No wonder you are stressed. It seems that the pastor's sermons make you think that Christian marriage is supposed to be perfect.

Faye: Yes, they do. Aren't most couples free from conflicts?

Gary: Unfortunately, no. Pastor Michael preaches about the biblical ideal not the human reality. Maybe we have been communicating a distorted message.

Faye: So other couples in the church have troubles too? I have been upset with James because he will not come to church. He says that I nag him all the time.

Gary: Yes, everyone has occasional problems. Are you saying that you pressure James and he resents it?

Faye: Maybe I have been nagging him a little bit. However, if he could only find the Lord I know we would be much happier.

Gary: Has this been a major cause of friction between you?

Faye: Yes. Ever since I became a Christian, we have fought about church attendance. He says I am putting pressure on him.

Gary: I can see that you are very committed to the Lord and want James to know Him like you do. But, if I am right, when you pressure him he actually pulls away from you and from God. It doesn't seem to be working does it?

Faye: No. That is why I am so frustrated. I am trying to witness like the church says to but it makes my husband and my children mad at me. Is there anything I can do? I want to please the Lord, but I can't please Him and my family both.

Gary: So, a root issue is trying to please both God and your family and you feel caught in the middle. It sounds like you are nagging James to please the Lord. Are there times when your relationship with James improves?

Faye: Yes, I think we get along quite well when I don't nag him about church. In fact, James really likes it that I am a Christian. He says that I have a better personality now except when I push him to attend cell meetings instead of working so much.

Gary: So, James is happy you have become a Christian? He doesn't resent Christ and the church just you're pressuring him to change. Is that it?

Several Affirmation interactions occurred in the dialogue. Immediately after Faye says she is sleeping better, Gary inquires about success in the marriage. He uses a simple, *exception question* "are there any times when things are better?" She recollects good times on holidays. Then Gary *Concretely* asks what is different when they are on vacation.

Gary also highlights marital strengths by affirming their discussions. This is *positive blame*. He says other couples in the church need to learn from her and affirms her commitment to the Lord while summarizing what is not working. This recognizes the reality of the problem while holding out hope for improvement. We never want to deny a person's pain by overly emphasizing the positive aspects of life.

Gary asked another exception question. "Are there times when your relationship improves?" and discovers that Faye appreciates James. All of these promote faith, hope, and clarity.

Exceptions provide a graceful context where both pain and potentiality are equally examined. We do not have to deny reality in order to have faith that God is at work.

God promises to empower us with His fruit of patience. However, waiting on the Lord's timing is one of the great challenges of helping. In Rom 2:4, St. Paul says, "The kindness of God leads to repentance." Kindness means to be mellow in our relationships rather than uptight. To patiently wait on God's timing requires an attitude of mellow expectancy. Waiting is worth the effort when it leads to repentance.

 ## Confessions of a Former Editor

The following story by a creative writer in Cincinnati tells how much a helping hand can mean to a struggling young student. Julia Sweeten Knispel writes movingly about her conversion from being a cutthroat editor with a quick red pen to a compassionate coach who is concerned about encouraging growth.

I confess. As a young, gung-ho editor in my twenties, I was oblivious to how fragile writers' creative dreams could be. I excelled at slicing and dicing their work into neat, grammatical rows that would march like obedient soldiers across the page. I prided myself on being the fastest red pen in the Midwest, leaving no awkward sentence or sloppy paragraph untouched. If a writer flinched at my editorial criticisms, I always assured him it was nothing personal. I was, after all, only trying to help.

What stopped my red pen cold was something a writer said to me after I critiqued a short story she had written. She respected my professional opinion so much, she said, that I helped her realize she didn't have what it took to be a writer.

When she had needed a pat on the back, I had given her a knock in the head. After that, I began to realize that telling a new writer everything she'd have to do to make a story publishable is like teaching a baby to balance books on his head while he's learning to walk. It doesn't take much more than a smiling face, some enthusiastic words of encouragement, and a little supportive applause to help them walk across the room for the first time. Giving too much advice—"Keep your head up! Hold your shoulders back! Stop wobbling around like that!"—will only convince a baby to sit back down and crawl.

When I was a writing tutor at Anderson University, a freshman student named Catrina came to see me. The first words out of her mouth as she slammed her way into my office were, "I hate writing!" I had already heard about her from the professors in the English department who didn't think she belonged in the writing program, and I knew they considered me her last shot at staying in school. It was pass or fail time.

When she read me her essay, "My Summer Job at Fifth-Third Bank," I knew we were in trouble. All the critiquing and editing in the world couldn't help her at that point. The professors had made it clear what she was doing wrong, but her work hadn't improved.

"See? I can't write. It's awful, isn't it?"

As she sat awaiting my verdict, I decided to take a risk. What did we have to lose?

"Actually, I can already tell that you're a creative person," I said. "You just have to learn how to bring that out in your writing and express yourself more effectively."

Her jaw hit the desk. The tough kid who had swaggered into my office with a chip on her shoulder broke down and cried. "You know," she said, "I used to love writing, before they told me I was so bad at it."

Her work automatically improved after that, before we even had our first lesson in thesis statements or topic sentences. By the end of the year, she was not only passing her classes, she was excelling in them. Amazingly, one of the same professors who had predicted she wouldn't last the first semester of college chose one of Catrina's essays for publication in a student journal.

Everyone needs help with their writing now and then, whether they're a budding beginner or a published professional. There's nothing wrong with taking or giving advice, and I still do both regularly. But these days I'm more aware of how fine the line is between giving a writer a leg up and kicking him down. I confess that I slashed a few creative dreams with my red pen in the past, but I'm mending my ways. I'm learning to heed the words of the poet William Butler Yeats, who wrote: "I, being poor, have only my dreams. I have spread my dreams under your feet. Tread softly."

Life Scan Summary

As we move through the CALM skills we have come to A for Affirmation. It allows us to consider a vision of life without the identified problem. Affirmation brings forth key information that is the essential raw material for constructing a solution that works.

The four basic tools of Asset Based Affirmation are *Miracle Questions, Coping_Questions, Exception Questions,* and *Positive Blame. Miracle Questions* propel us on a discovery journey using a hypothetical situation. They generate hope, faith, and wisdom. *Coping Questions* acknowledge the Seeker's courage, and resiliency in the face of adversity. Personal strengths are often hidden by a problem focus.

Exception Questions create conversations about successes and uncover patterns that work for the Seeker. The final tool is *Positive Blame* that gives us opportunities to celebrate and reinforce healing as well as highlight progress. All of them enable the Helper and Seeker to move towards *Ready to Change.*

TIPS for Life

Personal Reflection and Practice

- When do you practice affirmation? Have you ever used the strategies presented in this chapter? What happened?
- At the beginning of your day, consider how you can successfully express the skills of Concreteness and Affirmation. Predict on a 1-10 scale how well you will do that day. At the end of the day, place a scale in your journal showing how well you did with each skill and compare it with your predictions.
- In this chapter,

Name one key insight

What Assets did Gary discover with Faye?

How did he elicit information about Faye's strengths, and resources?

What strategies were employed to *Affirm* her?

How did she respond? Is she moving towards the *Ready to Change Stage*?

13

Looking For Good and God

All things work together for good for those who believe in God. Romans 8:28

When written in Chinese, the word 'crisis' is composed of two characters.
One represents danger, and the other represents opportunity. John F. Kennedy

In most counseling theories, the Seeker's personal circle of influence is not taken into consideration. However, it is an important dimension deserving special attention and hard work. A wise Helper discovers all the places Humpty gets support when he is away from us. We ask appropriate questions, affirm supportive people and refer him to places that offer encouragement. We try to find churches, recovery groups, co-workers, sports buddies and family members who will help Humpty change for the better. If Humpty spends an hour in counseling a week, he is away from us 167 hours. What happens during that time is more influential than anything we can do in a ministry session.

One of the ways to find areas of support is by asking questions that help Humpty think about good and God. For example,

---

- What is better since we last met?
- What has improved since the cell meeting?
- Did the Lord do anything good in your life since last week?
- Has the Lord said anything to you since we spoke?
- We asked the Lord to intervene, what did He do?

We fully expect to hear about good things that have happened. This builds the Seeker's faith, hope and positive expectations and showcases places of support he has not considered before. It allows us to *Affirm* not only Humpty but his surrounding influences.

Gary once counseled a man with clinical depression. Each week he would start by relating how depressed he felt and how badly the week had gone. However, after a couple of meetings, Gary began to ask him what good things had happened during the week. One time Tom began to morosely talk about the past week.

Gary: Hold it a second, Tom. You set a goal to have lunch with your dad. Did you get a chance to do it?

Tom: It may not be important but I did call dad and we had lunch on Wednesday.

Gary: Great. You have wanted that for a long time. I suppose everything went well at the lunch?

Tom: Well, I guess it did.

Gary: Was your father supportive and interested in talking with you?

Tom: Yes, after lunch we went to a small Catholic Church where he asked to pray with me. I know you are not Catholic so I wasn't going to say anything about that. I was afraid you might be upset.

Gary: I am happy, not upset. I am amazed. All you had hoped for was lunch and you got a prayer too? Man oh man! That sounds wonderful. What else happened?

Tom: Well it was neat. He also asked my forgiveness for being a poor father and I asked him to forgive me for being such a bad son and we prayed together.

Gary: Tom, that is one of the most wonderful miracles I have heard about in a long time. Tell me more about the ways God answered our prayers.

> *Hope*
> *is the*
> *melody for*
> *the future*
> *Faith*
> *is singing*
> *the song*
> *Love*
> *is learning*
> *to dance.*
> GRS

If Gary had not persisted in asking about the good things in Tom's life he would have neglected to bring them up. Seekers may think we only want to hear about their tragedy and pain. Perhaps they have been reading too many stories about Freudian and problem-centered therapists and have developed negative expectations.

We do not claim victories that are not there nor do we deny reality or see bright lights when things are dim. However, we look for miracles between sessions even when they come in small packages. Remember two things rarely happen: *everything and nothing*. God always brings about *something*. It is tragic when we miss the *somethings* of God.

Even Jesus had to grow in body, mind, relationships and spiritual insight. He began low on the scale of growth but He soon progressed to a higher level. Seekers may begin at a three or four on the scale of emotional maturity and will not get to ten with only a few meetings. We are convinced that they can move up the scale a point or two but *everything* rarely happens.

Research shows that counseling does indeed help people grow and change. Therefore, we are surprised if nothing good happens in the Seeker's support system and wonder if we missed God at work. Have the faith to actively seek the *somethings* of God.

Looking for Faye's support

The Seekers' support systems are not always apparent so we need to diligently search for them. We can do that by asking *who, what, when and where* to find the exact sources of encouragement. Gary and Faye model this process below.

Gary: Hello Faye, it is good to see you again. What helped you most this week?

Faye: Well let me think. I suppose it was a sermon on the topic of thanking God in all circumstances.

Gary: And how was that helpful?

Faye: Well, it got me thinking about all the good things in life. I have a good husband, wonderful children, a comfortable income and most of my life is great. Except for the fact that my family is not yet Christian and James works too much I am doing rather well. So, I started to count my blessings.

Gary: The sermon sure came at the right time.

Faye: Yes, in fact, I was laid off for a couple of days. I was really down about that and my marriage for a while. But, a friend from the cell group came over and brought me the sermon on tape. Actually, I now see that being laid off for a few days was a gift from God.

Gary: It is inspiring to hear the way the Lord gave you encouragement by sending her over with the tape. This lady must also be a very good friend.

Faye: Yes, she is. She has been through some difficult times herself but it did not get her down. I find that encouraging for me too. In fact, it reminds me of the song we've sung in church, "Count Your Blessings."

Gary: The timing was also amazingly important. Just after getting laid off the pastor preached on this topic and your friend brought it to you on tape.

Gary looked for positive things in Faye's life and she responded well. He asked a simple question about what had helped her most the past week, stimulating her to think of positive events. Second, he probed her answer about the sermon. This amplified and empowered the positive dimensions she reported. Third, it became obvious that Faye gets support from the church, cell group and friends. Fourth, Gary noted how the Lord provided the sermon at the right time. One cannot escape the notion that God is at work.

We have seen the devastation that occurs when a family or friend refuses to support a Seeker's change. A program in Cincinnati matches young people with business leaders who serve as mentors. The family system proved to be too strong for a mentee who dropped out of the program. He was pressured to stop his involvement because his parents were threatened by the youngster's connection with a "rich man from the suburbs." The program failed to involve the teen's parents who quickly destroyed all the progress made by the mentor.

Long-term growth depends upon finding people who will support us. Sometimes we involve relatives, pastors and friends directly in the counseling sessions to get them interested and involved in the process. At the very least we can help them understand and appreciate the benefits of affirming the changes they are seeing. It takes an entire village to rear a child and an entire village to change a Seeker.

The Lifeway Hospital Unit pioneered a family and community support process that significantly increased our effectiveness. We had three nights each week when the family could get involved in our groups. They learned good principles of family life, saw why support was necessary and bought into our goals. All of this is important in preventing a relapse and promoting work to maintain growth.

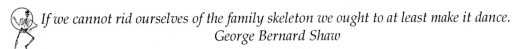 *If we cannot rid ourselves of the family skeleton we ought to at least make it dance.*
George Bernard Shaw

The simple act of calling us for help is a major step of faith. It means that people are already at step three on Prochaska's six-point scale so they have begun to count the cost of change. However, since Humpty is in the Complainant Stage, he will not think about or discuss improvements unless we ask him how things are better. He does not realize that there are steps in the change process or that he has already made great progress. It is up to us to educate him about how counseling works.

In a recent conversation about spiritual formation, Bill Hayes described the same kind of dynamic with a man he coached. Regardless of whether we call the process helping, counseling, mentoring or coaching, *Affirming* the works of the Lord is crucial. Far too often disciples are unable, on their own to identify the ways God is touching their lives. Bill, met Jay to help him discover how to best grow in the Lord. After some discussion, Jay agreed that there were three essential components to growth and he committed himself to become involved in all of them: worship, community with men and ministry to others.

Although Jay worked to practice the disciplines daily it was two steps forward and one back until he went to a fathers/son camp. There, the distractions were fewer and the opportunities greater to work on all three aspects. Upon his return, Bill listened to Jay talk excitedly about his experiences and how great they were and was able to remind him of their former discussion and the three issues identified as keys to spiritual growth.

We like to say that truth separated from experience will always remain in doubt. We can analyze our disciples with a temperament test and carefully prepare a chart to communicate our findings only to find that the connections are lost in the real world. Bill was able to Affirm Jay and his activities at the wilderness camp as a wonderful way to help him put it all together. Bill planted, the camp watered and the Spirit gave the increase. Jay was not quite ready for a *Commitment to Change* until he went to camp but Bill's support was also very important in the total process.

Jay missed the practical implications of the discussions with Bill. The words we use to describe spirituality are not always obvious in the practical situations of life so we must pointedly show people how they fit into our goals and objectives. Never assume that the Seeker knows what we mean when we agree on a course of action. Coming from a conservative church background, many believers are afraid of terms such as "accountability" or "commitment." They sound too much like formal religion or churchianity rather than life and peace and freedom. Help the Seeker by offering small steps of practical growth and Affirm the good things that inevitably happen.

> **Hope**
> *drives out*
> *despair,*
> **Faith**
> *reduces*
> *fear, and*
> **Love**
> *drives out*
> *helplessness*
>
> **GRS**

A recent consulting meeting with the staff of a growing church in California showed just how important this kind of clarification is. They asked us how to deal with a family in the congregation who refused to join the church and wouldn't allow the pastor to visit. The couple could quote scripture and attend cell meetings, indicating a move up the decision chain. They had not yet gotten to step four, *Committed to Change,* on the one issue of church membership. We suggested that the elders focus on the positive aspects of their involvement and see if Commitment came later.

Meeting and Measurements for Change

It is normal to spend at least one session on complaints before moving to Ready for a solution. Goal setting may require another meeting, the planning of which is an important part of the growth process. Planning a meeting indicates several positive things.

- Each person's time is valuable and must not be wasted.
- There is a purpose for each meeting.
- Meeting every week is not always necessary or best.
- Time between meetings can be used for homework.
- Difficult problems require time to resolve.

Faye and Gary model "Planning Another Meeting."

Gary: Faye, why don't we close our meeting now and resume our discussion later. You have a lot going on and we can't do it justice all in the next few minutes since we have to return to our jobs. Would you like to meet again?

Faye: Yes, I believe I need to discuss these issues in greater depth.

Gary: I am usually available on Wednesday at noon for a longer lunch hour. Are you interested in getting together again in one week or do you want to take more time in between our sessions?

The simple questions Gary asks will make a profound difference in the direction and tone of the discussion. First, he sets an important boundary by saying, "Our time today is over." This establishes the fact that each meeting has a beginning and end. Our time together has structure and boundaries. Time is precious so we make the most of it.

Second, he asked if she wanted to meet again. The statement does not assume Faye was interested nor did it put pressure on her to meet. However, Gary indicated he was willing to meet again. It also required Faye to make a decision to change, for *showing up is half the battle.* After revealing when he was available, he asked if she wanted to meet weekly or skip a week, requiring her to set a goal.

Faye: I prefer to meet next week if it is okay with you.

Gary: Yes, I can do that. However, I want you to do some homework before we meet next time. Spend some time thinking about when your relationship with James is good and when it is not so good. Pay attention to the pattern of communication and conflict between you.

Faye: Okay, I will write down my thoughts about James and our pattern of conflict. Would it be all right to call you when I get lonely?

Gary: I am sure you get very lonely during the week, but I don't think it is a good idea for you to depend too much on only one person. You need to continue to develop a circle of friends with whom you can share, so it is not a good idea to call me. Write down a short list of others you might contact.

Faye: Okay. I will try to talk with my friends at church.

Gary: I would also like to ask you to help me out by giving me some feedback. On a scale of 1 to 10 with 1 as very discouraged and 10 as very hopeful, where were you before we met today and where are you right now?

Gary structured the conversation in such a way that it set boundaries and gave her homework. He prepared her to discuss the positive and negative patterns of her relationship with James. No individual event or conflict is very important in itself, but a chronic pattern will reveal nuggets of gold to both the Seeker and the Helper.

Faye asked Gary to do something inappropriate. This can be very tricky for Helpers yet it established an important tone for the helping relationship. Gary set a boundary and refused to take her monkey. Paraprofessional Helpers should not give out their home address or phone number or agree to counsel in between sessions unless it is a crisis. Cell members, friends and family can provide the necessary spontaneous love and support during the week. Specialized Helpers operate within the boundaries of special meetings. Gary gently points Faye toward her normal social system for support and got her agreement to turn to them.

Measuring Progress

Gary also taught Faye to *Measure* how well she is doing. He asked her to scale her feelings before and after meeting with him. Any movement forward can be affirmed and á lack of movement can be investigated.

Scaling is a great way to be *Concrete* and helps us make the transition from *Complainant to Ready for Change*. It makes fuzzy issues clear, prepares us to set goals and changes the emotional flow of the *Cooperative Relationship*. Scales help us see the small changes that are occurring in life. Like the manna and unworn sandals to the Israelites in the desert, scaling helps us keep track of God at work. They allow us to visually renew our minds and become more realistic about growth. Everyone understands a scale.

We find scales useful to assess everything from the spiciness of food to the progress of Christian growth.

> *I long to accomplish a great and noble task, but it is my chief duty to accomplish small tasks as if they were great and noble.*
> **Helen Keller**

Q: On a scale of one to ten how spicy is that fish?
A: My fish is a seven on a scale where ten is very hot.

Q: How depressed were you when we began?
A: I was about a three.

Q: How much have you grown over the time we have been meeting?
A: I have grown a couple of points, from 3 to 5.

We use a series of these questions to get a better reading on when things are good and when they are not so good. This process helped Gary to a break through in a difficult situation in a western part of the USA. During a seminar, Pastor Doug asked Gary to meet with the parents of a troubled teen. Gary listened for about forty-five minutes while mother complained bitterly about how badly her son was acting. She wept profusely and complained in great detail about the teenager's rebellion, cursing, shouting and trouble making. Finally, Gary mentioned that there was not much time left so he wanted to clarify the situation.

1
2
3
4
5
6
7
8
9
1
0

Gary: On a scale of one to ten, how would you rank your child's behavior compared to other boys his age? Mother and father should rank him separately.

Mother: I think he is a six compared to other boys his age.

Father: I agree but he is even better than that so I gave him a seven. She is not as optimistic as I.

Gary: I am not sure you understand the question. How would you rank him with other boys his age? One means he is very bad and ten means he is very good. You both rated him above average. How can that be?

Mother: Oh, he is better than most kids his age. It is just when Jonathan and I argue that I think he is bad. He is really a good son.

Father: I agree. In fact, I think she is too hard on him.

Mother: When we hear about other couples' children we are happy about our son.

Gary: Okay, I see what you mean. However, why don't we look at him at his best and his worst? What has been the worst your son has ever been?

Mother: I think his worst is about a two.

Father: Well, for me, his worst is about a five.

Gary: Now, what would you say is his best would be?

Mother: I think his best is a six or seven.

Gary: So, a six point five would be about right?

Father: Well, for me, his best is about an eight or nine.

Gary: That is really high. Let's say an eight point five.

Mother: I think I am a bit low. He is probably an eight at his best.

Gary: What was happening when he is good and when he is bad?

Mother: Oh, that's easy. When he is allowed to be with his father and play on the computer, he is wonderful. He and I are the ones who fight.

Gary: When is he at his worst?

Mother: When I nag him to study. He yells and curses and we fight.

Gary: Are his grades bad? Is that why you nag him?

Mother: No, he does well in school but I don't think he is serious enough about learning. He would rather play on the computer and go to computer shows with his dad than study and that bothers me a lot so I scold him.

Scaling allowed us to unearth new and unimaginable facts that led the parents to change the way they related to this "troubled" son.

Gary: Do you think it would be possible for you two to agree on a way to work together with your son and keep your relationships on a positive level?

Father: Yes, we can do that. I have been trying to tell my wife that she is too hard on Jonathan but she would not agree. I think it is fine for him to work on the computer and spend time with me. After all, that is the way I make my living. I am a computer programmer and I think he has the same gifts that I do.

Gary: Mrs. Woods, can you agree that it is okay for Jonathan to spend time with his father and play on the computer?

Mother: Yes, as long as he gets his studies finished. I can see that the other way is not working so we need to come up with a better plan. I guess my husband is right but I may have some problems. He will have to help me talk with Jonathan.

Gary: I have some homework for you. After you decide on a plan to work with Jonathan call Rev. Doug and tell him what you have decided. He will help you stay on track in the future. Can you do that?

The parents discovered that there was a dysfunctional pattern in the relationship with their son. Neither Gary nor Pastor Doug knew what the patterns were. Most of the time, family problems are related to a chronic pattern and scales may reveal that pattern to everyone involved. Gary might have attempted to guess what the issues were but it was not necessary. There were two family experts in the room so all he had to do was ask them to describe the interactions. Nor was it necessary to blame and shame the parents. The scale revealed the truth and the parents made their own conclusions.

Prior to the meeting, all eyes were on the son. The parents, pastor and cell group members were all blaming Jonathan for the family's conflicts. The entire support system was caught in *the Complaint Stage*. However, the scaling process showed that the entire family had dysfunctional interactions. Amazingly, Mom and Dad both became customers who were *Ready to Change*. Once they reached this point, Gary simply suggested a action step with a simple goal and they saw its value.

Scaling with the Miracle Question

Scaling allows us to combine several processes. For example, we can use scales and the miracle question together.

Steve: On a scale of one to ten, you say you are presently at a three. What would be different if you were at a four or a four point five?

Janet: I would not be so sad and lonely.

OR

Steve: If you were now at a three on the scale, what would have to happen to get you above a five?

Janet: My husband would have to stop ignoring me.

This is a very effective way to encourage confidence and possibility thinking for the process seems less overwhelming. Anyone can move up by one point. Almost everyone has enough faith to take a small step in the right direction. Scales also provide us with an effective means of discerning a Seeker's level of motivation.

Steve: On a scale of one to ten with ten being totally committed to change the problem and one meaning no desire to find a solution, where are you today?

Janet: I am about a four. I just cannot get very motivated to try again.

Anything worth doing is worth doing poorly
until we can do it better. GRS

Scales and Moving to Change

Another way we use scales is to see how far one has moved toward *Committed to Change*. Those who move from *Pre-Conviction* to *Conviction* are twice as likely to reach the final goal of

Completion as those who do not move at all. Patiently supporting a slow client during the early relationship has important long-term consequences.

> **Steve**: When we first met a month ago what was your level of commitment to change and what is it today?
>
> **Janet**: When we began I was about a one. I only came because my pastor said I should. However, I am now much more open to think about doing something about this problem. I suppose I am at about a four.
>
> **Steve**: Have you thought about what it might take to get you to a five?

> *Do not grow weary in well doing.* Gal 6:9

Scaling Hope

We also use scaling to see how the Seeker is doing on developing faith, hope and positive expectations.

> **Steve**: On a scale from one to ten with one being no hope of change and ten being perfect faith that it will all work out, where are you today?
>
> **Janet**: I am at a five on hope. It seems some days that change is possible and some days that it is not so I guess that makes it about a five.
>
> **Steve**: Where were you before we began to work on the problem?
>
> **Janet**: Before I came in I was a zero or a minus ten! I had experienced so many disappointments that I was afraid to hope any longer.
>
> **Steve**: So you have made good progress. What was it that caused you change for the better?
>
> **Janet**: I have new insights about my husband, and myself and I see how things might get better if we tried real hard. So, I am hopeful that change can happen.

Scales are simple tools in the Helper's hand to facilitate easy understanding, promote greater hope and increase motivation. Even children understand scales and can benefit from their use. As you develop the use of scales in daily life we are sure you will see their power and ease of using as an intervention.

Life Scan Summary

This chapter completes the overview of the CALM acrostic with *Looking* for supportive systems and *Meetings with Measurement*. Wise Helpers look for places where Humpty can get support when he is away from counseling. Family and friends along with personal motivation provide some 40% of the encouragement toward positive change. If Helpers ask the right questions at the right time they usually find churches, recovery groups, co-workers, leisure and sports programs that will help Humpty grow.

Scales are an important part of a *Cooperative Helping Relationship*, especially at the transition from *Complainant* to *Ready for Change*. Scaling is also a special way to show

Concreteness. It makes fuzzy issues clear and prepares us to set appropriate goals. Scales can be created for almost any situation.

TIPS for Life

Personal Reflection and Practice

Where do you find support and affirmation?

- Draw three overlapping circles.

In the smallest circle, write the names of people with who you are closest and from whom you find the most comfort.

In the next circle write the names of people you like but with whom you spend less time. Underline anyone who you want to know better.

In the outer circle, write the names of personal acquaintances you do not know well. Are there people listed that you would like to know better and from whom you want more input?

14

Setting Good Goals

Forgetting that which lies behind I press on toward
the goal of Christ. Phil 3:13

Where do we want to go? This is the question that many ask but few answer. Determining a destination is half the battle of getting there. Without a clear idea of a destination, it is exceedingly difficult to develop clarity of purpose and the energy to find a solution to life's troubling matters. However, once we have decided on a destination, planning the trip is simply a matter of getting a good map.

You have probably heard about the man who wanted to go on vacation. He visited a travel agent and said:

> **Man**: I am planning a trip with my wife. How much will it cost?
> **Agent**: Where do you want to go?
> **Man**: I really enjoy travelling. Should I take an airplane or a ship? I could also drive. Which is best?
> **Agent**: But, sir, I do not know where or when you want to travel. I can't answer these questions if you are confused about where you are going.
> **Man**: I want to be comfortable. What kinds of clothing should I take? Is it warm this time of year or will it be cool?

Attempting to help a confused person is almost impossible. Unless he knows where he wants to go, he cannot figure how to get there. Nor will he be able to count the journey's cost, develop a road map to follow or discern how long the trip will take.

Such is the challenge facing Christian helpers. How can we possibly assist a Seeker unless we know his goals and objectives? Each person is unique with differing values, family structures and traditions. Finding a Seeker's motivating beliefs, deepest feelings and long-term goals is critical to having a good outcome.

> *You decide what it is you want to accomplish and then lay out your plans to get there, and then you just do it. It's pretty straightforward.* Nancy Ditz

Why Set Goals?

Setting well-formed goals can help us find good solutions. We are not interested in just seeing a change in ideas but also in making sure the ideas are acted out in life. There are many things we can do. We can give advice, offer to pray for healing, lead the person to confess, or call for repentance. The right intervention emerges from goals.

Setting goals has many benefits such as:

- Allowing us to decide whether the solution is biblical. Ministry involves making ethical decisions. Only by looking at a person's plan will be able to help him evaluate the ethics and morality of his decisions.
- Helping us evaluate progress. Changes occur one day at a time and one step at a time. It shows us what to scale.
- Enabling us to count the cost of change; to look honestly at the emotional, spiritual and relational energy accomplishing the goal will require. It may be friendships lost, habitual patterns altered, spouses incensed, family members confused or colleagues upset. Whatever the goal, there is a price involved and we must consider how to deal with it. We dare not close our eyes to the price one may have to pay to get healthy.

> *You cannot predict the future, but you can prepare for it.*

- Encouraging perseverance to continue the process of change when the going gets tough. Until the goal has been reached, the Seeker has a feeling of emotional discomfort called cognitive dissonance.
- Taking us from the abstract to the concrete.
- Breaking the journey down into small increments.
- Helping us develop a mental picture of what can and will happen.

The process of *goal setting* is an important opportunity to cement our alliance with the Seeker. Having goals helps one feel secure. When the goal has been reached, the person is able to celebrate his accomplishments and can move on to other issues.

Change is hard work for Helpers as well as for Seekers. It forces us to focus, be diligent with our follow-up and our follow-through. Inspirational advice is not enough. Preaching only begins the process, but setting good goals and keeping them current moves us into the future. Do not ask others to set goals unless you are willing to follow through and keep the account straight. Accountability keeps the momentum going.

Intervention Time

It is at this point that we are getting ready to intervene with prayers, advice, scripture, wise counsel, spiritual warfare or a variety of other actions. The patient listening and clarifying during the first two stages will pay off here.

Sometimes the intervention will focus on faulty thinking patterns. At times, the Helper and Seeker will analyze patterns in the family of origin and develop appropriate innovations while prayer for inner healing is the best alternative for some situations. This is the time to use our knowledge and techniques (*Content*) to assist the Seeker In finding a solution. The entire model comes together as process and the content converge.

Unless you try to do something beyond what you have already mastered
you will never grow. Anon

The SO SMART acrostic reminds us how to establish goals that are effective and complete. It combines ideas from business, strategic planning, management, psychotherapy, addictions research as well as Lifeskills' training. Since this is so much to remember, we have broken it down into several simple pieces.

S EEKER
O WNED

S MALL SIMPLE SPECIFIC
M EASURABLE
A DDITIVE
R EALISTIC
T IMELY

Seeker Owned Goals

Have you ever bought a product to regret it later? How did you feel about the sales person after the unwelcome discovery? Did you have anger or frustration? We sometimes blame the sales clerk for making us buy something we did not want or need. How many times do we try to sell a Seeker a solution they cannot achieve and do not really want? How can we tell if it is genuinely their goal or simply something they *should* want? If a person fails to follow through we can assume that it was not really his goal.

This does not mean that people will not work on a project without complete understanding. We sometimes carry out prescriptions because we trust the person who gave it. One man wanted a better romantic relationship with his wife and accepted our suggestion about listening to her before leaving for work. The idea made no sense to him but he valiantly carried it out. He trusted our wisdom and found success. This, however, is not the norm.

Sometimes our advice is wrong and we need to admit it. We were convinced that a certain intervention with an addicted husband would be good. However, the family resisted, and, we probed a bit farther. Finally, the truth came out. Our suggestion was in conflict with their religious tradition. It was not a biblical command but a strongly held value that we dared not challenge. Upon learning the reason for their resistance, we immediately withdrew the idea from consideration. It was fruitless to pursue it and could have led to a breech of trust between us.

We need to get specific enough to clearly evaluate the client's ideas and objectives according to biblical values. If the person sets a goal that we believe is inappropriate, we must do two things. First, communicate our gracious concern for the person. We accept them in love and respect their ideas. However, we refuse to agree to an unbiblical goal. We will not:

1. Treat others in an immoral or unethical manner.
2. Violate the Golden Rule
3. Carry a monkey
4. Do any harm

Other than these simple boundaries, we can go along with almost anything the Seeker wants to do. We may consider their goal frivolous but we can support it if the Seeker is committed to it. For instance, a client wanted to bring her dog to the counseling sessions. We knew the research about how much comfort a pet gives to people so we agreed with the request. The principle is, "don't sweat the small stuff."

Authority, Power and Influence + Prudence Revisited

> *The only people who want a change are wet babies.*
> Anonymous

Counseling and other forms of personal ministry are different from preaching and teaching. Although information can be important in counseling, the process is different. Christians have become so closely identified with proclamation that it may seem strange to employ any other style of Influence. Yet, when it comes to personal interactions, proclamation is the least effective way to bring about change. In fact, it may have the opposite of the desired effect.

Anytime we push against another person's will, the natural and automatic reaction is to push back. If we attempt *to motivate the unmotivated to be motivated*, we must take care lest we promote Seeker rebellion. For example, to use *authority*, we must be in a position of absolute control and have the ability to enforce whatever laws we make. Only in the armed forces is such an approach possible. Certainly it is far from normative in the church or the world.

Prudent Influence:

- Humbly admits we do not have all the answers.
- Recognizes that God's Spirit is present to guide us to the solution.
- Prefers that the Seeker take responsibility for both success and errors.
- Does not wish anyone to become dependent upon him.
- Realizes that the Seeker is the expert on himself and his situation.
- Recognizes that the client knows what will work and what will not work.

> *Do nothing out of selfish ambition or vain conceit, but in humility consider others better than yourselves. Your attitude should be the same as that of Christ Jesus who, being in very nature God, did not consider equality with God something to be grasped, but made himself nothing, taking the very nature of a servant, being made in human likeness. being found in appearance as a man, he humbled himself and became obedient to death—even death on a cross! Therefore God exalted him to the highest place and gave him the name that is above every name. Phil 2:2-9*

Sometimes our strong convictions make it difficult to *respect* the Seeker's ideas. However, even if we disagree, it is important to hear a person thoroughly for it reveals his motivation. We rarely disagree completely with a person's goals. If we have taken enough time to listen carefully, understand the root issues and have established trusting relationship, we usually discover some good ideas that we will be able to support.

Remember the Apostle Paul tackled the issue of controversial behavior in his first letter to Corinth. In Chapter 10, Paul gives advice about eating meat sacrificed to idols. Some of the members were eating the meat while others were scandalized by such behavior. Controversy erupted into a major conflict that could have split the young and passionate church. Paul was asked what to do. He writes to the leaders of Corinth and advises them to act with prudence.

Everything is permissible—but not everything is beneficial. Everything is permissible—but not everything is constructive. Nobody should seek his own good, but the good of others. Now, you may eat anything that is sold in the market without asking any questions about where it came from. Your con-science will not be harmed for, 'The earth is the Lord's, and everything in it.'

If some unbeliever invites you to a meal and you want to go, eat whatever is put before you without raising questions of conscience. But if anyone says to you, "This has been offered in sacrifice," then do not eat it, both for the sake of the man who told you and for conscience' sake—the other man's conscience, I mean, not yours. For why should my freedom be judged by another's conscience? If I take part in the meal with thankfulness, why am I denounced because of something I thank God for?

So whether you eat or drink or whatever you do, do it all for the glory of God. Do not cause anyone to stumble, whether Jews, Greeks or the church of God— even as I try to please everybody in every way. For I am not seeking my own good but the good of many, so that they may be saved. I Co 10: 23-33

Paul is sensitive about the Corinthians' theological, social and psychological state. Eating or not eating meat was not the question. More important to Paul was what would happen to family relationships. Are people drawn to God with peace? Then all things are permissible. However, if eating is offensive to others then we should be willing to deny ourselves food. Immature believers should be respected.

To the legalistic group he said, "All this is lawful but it may not be profitable." In other words, some things are not contrary to biblical standards but they are not wise. This is the case with drinking alcohol. It is lawful by biblical standards but unprofitable for the church because some will be offended. We will not drink wine if it offends a brother.

He goes even farther. *Feel free to eat sacrificed food with an unbeliever.* In other words, we are not to make an issue of an unbeliever's behavior. However, should the unbeliever inform us that it is "sacrificial food," making it a point of conscience we should refrain from eating it. Eating or not eating sacrificed food is unimportant. How we treat our family and friends is very important. Paul urges us to be sensitive to the feelings of others so we can witness to them about Christ.

If it works, do more of it. If it doesn't work, stop it.

This is also guides us as we set goals that are *Seeker Owned.* In the early days of our ministry, we became enamored with deliverance. After several years of exciting but unsuccessful power encounters, we decided to stop until we figured out why people did not get better and stay better. Our key insight was this:

People delivered against their Will are in the same old troubles still.

Jesus warned against casting out the "strong man" unless something else was put into the cleaned up house. Otherwise, the spirit would wander around and find seven more powerful spirits and the second condition would be worse than the first. Mt 12:29 We personally discovered the truth of this principle. James makes a similar point when he asks, *Are any of you suffering from evil? Let him pray. James 5:12*

The Seeker must willfully choose to stand against the enemy. He must want freedom from demonic influence and pray the prayers. In former days we acted without their expressed desire. Now we ask the person to pray for self-deliverance and affirm them for praying with power and pray with them to break the bondage of the evil one. Only then will he know how to fight with his own armor and the sword and remain free. Eph 6:10

Simple Goals

Simple goals are small, uncluttered, easily stated and clearly understood. Growth is difficult enough without setting complicated goals. Simple goals help us decide exactly what we are committed to do. Goal setting reveals our motives, drives, interests and commitment to find workable solutions. Some persons do not want to find a solution. They prefer to stay in the Complainant Stage *so we continue to listen, ask good questions and pray. Sometimes we get to the point where our patience ends and we refer the person to someone else or wait until they have decided to change.*

A well-formed goal will be "faith-sized" according to the Seeker's faith rather than the Helper's. We may wrongly assume that a faith goal must be big. Our vision is large but our goals must be small. A vision can be the loss of fifty pounds; the objective to lose one pound per week and a goal to stop snacking at night.

Making the simple complicated is commonplace; making the complicated simple, awesomely simple, that's creativity. Charles Mingus

Simple goals empower us to move in the desired direction. One research study concluded that having good goals increases the likelihood of positive change by a factor of two. To be able to double the chances of success by setting a good goal is a very good reason to work on this skill. There are great rewards from simple goals.

If you can't write your idea on the back of my calling card, you don't have a clear idea. David Belasco

Measurable Goals

Only by having a *Measurable* goal can we tell if we have made progress. Scales and specific action steps allow us to evaluate how well the Seeker is doing. For example, Faye wants a more loving husband and might say, "I will pray for James to become more loving." Despite the wonderful sound of this statement, it is not spiritual nor is it measurable. It also reinforces Faye's desire to stay in the *Complainant Stage* by keeping her focus on James while avoiding her own need for change.

A Measurable goal is, "I will do the following things to show my husband I care. I will stop nagging him about attending church. I will no longer leave tracts around the house." These are steps that we can follow-up and see if they have been accomplished. We could ask, "Faye, you said you wanted to stop nagging James. How successful were you? What good things happened?" Goals that are met will give her encouragement for the long journey ahead.

Clarifications and Examples

A recent workshop showed us how difficult it is for believers to accept the idea that counseling is more than preaching. We used the following analogy to explain the differences. Suppose a young father in the congregation was killed in an accident. How would a pastor most effectively minister to the widow? First, he must consider what to say at the funeral. Then he must think about how to comfort her when she comes for pastoral counseling. These are two distinctly different activities.

A pastor must confront the reality of death and bring hope to the survivors. A funeral service does that in very specific ways. It is designed to proclaim God's love, sovereignty and eternal care through singing, scripture, preaching, and eulogizing the deceased. Friends, family and clergy talk about God, resurrection and the hope of eternal life.

On the other hand, a grieving widow has very different needs. After the funeral is over she needs a safe place to pour out her pain and sorrow, anger and disbelief, confusion and bewilderment. We do not eulogize but carefully and empathetically hear the widow's struggle to honestly disclose her anger at the abandonment she feels as well as the loneliness she is experiencing. We do not rush to speak but allow her to tell the truth about her thoughts and feelings.

Worship services and proclaiming God's word are essential parts of growing the church but they serve a different purpose than equipping, pastoral care and counseling. Public meetings aim at inspiration while counsel aims at action. Preaching speaks boldly without hesitancy. Preachers speak faithfully about God's love, His providence and our hope. Counselors cry, listen, probe for truth and admit they do not know why bad things happen to good people. Preachers admit no doubts and fearlessly speak about God's eternal love and grace. Counselors tremble with confusion for a young widow with children and no money.

A certain radio evangelist famous for his brilliant and well-developed defense of the truth is a wonderful proclaimer of scripture. In a recent radio broadcast about Job, he departed from his normal pattern to tell how we should counsel a young, orphaned child. His advice was purely philosophical, ethereal and heady, nothing a child could understand. He said that although Job lost his family, he got everything back with interest. "This," he said, "teaches us never to worry about the loss of a family member but to look forward to God's faithful blessings." The preacher forgot to mention that Job's grandchildren could never replace their parents. Nor did Job's new children replace the love he had for those who died. This evangelist is a good theologian but this is not how we should counsel.

Humble Goals

St. Paul had a very large vision for his life but admitted that he had not realized it. The high calling of Christ was far off. So, he counsels believers to set more humble goals and give themselves grace when they fail to reach them.

> *I want to know Christ and the power of his resurrection and the fellowship of sharing in his sufferings, becoming like him in his day, and so, somehow, to attain to the resurrection from the dead. Not that I have already obtained all this, or have already been made perfect, but I press on to take hold of that for which Christ Jesus took hold of me. Brothers, I do not consider myself yet to have taken hold of it. But one thing I do: Forgetting what is behind and straining toward to what is ahead, I press on toward the goal to win the prize for which God has called me heavenward in Christ Jesus.*
>
> *All of us who are mature should take such a view of things. And if on some point you think differently, that too God will make clear to you. Only let us live up to what we have already attained. Phil 3:10-16*

Paul wanted to live above sin, sickness and weaknesses. He wished to live in the resurrection power of the Holy Spirit. Unfortunately, he and the rest of us, fail miserably at the perfection game. *I am not perfect*, he says, *but I push on to take hold of Jesus Christ. It is best to forget the past failures and keep our eyes on Jesus.* In an ironic coup de grace, Paul challenges his detractors to do the same thing. *I am not perfect* (mature) he says, *but I am perfect* (mature) *enough to urge the rest of you who wish to be perfect* (mature) *to adopt my strategy.*

Our paraphrase for counselors and pastors says: *I do not want you to think I know enough to tell others what to do, for I do not. However, I do have the following wisdom. Forget all the foolish and irrational things you have been doing and move on with Jesus. If you disagree, that is all right for I am convinced that God will reveal the truth to you some day. Just do not backslide and forget that which you have already learned.*

This reminds us that we do not have all the answers. In fact, we may not even know the right questions. However, we do have access to the One who knows how to search the heart and provide the answers. For those of us who nervously seek perfect responses to the great questions of life, take heart. If Paul was open to correction, we can be open as well.

Jesus left His followers with the promise of *a peace that passes understanding.* John 14:25-27 We seek an understanding that will provide peace for those troubled by loss, difficult children, abuse and other issues common to mankind. Peace comes from faith in God's provision, goodness and kindness in the midst of pain. Glib answers do not heal broken hearts or provide assurance to those who suffer. Peaceful people can communicate hope and offer a pathway to assurance of God's love.

Perhaps the greatest need of the evangelical church is to understand and act upon setting goals for step-by-step equipping of its members. No weakness is greater among small and large congregations. It is obvious that the training of Christians is less developed and thought through than a Wendy's or MacDonald's Restaurant. Flipping hamburgers is deemed more important than discipling believers to win the world to Christ. Even the largest and most famous congregations lack the most simple plan of training and depend upon high profile talkers who can say wonderful things and tell great stories. By learning to set good goals we can go a long way toward correcting this lack.

Life Scan Summary

Effective Helpers are prepared to engage in goal setting discussions when the Seeker is ready. The SO SMART acrostic reminds us of the seven factors in a good goal. In this chapter we covered SO (*Seeker Owned*) and SM (*Small & Measurable*).

Unless we understand where the Seeker wants to go, we cannot figure how to get there, count the journey's cost, find a road map to follow, or discern how long the journey will take. When a Seeker expresses his desire to change, the Helper must be ready to facilitate the small steps that the commitment to change will require. Goal setting motivates the Seeker to continue the process of change when the going gets tough by giving her a clear, mental picture of what can and will happen.

When the Helper and Seeker cooperate in goal development, the process itself reveals good solutions, allows them to discern if the change is biblical, provides them with a bridge from insight to action, enables them to see growth, directs them to count the cost of change, encourages them to persevere, and offers them a plan to move from the abstract to the concrete. This collaborative effort also is a bonding process that strengthens the Helper and Seeker alliance.

If the Seeker owns the goal the chances of attaining and maintaining it are high. If the Seeker sets an inappropriate goal the Helper should respectfully inquire if it will really work. A goal that works will bless others, edify the church, and respect family members. Setting goals that are too complicated, too vague, and too big is a barrier to growth. The goal must fit the Seeker's faith and be easily measured.

TIPS for Life

Personal Reflection and Practice

Think of a time when you set a goal. Analyze its *SO SMART* characteristics. Scale your progress with ten meaning it has become a habit and one meaning you are considering what will be the first action step.

15

Going on with Goals

_____

Him we proclaim, warning every man and teaching everyone in all wisdom,
that we may present everyone mature in Christ. Colossians 1:28

Goals are different from mission, vision and plans. A mission is an overall passion or call to serve Christ with all my heart, soul, mind and strength, but the vision is a picture of how the ministry will look. It is a picture that shows how we are to relate to others. Jesus is the model for us because we see Him as a brilliant, strong willed man who treated fragile people with gentleness and arrogant people with conviction. Filled with the Holy Spirit, He healed the broken hearted and set the captives free.

> *Vision without action is merely a dream.*
> *Action without vision just passes the time.*
> *Vision with action can change the world.*
> **Joel Barker**

A strategic plan is the specific way that one organizes his life so the vision and mission actually take place. Goals are the specific steps of implementing a plan that accomplishes the vision and mission. As Barker says, "Vision with action can change the world. Unfortunately, many of us have a hard time putting feet on our dreams and visions so we get nowhere. Goals are the shoes for our feet.

Hard Work

A good goal usually takes a great deal of hard work but is not impossible. A lack of difficulty may indicate that little or no real change is required. An established habit is difficult to alter and a lifestyle develops over years of daily practice. Setting and accomplishing worthwhile goals requires mental focus and a fair amount of elbow grease. This is one reason that those who protect others from discomfort by carrying their monkeys do not see growth for co-dependency retards transformation.

Additive Goals

In the last chapter, we discussed goals that are *Seeker Owned, Small, Simple, Specific and Measurable.* Now let's examine what it means to be *Additive, Realistic* and *Timely.* Additive goals are not just corrective; they are the start of something new. Instead of trying to stop a problem, we try to set goals that make problems less likely to occur in the future. Getting rid of a bad habit will leave a vacuum that can lead to relapse so we set forward-looking goals to prevent future failures.

People seek assistance because what they have been trying doesn't work. However, they may not know how or what to change. If they did, they would not need us. Humans can repeat dysfunctional behavior for many years. Unhealthy habits and lifestyles of frustration may seem obvious to an outsider, but to the Seeker it is the normal way of life. Just visit a friend's family reunion and watch how relatives interact with each other. Every family system has developed patterns and reinforcing habits that are the only reality to them. You, on the other hand, wonder how such patterns ever came into being. Counseling unravels these ironclad historical rules so people can make healthier choices.

ADDITIVE GOALS

Additive goals get people out of the pits of despair and move them toward the mountaintop of joy. However, we are climbing Mt. Everest so it will take hard work and wisdom to get to the peak. Faye's request to Gary reveals her willingness to perpetuate a negative habit pattern.

> **Faye**: I want to witness to James by placing booklets around the house. Do you know of any good tracts?

Faye has already said that her previous efforts to "witness" have backfired and turned her husband away from church. This goal, if pursued, would repeat that same unsuccessful behavior and have the opposite of its desired effect it would not be wise to support it. The goal is defective in several ways. It is not *Additive* because it repeats past futile, unworkable attempts to influence her husband.

Alcoholic's Anonymous long ago discovered the principle of affirmation instead of obsessing over negatives. They have used positive thinking with great success. For example, although the name of the group has to do with alcohol and they strongly promote sobriety from alcoholism, rarely do AA leaders discuss the evils of drinking or preach about the dangers of alcohol. They assume people already know that. They are most effective when one is already a *Complainant*.

AA does not emphasize quitting alcohol but starting sound new habits that are designed to eliminate all the old ones. Sobriety is their long-term vision and they have many good SO SMART goals designed to move toward that vision. They include daily prayers, working the Twelve Steps and attending meetings. They make use of many short, simple, easy slogans to remind members to practice these goals.

> - ***One day at a time***
> - ***Let go and let God***

Suiting Goals to the Behavior

Dr. Doug Reed developed a simple formula for understanding the difference between compulsions that arise from inner brokenness and dependencies that do not. He developed a formula to assess whether one is *Addicted, Compulsive or Dependent.*

Addictive Behavior equals Compulsions plus Dependencies: A B = C + D.

Compulsive behavior is a habitual reaction to negative events that are unconsciously designed to reduce inner pain. This includes guilt, shame, fear, anxiety or other emotional/spiritual discomfort. For example, some of us grew up in homes where we were not allowed to feel, think, ask questions or be honest about ourselves. Upon marriage and parenting we found that the habits developed in childhood did not work. This inevitably led to inner conflict and, sometimes, to the development of *Compulsive behavior* that include pornography, alcohol, eating, anger, spending or religion.

Dependent behavior, on the other hand, is habitually responding to a gratifying stimulant. It is not done to reduce inner pain but is designed to get a high. Although these two lifestyles may look a lot alike, their genesis and treatment are very different. Let us assume that Tony is drinking excessively in order to get a buzz. He has developed a lifestyle of alcohol *Dependency* that *is* not related to inner pain. In fact, Tony must feel guilt and shame before he will be motivated to change for he is not *Convicted* to change.

One may be *Compulsive* (reacting habitually to inner pain) without being *Dependent* (habitually getting a high) and, one may be *Dependent* without being *Compulsive*. Additionally, those who are *Addicted* are both *Compulsive* and *Dependent*. *Compulsives* cover up their inner pain with the behavior and *Dependents* medicate to get a high.

We must focus on ways to reduce the pain of a *Compulsive* person and avoid anything that will raise their fear, condemnation or anxiety. If a Seeker suffers from guilt we lead him through forgiveness and the liberating power of Christ to bring peace. If shame is a problem we work on renewal of the mind. Roots of bitterness, early childhood trauma, rejection, grief or self-condemnation are dug up and healed. Anything that increase his guilt, shame and anxiety is counterproductive. Every day and every week sobriety is a victory to be celebrated. Failures to stay clean are forgiven with hints about how to avoid relapse the next time.

> **Compulsives need goals that heal their inner pain**
>
> **Dependants need goals that form healthy habits**

Dependent people present a different challenge. They seek thrills and chills and hate the boredom of life. Adrenalin is a favorite American drug of dependency as is sex, food, the Internet and cocaine. Bored teens who want a high indulge in illegal drugs. Many will get *Dependent* and some will become *Addicted*. We need wisdom to discern when a *Seeker is Compulsive* and when he is *Dependent*. After assessment we work to heal the *Compulsive's* wounds and confront the *Dependent's* apathy about repentance.

Sexual habits are favorite snares of the enemy for it is easy to become *Dependent* and/or *Compulsive* with this very powerful stimulant. Sex can be distorted, abused and misused because it feels so good and can be easily practiced. However, since it is a gift from God, guilt and shame arise when misused. Even non-Christians may feel guilt and shame over promiscuity. Premarital sex often leads to explosive problems and irreparable problems many years into the marriage. This is an insight that has led us to counsel married couples to confess and forgive each other if they had sex before marriage.

However, sexual *Compulsions, Dependencies* and *Addictions* are no more difficult to change than any other destructive behavior. Additionally, they do not yield to exhortation and rebuke any more than *Dependently* overeating or *Compulsively* preaching too long. There is hope for change in all habits and emotional lifestyles, but the cost can be high so do not grow weary in ministry or give up if people relapse. Hope provides a powerful motivator for both Seekers and Helpers.

If we are working with an addict we must deal with both sides of the equation and set goals for healing the inner pain behind *Compulsions* as well as confronting the highs of *Dependency*. All grace without confrontation will not work for *Dependents* and all confrontation without grace will fail for *Compulsives*. To heal inner pain we need clear goals that eliminate true and false guilt. To overcome *Dependency* we need goals that show the *Seeker* how to substitute a healthy high for one that is destructive.

Robert Spitzer, M.D., a psychiatrist from Columbia University, recently changed his mind about whether or not homosexuals could become heterosexual. He had said many years ago that such a change was impossible. After hearing testimonies from Christians who had come out of the homosexual lifestyle, Dr. Spitzer did his own research study and concluded that he had been wrong. In his study of over 200 men and women, Dr. Spitzer discovered that sexual preference could be changed and the key to change was the Seeker's motivational level and a willingness to work hard.

Realistic Goals

Realistic goals are those that can reasonably be accomplished. If people set the bar too high, failure is inevitable. This was one of the problems with the man who was looking at pornography. To abstain for 90 days was such a large and distant vision that there were few daily rewards. *Realistic* goals focus on accomplishing sobriety one day at a time. It is almost impossible to consistently maintain a discipline of complete sobriety for three months but it is very *Realistic* when done one day at a time.

After encountering a heart problem in 1999, Gary was advised to do aerobic exercise every day for the rest of his life. That was long-term vision. He knew exercise was important to his health but it was too big to grasp in one bite. Now Gary has a goal to get the exercise he needs each day. He may miss day or two but he rewards himself for each of those daily successes. One can hardly imagine what daily exercise for 30 years looks like. However, aerobics one day at a time seems manageable.

Sometimes a person's expectations bring false guilt. By encouraging *Realistic* goals, we make sure that a Seeker gets rewarded for each step in the right direction. Scaling allows us to ask how many points a successful goal achievement will take them forward. Sometimes a Seeker will smile and admit that she set a large goal to impress us. It is better to set a small goal that can be easily accomplished than one so big it will cause the Seeker to struggle and fail. Although relapse is common the goal itself should not cause the failure. In fact, we may discourage a person from trying to accomplish too much. Imagine the following conversation between Gary and Jim.

> **Jim**: I see the light, Dr. Gary, and I promise to never watch porn again.
> **Gary**: That sounds like an awfully big step, Jim. Perhaps it is more than you want to try right now. Can we think about something more manageable?
> **Jim**: But, Dr. Gary, I have been delieverd from my addiction. God has touched me and I will never be tempted again. I can just see that all my problems are gone.
> **Gary**: I know that the Lord has touched you powerfully and you will always be different. However, we usually find it more helpful to think about being sober one day at a time. In fact, it is an hour-by-hour, moment-by-moment trust of the Lord. If you can live one day in sobriety you can feel good about your accomplishments. Can we work on a goal for staying healthy today?

Working on an issue one step at a time is not easy for us. We like instant oatmeal. Just put it into the microwave and, Zap, it's finished and ready to enjoy. However, getting it ready for the microwave is a long process. First, a farmer must buy the right seeds at the right time, till the ground in the appropriate manner, plant the seeds at the correct depth, treat the ground with the fertilizer, water the plants, weed the field, harvest the crop, take the oats to market. Next the oats must be turned into oat meal, packaged and taken to a store.

Then we arrive on the scene to purchase the package; take it home; put the oatmeal into the microwave-safe bowl and mix it with sugar, milk and salt. Finally, we turn on the microwave for exactly the right amount of time; take the hot bowl out of the oven; get the spoon and eat it.

The final zap actually takes several months and the cooperation of hundreds of people. All these small, evaluated and successful steps are necessary before the meal is ready. We must be prepared to work on many small tasks to fully disciple a believer. The process includes preparation to witness to an unbeliever, leading a person to Christ, discipling him in the basics of the faith, nurturing him in grace, healing his wounds and bringing him to maturity. There are many things to accomplish before we have an "instant oatmeal Christian".

In the Beginning

Good goals focus on the *beginning* of the change process, not its end. To say, "I will never be angry with my family again," points us toward a vision that is not *Small, Simple, Specific or Realistic*. It may be a final dream to be a calm, peaceful and patient father and husband at all times. However, for those who struggle with temper, it is too great an intention to achieve in one step. A good goal for Faye would be something like:

> *I will deal with my anger today by renewing my mind and thinking positive thoughts about my husband. I will begin the process by asking James to forgive me for scolding him last night.*

These are *Realistic* goals that are *Additive* at the *beginning* not the end. Their successful completion will allow us to reward the Seeker several times as he journeys toward a peaceful lifestyle. After many days, weeks and years of success we can see the final plan take place. After 30 years of pastoral care we can think of only a few persons who have experienced dramatic events that completely changed their lives. However, there are thousands who have taken *Small, Additive, Realistic* steps forward on their journey to maturity. Most of these steps forward have been taken without the benefit of counseling experts or pastors.

Timely Goals

 Timely goals encourage Ad*ditive, Realistic* changes by setting a reasonable date for their completion. By imposing a time boundary, we are more likely to develop the discipline necessary to alter those destructive old habits. Open-ended goals put no positive pressure on us to seize the day and make the most of the time. For example:

> **Esther**: *Some day I am going to stop eating fatty foods and lower my cholesterol level so I do not have a heart attack.*

This is not a goal but a fond hope. This is how a *Convicted Complainant* talks for she has not yet counted the cost or decided to change her diet. When one is *Ready to Change*, the language of setting a good goal would be something like this:

> **Esther**: *I will eat salad with a low fat dressing and no dessert at dinner.*

The second comment allows Esther to evaluate how she is doing each day at dinner. By choosing a low fat dressing she can reward herself with positive affirmation. Should she fail by eating dessert or a fatty dressing, the lapse is not overwhelming or fatal for she can be successful the very next day. This goal is SO SMART for it contains all the elements of our acrostic.

> *Sow a thought and reap an act*
> *Sow an act and reap a habit*
> *Sow habit and reap a character*
> *Sow character and reap a destiny*
> George Munzing, <u>Living a Life of Integrity</u>

Modeling SO SMART Goal Setting

In the following dialogue, Gary and Faye develop small goals to accomplish Faye's vision of living in a harmonious Christian family.

Faye: I am so frustrated! I have been trying to witness to my husband like the church is telling me, but it just doesn't seem to work. What can I do? Do you have any suggestions?

Gary: So, despite doing everything the church is telling you it doesn't seem to be working. I can see why you would be frustrated. Tell me more about what you are doing. Perhaps we can find a more successful approach.

Faye: Maybe I'm doing something wrong. I try to talk about God to my family but we get into arguments and it ruins everything. I just can't please anybody. My husband doesn't think I am very loving even when I say I have the love of God in my heart.

Gary: So you both want to have a loving relationship. Has anything come to mind as you thought and prayed about what might work?

Faye: Well, yes. Maybe I need to show him my love instead of talking so much. The pastor said last week that action is more important than words.

Gary: Sounds like the Lord has already spoken to you about this issue. What kinds of things did you did you think about doing?

Faye: Well, he goes into work early to get things done before everyone else comes in and interrupts him. I complain about him leaving so early. I guess I could stop being so negative. That might be a good witness.

Gary: It could be a good start. I imagine he doesn't feel your love when you complain. Have you considered what else you could do? You are thinking about eliminating a negative action. Is there a positive step to add to it?

Faye: He always starts the morning with hot tea. I could get everything together the night before and have it ready for him in the morning. It doesn't sound like much but I think he would really like it. It would prove that I am trying. But, it isn't very spiritual.

168

Gary: Serving your husband tea seems pretty spiritual to me. You're trying to show God's love in his language instead of yours and that is a very biblical thing to do.

Gary empathizes with Faye's frustration and guilt. He affirmed that both she and James want a loving relationship. Gary could have confronted her critical comments but Affirmed instead. He asks if anything has come to her mind about how to change assuming she is praying about a solution. When Faye develops a negative goal Gary asks for something positive as well. A small step is almost sabotaged with negative thinking that "it is not very spiritual" but Gary affirms serving. It's an interactive process of AS I GREW CALM.

Faye: I am not sure it is enough though. Maybe I should get up and fix his breakfast too. I am not a morning person and he would be shocked if I got up early just for him.

Gary: That is a big step. Could you do it with a good attitude?

Faye: I think so. It wouldn't do any good if I got up early and nagged him the whole time, would it?

Gary: (Laughing) No, it sure wouldn't. But, if you could do it in a cheerful manner, it might really be impressive, showing that you want to support him in his work. You could send James off with a positive attitude.

Faye: I don't have a positive attitude because I am angry that he travels so much. Maybe I need an attitude adjustment. Sometimes he is away the whole week when he travels overseas. Now he is going in early to train new workers.

Gary: So you are still upset about his schedule. Is this the right time to try something like fixing breakfast? Can you do it without an attitude adjustment?

Faye: I suppose I can try it. Maybe we can pray about my attitude today. I could just fix his tea, and get the cereal out while he is showering. I can sit with him during breakfast until he goes to work. Then I can have my quiet time later.

Gary: That sounds like a good plan. You seem to have mapped it out and know how you will set it up. When will you start this experiment?

Faye: I will begin tomorrow morning. He has to be downtown at seven to train the new salesmen so I know he will be in a big hurry to get everything organized.

Gary: Why don't we pray about your plan right now? It is a good first step toward a plan of witnessing to the family by deeds rather than words. Is there anything you want to ask the Lord to specifically bless?

Faye: Ask the Lord for a good attitude while I am serving him and for the Lord to show me how to be more thankful for James and his good job.

> *We need to help people become owners of their own solutions rather than renters of ours.*
>
> GRS

Faye worked hard to set good goals and choose ones that would be reasonable. By making her own decisions, Faye was empowered to take personal responsibility for her part in the relationship. Gary attempted to influence her by listening, clarifying and making suggestions. By asking good questions, affirming specific plans and offering his ideas, Faye made progress toward rebuilding trust with James. He used the power of positive blame by rewarding her each time she took a step forward and ignored things that did not build the relationship.

Gary also challenged Faye to consider whether she was ready to set a goal to fix breakfast. They examined her need for an attitude adjustment and discussed the fact that nagging would destroy her good intentions. This led to Faye's honesty about being angry. It is the first time she clearly faced her own need to change and did not put all the blame on James.

The goals set during the conversation were small, simple, specific and measurable. Both of them knew the exact nature of the goal and could later test whether or not it had been reached. Faye agreed that she would do something different and specified the nature of the change. They established a SO SMART goal. Should Faye not succeed in accomplishing everything, it was small enough to try again. Toward the end, Gary asks Faye to evaluate her relationship to James.

> **Gary**: Faye, scale your loving behavior toward James right now.
> **Faye**: Well, I think I am below average for a Christian so I will say, 4.0.

> Low   Medium   High
> 1-------2-------3-------**4**-------5-------6-------7-------8-------9-------10

> **Gary**: How far up the scale would you move if you make his tea?
> **Faye**: I think it will pull me up to about a 5.0, at least. Don't you?
> **Gary**: So, this step will move you forward toward accomplishing your overall purpose of showing James more love.
> **Faye**: Yes, I think so. It doesn't get me to ten yet, but it is a step forward.

At the next meeting, Gary helps her evaluate how well she did. He also asks about *Positive Support Systems* and searches for ways to *Affirm* Faye for taking steps toward resolving her marital problems.

> **Gary**: We established some clear goals last week. What good things happened?
> **Faye**: Well, I didn't do so well. I did manage to get up and fix James' tea but I don't think I was very pleasant.
> **Gary**: Despite being imperfect, you did get a good start. What did you do well?
> **Faye**: I got up early despite my aversion to mornings. And I fixed his tea and got the cereal out for him.
> **Gary**: How did he respond to that? Was he happy, sad, or upset?
> **Faye**: He was shocked and pleased. He looked at me in a very strange way and protested that it was not necessary for me to get up so early because he knew I liked to sleep late. I could tell that he was happy, although he was surprised.
> **Gary**: Are there any other good things you did?
> **Faye**: I apologized later that morning about being so grumpy, but he said he did not notice it at all. In fact, he brought me flowers the next day.
> **Gary**: Flowers! That is wonderful. How often does that happen?
> **Faye**: Not very often. I guess I accomplished my goal to put my love in action.
> **Gary**: On a scale of zero to ten, how successful was your venture?
> **Faye**: About a seven. I still need to be in a better mood and I am still a bit frustrated with his travel. But I asked the Lord to help me change. In fact, He nudged me the other morning to be more thankful. James is a good father and a good provider.
> **Gary**: The Lord is certainly at work in your house in a number of ways, not the least of which was doing an attitude adjustment in you. I can see that you are more

encouraged now than when we began to talk and for good reason. You have already made some positive changes.

It was easy to affirm Faye for accomplishing several positive changes and for meeting her goal. Despite her confession of inadequacy, the plan went off quite well. The entire conversation and tone of her thoughts are different now. He attempted to integrate all the AS I GREW CALM and SO SMART skills and *Influence* Faye to take small steps toward improving her marriage. Once the snowball of healthy thinking, feeling and behaving begins, it will pick up speed and build into an avalanche of love.

Life Scan Summary

This final chapter discusses the remaining keys of *Additive, Realistic and Timely* goals. *Additive* goals describe what is new and different from past behavior. It points to a positive behavior that heretofore has been underutilized, neglected, or forgotten. Members of A.A. focus on reaching the presence of sobriety instead of the absence of alcohol. Good goals *add* to the Seeker's life.

If fear is cultivated it will become stronger, if faith is cultivated it will achieve mastery.
John Paul Jones

A good goal is based on the *Realistic* assessment that it can be achieved. Setting unrealistic goals is worse than having none at all. *Timely* goals set boundaries and allow us to be accountable. It indicates that the goal is more than an abstract idea, but will be part of the Seeker's life by a definite point in time. It says the Seeker has faith that his life will start to change in real time.

TIPS for Life

Personal Reflection and Practice

- Reflect on a recent goal that was not Realistic.
- Can you make it Small, Realistic and Timely?
- Use a scale to analyze your growth in the use of the SO SMART skills. Do a before and after scaling to see how far you have come.

Look at a stone cutter hammering away at his rock, perhaps a hundred times without as much as a crack showing in it. Yet at the hundred-and-first blow, it still split in two, and I know it was not the last blow that did it, but all that had gone before.
Jacob Riis

One may miss the mark by aiming too high, as too low.

Thomas Fuller

Appendix

LIFE  WAY

4015 Executive Park Drive, Suite #305
Cincinnati, OH 45241
(513) 769-4600 or (800) 334-8973

Depression Checklist

Please answer yes or no:

1. I often feel downhearted and blue.
2. I often cry or feel like crying.
3. I have trouble falling asleep & sleeping through the night.
4. I have: lost interest in eating, do not eat as much as I used to, or am eating more than usual.
5. My mind is not as clear as it used to be.
6. I have no hope for the future.
7. I am more irritable than usual.
8. I do not enjoy the things I used to enjoy.
9. I have difficulty making decisions.
10. I am tired for no reason.

If you have answered yes to 3 or more questions, you should speak with a counselor.

Gary Sweeten and Steve Griebling

LIFE ❤ WAY

4015 Executive Park Drive, Suite #305
Cincinnati, OH 45241
(513) 769-4600 or www.lifewaycenters.com

Marital Happiness Assessment

In Column A, respond to the statements that best describes your feelings and in Column B, your spouse's likely response.

A		B		
Self		Spouse		
Yes	No	Yes	No	
_____	_____	_____	_____	1. Marriage expectations are being met.
_____	_____	_____	_____	2. My spouse meets my personal needs.
_____	_____	_____	_____	3. Household responsibilities are satisfactorily shared
_____	_____	_____	_____	4. We often have times of small talk.
_____	_____	_____	_____	5. We have good memories together.
_____	_____	_____	_____	6. We successfully resolve our conflicts.
_____	_____	_____	_____	7. We enjoy our sexual relationship.
_____	_____	_____	_____	8. We handle our finances well.
_____	_____	_____	_____	9. We share common spiritual values.
_____	_____	_____	_____	10. I like the quantity and quality of our time together.

NO answers to more than two of these questions are a warning that problems may become unhealthy or damaging to your marriage. More than four NO answers indicate an immediate need for counseling.

Assessment Checklist Cards/Server/Mkt Ext/1992/ab

LIFE WAY

4015 Executive Park Drive, Suite #305
Cincinnati, OH 45241
(513) 769-4600 or www.lifewaycenters.com

Is Your Child Angry?

Please answer Yes or No

_____	1.	Blows when pressure builds
_____	2.	Can't handle change and stress
_____	3.	Shows rage at times of loss, pain, frustration or disappointment.
_____	4.	Turns anger into shouting, tantrums, or aggression
_____	5.	Can't calm down when he or she is angered
_____	6.	Fights with others frequently
_____	7.	Uses words as weapons
_____	8.	Blames others
_____	9.	Thrives on revenge
_____	10.	Refuses to take self-responsibility.
_____	11.	Lacks self-control
_____	12.	Has a low self-confidence
_____	13.	Does not care about the feelings and rights of others
_____	14.	Will not compromise or negotiate
_____	15.	Cannot forgive others

If you have responded Yes to several of these items, call for an evaluation.

Pictorial Chart of Lifeway Principles

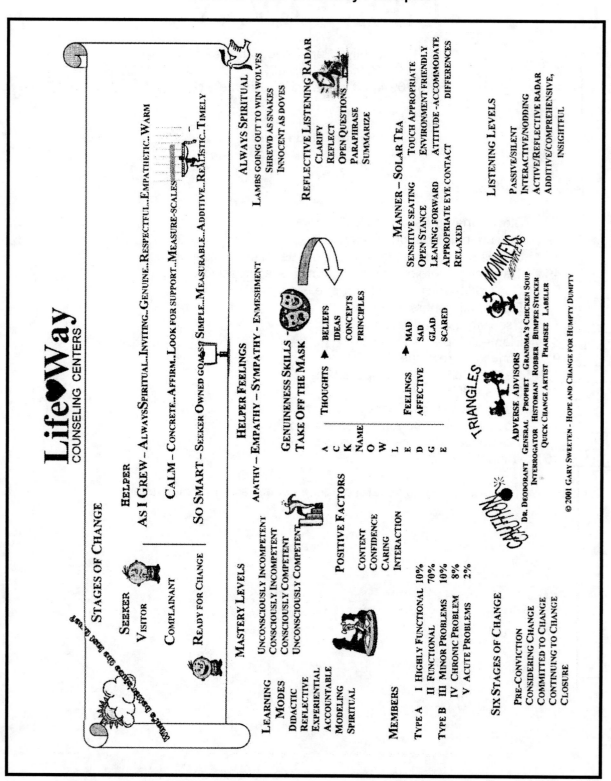

Chart Outline for <u>Hope & Change for Humpty Dumpty</u> by Brenda Dyer

A Structure for Equipping the Local Church

Church leaders need a simple system in which to place their equipping strategy. In the early seventies, we began to develop a church wineskin that could hold the new wine of the New Reformation. Alive churches continually bring people into the Transformational Process so equipping is a continual, ongoing, vital part of growing. It takes advanced planning to prepare a person to be ready to be involved in lay ministry. From entry at the New Member's Classes to graduation from a specific training program will take two to three years of learning and growth.

Pastors Oversee Equipping Processs

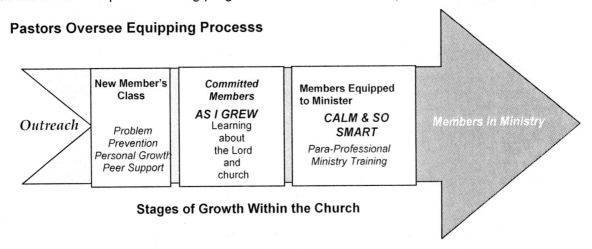

Stages of Growth Within the Church

This simple flow chart indicates how people are won to the Lord and come into the church to proceed along a predetermined path toward maturity in the Lord. First, we need a planned outreach process to involve equipped members in witnessing to unbelievers and the un-churched. We suggest that you look up Steve Sjogren's web page, www.kindness.com

New members need an inquiry class that informs them about the Lord and their particular congregation. It should be led by equipped members answer the following questions for those inquiring about membership.

- How do I become a Christian?
- What does it mean to be a Christian?
- What does it mean to be a Christian in this particular congregation?
- What can I expect from this congregation's staff and lay leaders?
- How do I get involved in learning/growing?
- How do I get involved in ministry?
- Here is a small group to support you.

Committed Members Trained by equipped members at Level 1 for Prevention of Problems, at Level 2 for Personal Growth into holiness and right living with God and neighbor, and at Level 3 for Peer Support to encourage, nurture, friends, family, fellow small group members and co-workers. This equipping is for all members who want to grow in normal, daily Christian living. (See Chapter 2 Healing Community)

- Truth: Cover the basics such as who is God, what is salvation, how to pray and have devotions, who we are in Christ, what is the church? The Apostle's Creed, Lord's Prayer, the sacraments. In Lifeskills, <u>Renewed Christian Thinking.</u>

- Gifts of the Spirit. Understand gifts, talents, skills, call and how they can be used for ministry.
- Fruitful Relationships. Premarital, Parenting, Prenatal preparation. The AS I GREW skills.

Members Equipped for Level 4. Paraprofessional Ministry by Pastors. For all those who are mature and called to a specific ministry such as small group leadership, lay counseling, home visits. Select those who are competent in the basics of Truth/Fruit/Gifts noted above. Train them in the ministry skills that are specific to Paraprofessional Care and Counsel. (10-20% of the church)

- Add the CALM and SO SMART skills to AS I GREW
- Small group leader training
- Can apply Renewed Christian Thinking to others at the right time.
- Inner Healing Prayer
- Ethics and Confidentiality
- Sharing the gospel

How do We Recruit Paraprofessional Helpers?

The most common way to think about recruiting laity for the church is called, "The Warm Body Approach" for it focuses on getting people to "volunteer" for all the ministries. The giftedness, level of maturity, skills, knowledge or training is not thought to be very important.

We tried the Warm Body Approach and found it to be wanting-severely. When we first established the Bethel Bible Program, we followed their approach to recruiting teachers and opened the doors to everyone who wanted to be a Bethel Teacher. It did not take us very long to discover the folly of such a plan. At the end of an arduous training program, we discovered that about half the class, all of whom had been promised a slot as a teacher, had neither the gifts, call, ability or emotional/spiritual maturity to teach.

They loved the scripture and were committed to God. However, they were not called to be adult teachers of the word. This led us to the difficult task of telling these willing workers they could not work in our ministry. It was one of the hardest things I ever did, but it led us to develop a better system of recruiting teachers and Helpers for the Teleios Ministry.

Why We do not Recruit from the Congregation

There are several reasons why we strongly suggest that it is not wise to recruit directly from the congregation.

- At least one half are there to get counseling for themselves
- Many are immature as persons
- Many of them have no gifts of personal ministry.
- Some are on a "power trip" and want to control others.
- Many are co-dependent and need to rescue others.
- Most do not have the basic knowledge of scripture, relationship skills or a balanced approach to healing.

- It will necessitate our having to remove people from the ministry after they have completed the training.
- It will take longer to establish a quality Helping ministry.
- It will communicate to the congregation that anyone can be a Helper and lead to lower levels of trust in the Helpers.

Wise recruiting and faster equipping will occur if we slowly develop a congregational equipping program first and recruit our Paraprofessional Helpers from those persons who successfully complete that segment.

- Start by equipping the Committed Members in AS I GREW skills, Renewed Christian Thinking and personal prayer.
- Observe those who are talented, gifted and skilled.
- Ask them to come with you for the next training program to observe and assist in equipping.
- Take them along with you to minister so they can observe you.
- Include them in classes for CALM and SO SMART skills.
- Include them in the tutorial classes to apply the skills.
- Send them out to minister in teams of two.

How to Set Up a Lay Helping Ministry

Develop a clear plan with a mission, vision, values, strategy and work it through the staff, elders, deacons and informal church leaders. Inform them of your time line. Get feedback and keep it flexible. Educate them about why this plan differs from others.

- Start the congregational equipping phase. Do not call it a counseling program lest the term misrepresent your intentions.
- Recruit trainers and Helpers from this group. Take them through tutorial classes to develop skills at an "Unconsciously Competent" manner.
- Take your recruits through a Facilitator and Teacher Class.
- Have them assist you in teaching and leading the small groups.
- Start congregational equipping classes taught by the recruits who have been trained in Ministry Skills.
- Recruit a wise gatekeeper who knows the AS I GREW SO SMART skills, how to assess the level of problems and pain and how to refer the bottom 10% to Professionals. Develop a list of Professionals in the community.
- Establish a financial education ministry to help people with money for doctors, attorneys, dentists and counselors. Only help pay for services of those who get financial counsel.
- Establish a private place where the Helpers can meet to listen.
- Advertise by alerting the staff and elders. Do not broadcast widely lest it become overwhelmed. Build Slowly, Build Solidly, Build Spiritually.
- Remind everyone that the most powerful source of healing and growth will come from the classes and small groups not from individual counsel.

Group Questions, Exercises & Real Life Models

Use these questions and exercises in your small group as the Experience and Accountability parts of DREAMS. As you discuss the questions and practice the exercises, you will increase your level of confidence and competence in the AS I GREW CALM and SO SMART skills. Practice makes permanent, not perfect. Support and affirm one another as you apply these skills.

The *Real Life Models* section will aide you in observing concrete examples of the principals and processes described in each chapter. You will do the tasks between group sessions and then share your observations with the group. If you are reading the book and are not in a training class, the tasks will assist you in discovering practical applications. Seeing someone model the concepts and skills can deepen your understanding and prepare you to be an effective Helper.

Chapter 1 - Searching for Solutions

- Introduce yourself to the other group members. Share your role or involvement in church or ministry organization.
- What do you want to learn? What goals do you want to accomplish?
- As a group, write on newsprint the expectations you have written. Choose a spokesperson to share the group's list with the other groups in the class. Save the goals for later use.

Real Life Models

- When you read magazines, newspapers, watch TV, or surf the web, keep an eye out for churches or Christian groups that encourage healing and growth. What are there methods? Can you identify their principles and processes?

Chapter 2 - The Church as a Healing Community

- How does your church promote the growth and healing?
- Cite examples of Truth, Love, and Power encounters.
- How is your congregation like a family?
- On a scale of one to ten, rate your church family's overall health. Use one as the worst possible dysfunction and 10 as optimum wholeness. How would you know that the church had improved by just one point on the scale?
- What does your church offer for Prevention, Personal growth and Peer support?
- Describe a relationship that encouraged you to grow.
- How can this group help you grow? How can you assist others to grow?

Real Life Models

- Which of Jesus' healing encounters is your favorite? How did Jesus interact with the Seeker? How did it affect the Seeker's inner life, social life, or family life? Did Jesus use it as an opportunity for teaching?

Chapter 3 - Four Factors of Helping

- Discuss your reaction to the four factors.
- Share examples of the factors and how they worked in a helping relationship where you were either a Helper or Seeker.
- The Seeker's Context is the most influential factor in helping. How can you grow in awareness of Context?
- With a partner from your group, share about a habit you changed. It can be a spiritual discipline, a lifestyle change, or a pattern of relating with others. Identify the six stages of change.
- Share one example of the six stages with the group.

Real Life Models

- Read Acts 10 and reflect on how Peter changed. Define Peter's problem. Who wants him to change? Does Peter think he needs to change? Identify the six steps. Who supported Peter? What was the result of his changes?

Chapter 4 - A Roadmap for Helping

- Share the key insight you gained from this teaching. Explain how it can be applied in your helping relationships.
- Select two persons to read the following conversations aloud. Discuss each interaction and decide if the pair is in the Visitor—Host, Complainant-Listener, or Ready to Change-Solution Focused stage.

Conversation A

Parent: How was your day at school?

Child: It had its' ups and downs. I am really satisfied because I did well on my history test. It was easy. I knew every question and finished in plenty of time. It's a relief to have that finished.

Parent: Congratulations. I know you read your assignments and review your notes every day. I'm glad your preparation and hard work paid off. You are learning quite a bit about history.

Child: Yea, but then there is math. We had a pop quiz and I was totally lost. I did the homework, but I just don't understand what he wanted. I couldn't figure out most of the problems. I'll be lucky not to get a failing grade.

Parent: Oh no, I guess it was frustrating because even though you completed the homework, the quiz did not go very well. That must be the down part of the day.

Child: Math is driving me crazy. I just want to give up. I want to understand it but I'm always making dumb mistakes. Sometimes I put off doing math because I'm afraid I won't understand the concepts.

Parent: It seems to be your biggest challenge this year and I know you are anxious about this not getting any better.

Child: Yea, exactly. I wish I could do something to gain confidence in that class. I really don't want to give up. I need to learn it for next year's science class.

Parent: This is tough and it's got you confused. Besides your study habits, is there something else you could do that would help? Have any ideas.

Child: Well, I like my math teacher. He is excited about teaching us the concepts, but I guess my pride gets in the way and I don't ask for help.

Parent: Yes, you are so used to being independent with schoolwork, you haven't had a lot of practice asking for help from your teachers.

Child: He tells us we can ask to meet with him anytime. In fact he has his conference times when I'm in a study hall. I guess it's time for me to go have a conference and try to figure out what I'm missing.

Parent: So will you pay your math teacher a visit tomorrow during study hall or wait awhile? You seem to think he would be glad to help you.

Child: Yes, I'll see him tomorrow. It's time to move on this before I get too far behind. Thanks for talking. This helped me. I just need to move my pride out of the way and get some help.

Conversation B

Parent: How was your day at school?

Child: Fine

Parent: What did you do?

Child: Nothing much.

Parent: Well did you get some homework?

Child: You know we always do. They don't let us out without homework.

Parent: Yes, I guess it would be nice to have a break from it once in a while.

Child: It sure would, but that will never happen- at least not with my teachers.

Parent: I thought you might be hungry so I made a snack. Want to eat now?

Child: Sure. What is it?

Parent: I made your favorite fruit dish and some chocolate chip cookies.

Child: OK, but I want to call Jim first to see if he wants to get together later.

Parent: Make the call and I'll get the snack on the table.

Child: Thanks, I'll be done in a minute.

Conversation C:

Parent: How was your day at school?

Child: Mostly, bad. These teachers can ask the weirdest things on tests. They just want to trick you instead of really finding out what you have learned.

Parent: Wow, what happened today to make you so angry?

Child: Oh, I just get so frustrated when I do my work, but it doesn't seem to get me anywhere in math class. That teacher makes you feel so stupid.

Parent: I know math has been a real challenge. Did something happen in class?

Child: Oh, we had a pop quiz today. Which should not be a big deal. But I don't know where he came up with some of these problems. I felt like I had never been in his class before. It's just not fair!

Parent: Maybe you need to have a conference with your teacher to figure out what happened. You seem pretty confused by the quiz.

Child: The homework on the stuff we learned yesterday was easy. But the questions he gave us today were off the wall. I never heard of a couple of the words that he used. I had no idea what was going on. Someone needs to teach him how to make tests that are about the material.

Parent: So, you think your teacher will not get an accurate picture of what you are learning because the questions didn't reflect the material you have been studying, and this is really maddening.

Child: It's like he forgot what he taught us yesterday or got his plan mixed up. I don't know what he messed up but it sure ruined my day.

- Discuss these three role-plays. Which can you identify with? Do they seem real?

Real Life Models

- Review the story about Peter in Acts 10. When was he a Visitor? A Complainant? What moved him to Ready for Change? How did God cooperatively help Peter?

Chapter 5 - AS I GREW

- How have you focused on God in this group? How have you been spiritual?
- What do you want new members at your church to do? Become like other members or grow in Christ as individuals?
- How is your ministry inviting to others. How could you improve it?
- If Josh came to your small group for help what would you do? Come up with a plan for him. Share your plan with the other small groups.

Real Life Models

- Write a list of the Adverse Advisors you encounter daily. After a week, look for patterns. Where do you most frequently run into them? Is there one who appears many times? What one is most common? How do you cope with them?

Chapter 6 - Genuineness

Share one belief or conviction with others in the group.

- I believe_____. I think_____.
- Identify, acknowledge, name, and share the feelings you experienced as you shared your conviction. Ask others to describe their perceptions about you.
- Recall a time when you were struggling to effectively help a friend. What were your feelings? Write the feeling words down and share them with other members.

Real Life Models

- How has your trainer expressed Genuineness? Identify genuine characters in movies. How do they express their honesty? How does their genuineness affect other people? Think of a person in your life who is highly skilled at genuineness.

Chapter 7 - Warmth

- Follow the scaling instructions from the *Personal Reflection* and then share with other group members.
- Divide into 2 pairs: A. Helper and Coach B. Seeker and Coach

1. Confer with your partner about preparing for a role-play
2. The Seeker shares a positive experience to the Helper.
3. The Helper listens with SOLAR TEA skills.
4. The Seeker Coach observes the Helper-Seeker interaction for 3 minutes.
5. The Helper Coach observes and consults with the Helper if needed.
6. After 3 minutes the Seeker shares his experience and feelings.
7. The Coaches share positive observations about the Helper's warmth.
8. The Helper rates himself on the 1-10 warmth scale and explains why.
9. Helper states what he could do differently in the future.
10. Each group member takes a new role and repeats the exercise.

Real Life Models

- Recall an instance when a person was too warm. What did you think, feel? How did you respond?
- Name the people who consistently express SOLAR TEA?
- Was Jesus warm? When? With whom?

Chapter 8 - Understanding Others

- Refer to the tasks described in the *Personal Reflection and Practice* section at the end of the chapter, and take turns sharing your experiences with the group.
- Identify and write the feelings others describe? What thoughts and circumstances are attached to the emotions? Sharing insights about the feelings and thoughts you heard from each member. How accurate were you?

Real Life Models

- On notepaper create five columns with headings: Callous, Apathy, Empathy, Sympathy, and Enmeshment. Every day mark the appropriate box when you observe one of these happening. Analyze the results after several days. What is the most frequent manner of relating? When did empathy and sympathy occur? How were they demonstrated? Name those who consistently empathize.
- Compliment people that show empathy and sympathy. Tell them you are trying to improve you skills and ask what helped them.

Chapter 9 - Respect and The Golden Rule

- Discuss the following questions about the first video role-play.

  1. In the first role-play what was Steve's problem?
  2. How did Gary respond?
  3. How did the Gary follow the Lead and Stone rules, ignoring the Golden Rule?
  4. What was the Seeker's reaction?
  5. What did Gary do differently the second time?
  6. How was he trying to be respectful with Steve?

- Discuss the second role- play.

1. What Monkey did Steve try to give Gary?
2. How did Gary respond?
3. What did Gary do differently in the second role-play?
4. How did Steve respond?

- Practice your warmth and empathy skills by taking turns being a Seeker and Helper. The Seeker will share a light concern or problem. Before the role-play begins the Seeker and Coach will discuss how to be genuine with feeling words. The Helper will review key aspects of warmth and empathy with the Helper Coach before listening to the Seeker. The goal is for the Helper to use SOLAR TEA and respond with at least two reflective, paraphrased statements.
- The Seeker Coach will stop after 5 minutes. The Helper will ask the Seeker for feedback: Rate me on the warmth scale. Was I too cool or too hot? What helped you realize that I was paying attention and cared? Did I accurately reflect your thoughts and feelings? The coaches may then comment on what they liked about the role-play. Repeat the process with a different Seeker and Helper.
- Practice respect skills. The facilitator will be a Seeker and choose a person to be a Helper. He will attempt to give the Helper his monkey who is to identify the problem, who owns it and affirm the Seeker's ability to carry his load. The Helper can call a time out to consult with the group about how respond to the monkey. Each role-play should last 10 minutes. Discuss what promoted respect. Repeat the role-play with another group member as Helper.

Real Life Models

- How was a tiny Albanian in India transformed from being hated and mobbed to having millions honor her death? The answer is Respect. This was at the core of her ministry and her sisters Respect the poorest of the poor around the globe.

One man was found in a gutter of lying in a pool of sewage, covered with sores. The sisters took him in for his final days, cleaned his wounds and covered him in soft new clothes. "I have lived like a dog but today I will die in the arms of angels," he said. Mother Theresa promoted the Golden Rule.

However she was extremely competent at avoiding the Stone Rule. Some journalists were overwhelmed with all the dying, hopeless people and asked why she continued her work. "It is so fruitless, because so many people are beyond saving." She answered, "When we die is God's business, my business is to obey Him by loving all people-even the dying." Mother Theresa understood she was not omnipotent, omniscient, or omnipresent and she would not attempt that which only God could do. This kept her ministry focused on doing "small things with great love" and having faith that this would change the world.

Chapter 10 - The Visitor-Host Relationship and Modeling GREW

- Discuss Faye's stage of motivation. Give examples. Were there any hints that she was beginning to move forward?
- How did Gary cooperate with Faye's stage of motivation and build trust with her?

- Discuss examples of the AS I GREW skills. Rate the Helper on a scale of 1-10 for each skill. What would you have done differently?
- As a group, create a Seeker-Helper scenario about a Visitor-Host relationship. The Seeker will prepare with a Coach and a Helper with a Helper Coach. The Seeker will be a Visitor and the Helper will practice the AS I GREW skills as a Host. Use at least one reflective, feeling and thought statement. Pause the role-play at any time to consult with the Coach. The role-play is to be 10 minutes.

Once completed, give the Helper positive feedback and affirm the skills you observed. The Helper should disclose what he/she was feeling and thinking and scale himself on Hosting and what he would do differently the next time. The Seeker will share about his/her experience as a Visitor. Change roles and repeat.

Real Life Models

- Look for Visitor-Host relationships. You may find them in your family, at work, at church or leisure. You may also see them in the movies or on TV. Write a brief description of one. Note how the Helper responded. Was he an adequate Host?

Chapter 11 - Mixing the Concrete

- Discuss the questions you have about the content of the chapter.
- Do a mini fish bowl with your group. Your facilitator will be a Seeker. The rest of the group members will all be Helpers. The Seeker will begin as a Visitor but talk about a complaint before long.

Sit in a semi-circle, facing the Seeker and a second empty chair. Group members will take turns sitting in the empty chair as the Helper.

The group may call a time out at anytime to consult with each other on how to best listen to the Seeker. End after 20 minutes. Real life practice of the AS I GREW skills and Concrete questions is the goal. Identify the main themes of the interaction. Note any transitions and good uses of the skills.

The Seeker will share his/her experience and describe what was helpful. The other participants share what they thought and felt when they were in the Helping chair. Affirm good skills and suggest areas of needed growth. Did specific information increase as the relationship proceeded?

Real Life Models

- Who helps you get specific? Is it someone at work, a family member, an instructor or a friend? How do they help you clarify and focus?
- Are you learning to be more concrete?

Chapter 12 - How to be a Blessing

- Relate how this course is affecting your inner life and your relationships. What is happening as you use the AS I GREW & Concrete skills?
- Choose a partner. One will be Seeker who has a complaint the other will be a Helper. The Helper will listen to the problem with AS I GREW skills. Then the

Helper will try to make a reflective, summary statement about the problem. The Seeker will acknowledge if the Helper has accurately understood him.

- The Helper should look for an opportune time to ask a Miracle Question.
- Discuss the effect of the Miracle Question. Trade places and repeat.
- Do a fish bowl or Seeker- Coach, Helper-Coach format. Use the same Seeker problem/scenario that you started in the last chapter. This is your second meeting. Helper's are to try Affirmation along with the AS I GREW C.

Real Life Models

- Who has been the greatest affirmer(s) in your life? How did they interact with you? What was the result of affirmation? Did the relationship promote changes in your life? Are you grateful? Thank God for the person. Contact the person and express your appreciation. How does God affirm you in daily activities; in relationships, scripture, worship, and ministry?

Chapter 13 - Looking for Good and God

- Choose roles—Seeker, Coach, Helper, Coach. The Seeker and Coach will meet to create a problem scenario to present to the Helper. The Helper and Coach will prepare to practice the AS I GREW CA skills and ways to ask about support systems. The Helper will decide what Looking skill he wants to practice. The Seeker should discuss his support system.
- The Helper should ask a pre-session change question and who, what, when, and where questions about sources of encouragement. (What helped you most this week?) The Helper will end the by asking to meet again. Go 30 minutes.
- Using a Fish Bowl to do a longer role-play. Continue with the problem you were working on in the last two teachings. Practice AS I GREW CALM. Ask scaling questions. Discuss the skills used, what worked, and possible improvements.

Real Life Models

- Who do you know that possesses a robust emotional, spiritual health? How would you scale them on a 1-10 scale (10 is Type A, Level 1 & Zero Type B, Level 5.) What characteristics put them at this point? What is it like to be with them? How are they different from people lower on the scale?
- Interview the person. Relate your involvement in the Humpty training the interview is an assignment. Tell them what you admire about them. Ask the what, who, when, where, and how's of their growth and development. Inquire about how God supported them during their journey.
- Without revealing the person's identity, discuss what you learned.

Chapter 14 - Setting Good Goals

- Take 10 minutes alone to work on the Personal Reflection and Practice questions. Share your goals and observations. Practice all AS I GREW CALM skills. Avoid giving advice. Describe the feelings you had. Members discuss how well they employed the skills on a 1-10 scale, with 10 being superior use of all skills. How will you know you have improved by one? Share feelings you had while listening. The speaker can provide feedback on which skills were helpful to him. Pray for the person and his goal.

Real Life Models

- At the beginning of the course your group wrote down learning goals. Review them. Which have you reached? What factors helped you?

Chapter 15 - Going on with Goals

- Seeker and Coach develop the character for a role-play while the Helper and Coach review SO SMART goal setting. Assume that the Seeker and Helper have met several times. The Seeker is Ready to Change. Before the role-play begins the Seeker will summarize for the Helper the problem that has been discussed in previous meetings.
- The Helper begins by asking, "What is better since the last time we met?" As the role-play proceeds, the Seeker-Coach will write out all the goals that are considered and circle the one(s) that the Seeker finally chooses.
- The Helper Coach will write AS I GREW CALM in columns and will scale the Helper's skills from 1-10. The Seeker or Helper may call for a time out and consult with their coach. The group facilitator will decide the time.
- What was most helpful? The Seeker Coach will present the various goals that were discussed and if the Seeker chose one. Members will analyze the goal to determine how it fits the SO SMART criteria. The Coach can share his scales for AS I GREW CALM. Then repeat the process with new people.

Real Life Models

- Consider a situation when you received help. Who was involved? Were the AS I GREW CALM & SO SMART skills in evidence? Did you develop a goal? How? What was the goal? Did you make progress? How did the Helper bless you?

References

<u>A Layman's Introduction to Christian Thought,</u> James Kallas, Westminster Press

Changing for Good: A Revolutionary Six stage Program for Overcoming Bad Habits and Moving Your Life Positively Forward. Prochaska, James C., Norcross John C., Diclemente, Carlos C., Morrow, William, & Co., 1995

<u>Circle of Quiet,</u> *by Julia Sweeten Knispel*

<u>Clues: Investigating Solutions in Brief Therapy,</u> de Shazer, Steve W. W. Norton, 1988.

<u>Conspiracy of Kindness,</u> Steve Sjogren, Servant Publications, Ann Arbor, MI, 1993

<u>Escape from Babel: Toward a Unifying Language for Psychotherapy Practice.</u> Miller, Scott D., Duncan, Barry L., & Hubble, Mark A., W. W. Norton, 1997.

<u>Healing Souls, Touching Hearts: Counseling and Care in the Cell Church,</u> Sweeten, Gary and Griebling, Steve, TOUCH Ministries International Pte Ltd, 2000.

<u>Helping and Human Relations, A Primer for Lay and Professional Helpers, Volume 1 Selection and Training,</u> Carkhuff, Robert R., Holt, Rinehart and Winston, Inc., 1969.

<u>Human Relations Development, A Manual for Health Sciences,</u> Gazda, George M., Walters, Richard P., Childers, William C., Allyn and Bacon, Inc., 1975.

<u>Natural Church Development: A Guide to Eight Essential Qualities of Healthy Churches,</u> Schwarz, Christian A., C & P Publishing, 1996.

<u>Power Shift,</u> Alvin Toffler, Bantam Books, New York, 1990.

<u>Psychotherapy with "Impossible" Cases: The Efficient Treatment of Therapy Veterans,</u> Duncan, Barry L., Hubble, Mark A., and Miller Scott D., W.W. Norton, 1997.

<u>Revolution in Leadership,</u> McNeal, Reggie, Abington Press, Nashville, Tn 1998.

<u>The Broken Heart; The Medical Consequences of Loneliness,</u> Lynch, James J., Basic Books, Harper Collins, New York, N.Y., 1977.

<u>The Mystery of the Holy Spirit,</u> Sproul, RC, Tyndale House Publishers, Inc. Wheaton, Il, 1990.

<u>The Tipping Point, How Little Things Can Make A Big Difference,</u> Gladwell, Malcom, Little Brown and Company, 2000

<u>True Spirituality,</u> Schaeffer, Francis, Tyndale House Publishing, Inc., Wheaton, Il 1971

<u>Working With the Problem Drinker; A Solution-Focused Approach.</u> Berg, Insoo Kim, & Miller, Scott D., W. W. Norton, 1992.

<u>Christianity Today,</u> *A Century of Growth*, November 16, 1998.

"Responses to Nervous Breakdowns in America Over a 40-Year Period": <u>Mental Health Policy Implications</u> Ralph Swindle, Jr. May 2000, <u>APA Monitor</u>

<u>Web Pages of interest</u>

Faith Community Baptist Church, Singapore http://www.fcbc.org.sg/links3.htm

Touch Ministries International, the international arm of Faith Community Baptist Church, and supplies books, tapes and materials on cell ministry. You can order our book, Healing Souls here. http://www.tmi.com.sg/homepage_ctnt.htm

Research on the American church. George Barna http://www.barna.org

The best research available on counseling effectiveness. Dr. Barry Duncan http://www.nova.edu/~blduncan/whatsnew.htm also Institute for the Study of Therapeutic Change: www.talkingcure.com

Interesting site on contemporary businesses.

http://www.fastcompany.com/online/34/listenup.html

About the Authors

Steven J. Griebling, M.S. has served as a clinical counselor in private practice with specialties in marital and family therapy, drug and alcohol addiction and brief therapy. He directed a lay counseling clinic and was Minister of Counseling in Columbus, Ohio before coming to Lifeway Counseling Centers as Clinical Director. He co-authored *Healing Souls, Touching Hearts: Pastoral Counseling and Care in the Cell Church.* Steve consults with leaders and church groups around the world.

Gary R. Sweeten, Ed. D. is a pastor and clinical counselor whose specialty is equipping Christians to care and counsel. He founded a lay counseling center at a church in Cincinnati, Ohio called, The Teleios Center and took its principles around the USA and into Norway, Sweden, Denmark, Russia, Singapore and Taiwan. He is the founder of Lifeway Counseling Centers, Lifeway Ministries Inc. Int. and the Lifeway Institute. Publications include, *Listening for Heaven's Sake, Rational Christian Thinking, Christian Care and Counsel and Healing Souls, Touching Hearts* and numerous articles. Gary also serves as a pastor of pastors in several congregations.

Lifeway Counseling Centers operate several clinics in Cincinnati, Ohio, USA. Founded in 1989 as an in-patient hospital for adults and adolescents, Lifeway treats hundreds of persons each year in an outpatient setting with a wholistic integration of psychotherapy, prayer and medicine.

Lifeway Ministries Incorporated grew out of the Lord's call to equip the saints for care and counseling. LMI and its predecessors have established international centers in Norway, Sweden, Denmark, Russia, Singapore and Taiwan and equip Christian leaders in many other countries. LMI cooperates with missionaries, churches, denominations, cell group movements and apostolic networks as consultants, coaches and care/counsel trainers.

Central addresses:

4015 Executive Park Drive
Suite 305
Cincinnati, Ohio 45241
513-769-4600
513-769-0304-fax
www.lifewaycenters.com
Lifeway@lifewaycenters.com

Printed in the United States
1119000002B